# AS THE PRO FLIES

**Books by John R. Hoyt**

ASSOCIATE FELLOW, I.AE.SC.
AOPA NO. 175071
*FORMERLY*
AVIATION SAFETY AGENT, CAA
NAVAL AVIATOR (COMDR.) USNR

AS THE PRO FLIES

MANUAL FOR AVIATION CADETS

SAFETY AFTER SOLO

# AS
# THE
# PRO
# FLIES

JOHN R. HOYT 1908-

*...flying expertly, in a professional manner*

*Technical illustrations by MARY N. HOYT*
*Cartoons by MEL LAZARUS*

McGraw-Hill Book Company, Inc.

NEW YORK    TORONTO    LONDON

**AS THE PRO FLIES**

# PREFACE

WRITING this book has been fun; let us hope that the reading of it is too. Certainly reading is less fun than actually doing what the book is about: flying expertly, in a professional manner.

Flying is now a business, but it still has elements of romance. I remember once writing a yarn about getting up at 0400 for a carrier take-off, remarking that it was as romantic as arising prematurely to evict an unhappy cat. To which my shipmates replied that the whole story was a romance, and that they could see through me as easily as looking through the Seventh Veil.

'Tis true. Once a man flies, he always wants to fly, whether his destination is someplace on Earth or the stars, whether he is looking back at 0400 dawn patrols or ahead to interplanetary travel. Romance is always there.

But romance and basic principles fly together, and the same basic principles will always be used: the safest pilot today or tomorrow is one who thinks, who thinks ahead, and who develops that mysterious Quality "X" which is the subject of a few chapters. Add that to the ability to use some practicable aids to practical flying and you behold the professional, accomplished pilot.

To *Flying*, for permission to use material which was previously published and for nearly twenty years of cordial, pleasant relationships, my many thanks. To AOPA's *Pilot* and to Max Karant, for helpful criticism and permission to use published pieces, my deep appreciation.

To Mib, for her work on the manuscript, her technical drawings, and her devotion, my boundless gratitude.

To the average pilot who wishes to become an expert and to fly with professional techniques, the very best of encouraging good wishes.

J.R.H.

v

# CONTENTS

# 1 : GOOD–BY TO ROMANCE

NOW that aviation is well over fifty years old there are many old-timers who reminisce sadly and assert that the romance of flying is gone. This is to be expected when fifty-odd years have gone by; certainly we'd look askance if the old-timers had symptoms of romance at the age of fifty plus.

What they are really saying is that aviation is no longer in the romance stage. Those once devilish-looking, oil-spattered, begoggled pilots of open-cockpit days have been superseded by businessmen who are flying twin-engined cabin jobs from mile-long airports. But ask either of them about flying and you'll find it's a mutual love, and where there's love there's romance.

What the reminiscers actually mean is that the ratio of romance has changed. Flying used to be 90 per cent romance and 10 per cent business, and anyone could have transported himself more quickly (and safely) on roller skates than by air.

Nowadays flying is mostly business, and with jet airliners we'll be able to breakfast in New York and arrive in Los Angeles in time for the coffee break. This reverses the ratio, leaving only 10 per cent for romance, a regrettably small figure indeed.

But it doesn't mean that we must say good-by to romance! Flying can still be romantic as one exults during an early morning take-off, feels the surge of power as he opens the throttle, and experiences the elation of aerial freedom. As he relaxes, the romance ratio increases, and as it increases he soon learns that there *is* a point at which he must say good-by to romance and seriously consider the business aspects of flying—the business of knowing how.

And that, in brief, is the topic: knowing how to fly in a professional manner. Flying isn't difficult; it merely requires better techniques than are used in other mechanized pursuits. To be sure, anyone can steer an airplane around the sky by just sitting in the cockpit and letting the plane fly him, but such pilots have been eliminated by firm, if unkind, measures. Just sitting, behind the controls of a moving airplane, is not healthy.

It would seem that the remedy is to learn how to sit. An example of this is The Case of the Sitting Pilot, whom we will refer to as Student Pilot Bumski, who once sat behind me in a Stearman biplane for fifteen hours of tortuous dual instruction. It is not known which of us was tortured most. Normally, eight hours of dual instruction prior to soloing was sufficient if the student purchased the time himself. As this was military time, it took more.

We were practicing stalls at 3,000 feet—it was not the first time we'd practiced them, but it was to be the last. As every pilot knows, stalls are required prior to solo in order that the student may recognize them and know how to recover promptly should he inadvertently stall.

Student Bumski never stalled inadvertently—he just stalled. He never sat and thought about what he might do—he just sat. Then, with a jerk, he'd come to life and do something quickly to prove that his reaction time was that of a fighter pilot. There were no illusions in my mind about what would happen to Bumski if I soloed him. Heaven knows *he* wanted to badly enough, but what with the airplane shortage in those days it just didn't seem the thing to do.

Of course, it can be maintained that Bumski would have soloed more easily and quickly with better instruction, but the best would have been none too good for Bumski. On the day in question he actually did his stalls correctly. He did five or six with reasonably acceptable technique, reaction time, and good sense (presumably he'd had a good night's sleep). He recovered with the time-honored method of pushing the stick forward to lower the nose, pick up speed, and resume safe flight. I rejoiced, turned the plane around, and let Bumski fly me home, intending to put him up for solo.

All went well until we arrived at the field. We entered the traffic pattern at an altitude of 500 feet, from which a freely falling body can reach the ground in about six seconds. The point was not that Mr. Bumski was thinking about jumping; he was supposedly thinking about flying the plane, watching for other planes, and making his approach correctly. Diversified thought was not his specialty, and after the first turn he slowed the plane to a stall. Not wishing to have him fall off into a spin, I informed Bumski with assumed nonchalance that he was stalling.

It is entirely to his credit that his reactions were prompt, but his promptness was exceeded by his vigor and determination. He pushed the stick forward so rapidly and so hard that we immediately assumed a vertical position—straight down. I pulled gently back on the stick

We recovered promptly from the stall.

... nothing happened. I pulled back harder, but Bumski was adamant: he was going to recover from that stall or else. He was also no weakling. With a mighty heave and by bracing my feet against the rudder stirrups I got the stick back just before we both became a couple of statistics.

It didn't take long to land and write out my recommendation that Bumski be made available for making airplanes rather than wrecking them. The papers were duly forwarded to the Commanding Officer and I went to the BOQ for what I needed.

Next day, the CO called me in. He reminded me that the country needed pilots badly, that *anybody* could be taught to fly, and that he was going to get Bumski through the course even if he had to teach the lad himself. I replied that only the CO's superior sagacity and skill could accomplish that impossibility, whereupon he offered to wager that Bumski would graduate and get his wings. This wager I snapped up, because I knew what kind of wings Bumski would get.

At that point orders came for me to report for duty at a faraway station—far away from instruction. This was the occasion for much rejoicing, both on my part and Bumski's, and I forgot the incident until a wire was received from the CO. It read: YOUR STUDENT BUMSKI JUST WASHED OUT. PAY UP.

I knew what kind of wings he'd get.

This eliminated forever my small faith in wagering with CO's. Because the wager was not in writing, there was no way of proving that the CO had wagered Bumski would *not* wash out, so there was very little I could do. After serious reflection about the considerable distance separating me from my former CO, that is just what I did do.

The Case of the Sitting Pilot is not romantic, but it does pose these problems. If he couldn't be taught to fly with supposedly good instruction, how can you, the reader, expect to fly better after reading this book? Or is it true that correct instruction will enable any student to pass, or that Bumski was only scared? Would he have become the world's foremost ace after fifty hours of dual? Can anyone tell if another person can or cannot fly?

First of all, the chapters to follow are for those who have already soloed and who therefore possess a certain aptitude for flying planes.

You must be interested in flying or you wouldn't be reading this, and if you're interested in flying you undoubtedly wish to fly better. But how can you decide whether you can or cannot fly better? Are there tests to determine if you are a good pilot who can become an expert?

The armed services give aptitude tests that eliminate some applicants prior to flight instruction, but every now and then someone who has passed the tests fails, or someone who fails the tests takes private lessons and eventually flies very well. To make excuses for this by solemnly asserting that we all make mistakes is no consolation to test-failers. But no test and no check pilot can tell definitely that *you* are perfectly safe or that you will never "dope off." No one can promise that you will always do the right thing at the right time. Much of the testing or the evaluation of the tests is up to you.

There *is* a way to determine whether one can do all the flying he wishes to in *this* world, and this is where self-analysis and books can help when all the objective tests in the world cannot. Too often, tests don't separate the slow learners who become experts from the fast learners who are dubs; many tests merely eliminate the never learners, or they set up an impossible criterion for aptitude.

Consider, for example, the test a commercial instructor gave to Edward Eager. Ed was eager but a slow learner, and after his second or third commercial flight the instructor took Ed into the Ready Room to discuss the facts of life. The facts, according to the well-meaning instructor, were that Ed simply couldn't fly, and in telling Ed this after only three hours of dual instead of eight he displayed an honesty beyond all cavil. To prove his point he placed a coin on a square piece of paper so that the edges of a corner were tangent to the circumference of the coin. Then he asked Ed to duplicate what he'd done. Ed carelessly placed the coin near, but not precisely upon, both edges, whereupon the instructor announced that Ed had "tunnel" vision and could never, positively never, fly. Tunnel vision had nothing to do with Ed's piloting ability: he was a slow learner at first, but rapid enough later to satisfy other pilots. In about a year and a half Ed landed a military fighter on the field to show his instructor how incorrect the prognostication had been. Was the instructor chagrined? Not at all. He was absent, having been inducted.

The point is that people are difficult to categorize. Ed couldn't possibly have proved to a prejudiced instructor that he had something else beyond the mere ability to manipulate the controls. His case does not prove that all instructors are wrong, or that aptitude tests can or cannot predict success in flying. No test can definitely prove that a student is inept and that the only mechanized equipment he's capable of soloing is a slow tractor on 40 fenced-in acres.

There must be something else, something within us that can be

He was supposed to have "tunnel" vision.

found by self-examination. Truly, much of our success or failure is due to ourselves; thus, if almost anyone can steer an auto or a plane, the multiplicity of accidents must not lie in the faulty manipulation of the stick, rudder, or throttle. There must be another answer.

Two more examples should suffice. Read about Student Pilot Aloysius, who got into an airplane one day with all the enthusiasm of a small boy opening his Christmas stocking. His air work was bad and his landings were worse: he persisted in trying to land the plane at either hangar height or subterranean depth. The instructor wept, cajoled, explained, and cursed, running the gamut of tutelage from Buzz to Zoom. Finally, after Al had been awarded extra time with another instructor, it was decided that Al was not a fitting candidate for three-dimensional activity.

Aloysius promptly went to a nearby civilian field and purchased eighteen or twenty hours of *good* instruction, eventually soloing. He then took himself over to the military airfield and showed his instructors how it was done. At this proof of their incompetency the instructors did not put their arms around each other and weep because, in the meantime, they had each turned out many students who were more apt than Aloysius.

But he had finally analyzed himself and learned to fly—too slowly for military purposes, but safely. Who was wrong? Was Aloysius right? Who is to be trusted, the person who thinks he can fly or the one who says he can't? A beginner can fool not only his instructor but himself, which is another way of saying that it's hard to tell whether a student has that enigmatic quality that permits flying to be mostly romance and partly business, or vice versa.

The finest example of the correct proportion of romance in flying was given by a military pilot called Mose. Mose had 350 hours to his credit and regarded himself as an Ace. He was so over-confident that he was no longer flying his plane—*it* was flying him. And the hazards of such flying are comparable to playing Russian roulette with all six chambers of the revolver loaded.

One evening after night flying Mose began to count his virtues, a trait suspiciously akin to bragging. Bragging is good for the ego, mostly the owner's, and is not particularly endearing to an audience. "Just think," said Mose enthusiastically, "here I've got 350 hours and never so much as scratched a plane. Who said flying was something special?" He didn't knock on wood, although there was plenty of it within reach, and when we reminded him of his omission he derided our remonstrances as a tale without supporting statistics.

Although it is true that science does not attribute validity to the wood superstition, Mose contributed some statistics. The very next day he came in for a landing with excessive nonchalance and a variable wind. It hurts to tell this, but before he knew what was happening his airplane had veered off to one side and had whipped around like a top, ground-looping a wing off.

But it was the last accident Mose ever had. He learned his lesson and became an expert pilot, a pilot who knows how to keep the ro-

mance and business of flying in proper proportions; he showed that
he possessed the same attribute that had benefitted Aloysius.

What is the answer? It seems to me, after thousands of flying hours
in both military and civil aircraft, hours spent in dive bombing, in
primary dual, and in flight checks as a CAA—now FAA (Federal
Aviation Agency)—inspector, that no test and no inspector can be
depended upon to predict one's aptitude for flying. There are too
many variables, too many factors in human nature; some students
learn slowly and become very adept, others learn rapidly and never
completely assimilate what they've been told. Some airline pilots
pass flight checks with high grades, only to fly away and commit
unpardonable blunders.

There is some other factor which we have not, thus far, been able
to test. It may sound silly, but the best time to ascertain whether one
can fly is after he's learned to fly. For example, place a simian in the
cockpit and note what a creditable job he does in a stable airplane.
But the ape cannot dodge cumulo-nimbus, avoid other aircraft, or
make a forced landing. In the same manner, any instructor can teach
the rudiments of flying so that a student can herd a plane around the
sky—but he *can't* teach him to become an expert pilot. He can teach
him the mechanics of flying and he can say, "Yes, you seem to catch
on quickly," or "No, you don't seem to react promptly to changing
situations;" but he can't make an accurate forecast of flying ability,
because a person learning to fly is so occupied with movements of the
stick and rudder that there isn't room for instructor analysis.

Even later on, after you've become a Private Pilot—or an Airline
Transport Pilot—he can only test you for complete mastery of flight
techniques, but he still won't know much about the pilot you are inside. And that is the important point: an instructor or check pilot can't
guarantee anyone's reaction, especially when the other person is flying on his own and more particularly when the unexpected arises
during solo flight.

How, then, is anyone going to learn to fly expertly, in a professional
manner? How can he tell if he's got that quality that separates the
dubs from the experts, the amateurs from the professionals? How
may one train himself and acquire that quality?

The answer is that *you* are the only one who can ever judge whether
or not you possess that indefinable quality or ability that will enable
you to enjoy the maximum amount of romance in aviation with the

least amount of business. The other question, "Can I acquire it?" may be answered by saying that you not only can but must. Finally, you can learn to fly expertly, in a professional manner, by acquiring that certain ability and by learning a few of the techniques described below.

But, prior to studying the techniques—those short cuts and easy rules to professional flying such as better techniques for take-offs, glides, landings, cross-country flying, transition to new planes, the ADF, the ILS, the Omnirange, night flying, and instrument flight— prior to studying these techniques which will enable you to fly *As the Pro Flies*, let's begin by reading about the indefinable quality that expert pilots possess. Then, after reading a few examples which will enable you to analyze yourself, we may go on to more advanced work and acquire the polishing touch that is needed to mold the average pilot into an expert who flies with the finesse of a "pro."

So, if you're interested in finding out what it is that all expert pilots have—that seldom-described factor which enables them to fly safely without having to say good-by to romance—read Chapter 2.

# 2 : EXPERT PILOTS HAVE IT—DO YOU?

A PILOT can instruct students for years, dodging other planes and avoiding cumulo-nimbus, answering questions until his verve declines to an all-time low and he thinks he's heard them all. Students ask questions that make an instructor wish he'd memorized a flying encyclopedia and a world almanac, but the day eventually comes when some enterprising student asks The Question that makes him reflect and consider.

That question is: "What is the greatest attribute a pilot can possess?"

There are those pilots who will immediately say smoothness is that virtue. As far as airplanes, which are of feminine gender, are concerned, smoothness is indeed a trait *par excellence*. Certainly we all want to fly without kicking the plane around.

Then there are other pilots who hold for good approaches and gentle landings. Although they are least noteworthy of admirable pilot traits, it must be conceded that we all like easy, greased-on landings that melt into the runway like a chunk of butter on hot buckwheats.

Also recommended are non-skid turns, feel of the plane, cross-country ability, aerobatics, and good instrument flying. Any one of these may be what we're looking for in a top-notch pilot, or it may not.

Take, for example, the case of Applicant A, who presented himself to me for a Private Pilot's ticket. Mr. A took me aloft and performed all the items on the grade sheet except one. Result: failure. A few weeks later he appeared again, and still this single shortcoming seemed almost on the good side of bad, but not quite. It need scarcely be stated that there was no doubt in the mind of this applicant that he should have passed. There was also no doubt in my mind, so he didn't. However, on the third flight I signed the ticket that gave Mr. A his permission to take off with passengers and tempt Fate.

Next is the example of two applicants who wanted their Airline Transport Ratings. In that postwar era we took them two at a time, which was easier for them and infinitely easier for us. The one who flew first was the one who lost the toss of a coin, thereby giving the other applicant an opportunity to watch the flight test and see just how tough the inspector happened to be.

Pilot Y, who lost the toss, got into the left seat. His companion sat back to watch every maneuver, figuring on being better prepared when his turn came. Both pilots were neither more nor less nervous than the average applicant (everyone gets checkitis during flight tests, but inspectors make allowances for this). We took off, climbed, and completed the high-altitude work first.

By the time a pilot is ready for an ATR ticket—the highest he can obtain—the mere technique of flying has long been mastered, and he should have some idea of what counts most in an airplane. But even having one pilot observe while the other flew didn't help, because one of them didn't have "it." Here is what happened.

Pilot Y kept me awake because his handling of the plane was marginal. He was rough but passable. If there was a bump in the air, he not only knew where it was and found it, but helped it along a bit. After bumping around for an hour we did our low-altitude work, which consisted of a simulated 400-1 shot (a 400-foot ceiling with a visibility of 1 mile). Pilot Y was good enough to pass but not to congratulate. He ended the flight test by treating us to a landing, the kind that is not rough enough for a failing grade but is bad enough to remember.

Pilot X, in his turn, flew some very smooth maneuvers under the "blind-flying," or instrument, hood. He had the feel of the airplane, his turns were bubble-centered, and he recovered accurately on headings. During steep turns he held his altitude within a few feet, and when the routine emergency occurred (one of the engines is always killed during this flight test) he was calm and collected. He recovered from unusual positions promptly and without any confusion.

*But each pilot was given a certain problem during the test,* a problem that occurs frequently in actual, real-life instrument work.

Their actions during the problem weighed heavily in determining their qualification. Pilot Y, the Rough Rider who had flown first, was told that he had passed, while Pilot X received a try-it-again slip. Being a smooth instrument pilot, he couldn't understand why he'd failed; he regarded the *billet doux* as unwarranted and offered the opinion that to be flight-checked by me was a Fate Worse than Death.

As the critique below will show, there was an adequate reason for Pilot X's failure; but pilots who fail don't say why they failed, because they don't ask themselves such a question in the first place. They *know* they did a good job and that next time (with a better inspector or check pilot) the result will certainly be a passing grade. It takes a long time for most failers to realize that they were unprepared, were trained poorly, or didn't have Quality X. There is hardly an applicant who blames his own shortcomings for failure; the only thing that convinces him is that ultimate proof—a crackup.

To crack up fatally in a mechanized vehicle is not difficult; it is done about 40,000 times a year in automobiles. Why drivers crack up is attributed to inattention, carelessness, inaptitude, or incompetence, but no one ever says that those who crack up lack a certain quality, inasmuch as that quality can't be defined.

This quality applies particularly to pilots, but it's just as indefinable. Take, for example, Pilot Z, who wanted an instrument rating. Everything went well during his flight test until he was given a homing problem on a radio range. Because he'd done his turns, timed turns, steep turns, climbs, glides, and whatever very nicely, he felt quite sure of himself. The range problem—tuning in Los Wages range and homing on it—would be simplicity itself.

Los Wages has distinctive Morse code signals called identifiers; so do all the other ranges in the United States, as anyone can hear if he *listens* to them. The applicant, for some unfortunate reason, tuned in a loud signal and homed on it, forgetting to identify the station. Because we were far away from the station he'd tuned to, it took him a long time to identify the sector he was in, and by that time we'd almost "had" it. Fortunately, a check pilot was along: at the last possible moment the hood was removed so that the pilot could see for himself. There, less than thirty seconds away, was a bristling, unmovable mountain.

Was the applicant dismayed? Of course not. He indignantly

averred that he was about to turn around anyway and, besides, he had never erred in that manner before. The latter was undoubtedly true—such a mistake is made only once during a solo instrument flight. The next question was: Should he *ever* be permitted to fly on instruments without a check pilot?

He had never made *that* mistake before.

The answer indubitably is "yes," because no check pilot can tell if a pilot really erred, was inexperienced, or will learn by experience. Suffice it to say that the next time he flew the test he did tune in the right station, homed on it, and proved he could do it.

But he too *had* indicated he lacked that something which is hard to pin down and which is impossible to use in disqualifying an applicant. It is probably a good thing that it can't be used, because check pilots can be wrong in judging applicants. If a check pilot is wrong and the future airline pilot turns out to be adept, the check pilot says nothing and hopes that no one else says anything. If the check pilot is proved right by the accidental death of the applicant and his passengers, the check pilot had *better* say nothing.

An inspector is compelled by law to issue a certificate if the minimum standards for maneuvers are met. This is fair enough, because otherwise there would be a lot of arbitrary check pilots, examiners, and inspectors. There are enough of them as it is. But they aren't always wrong, and they sometimes feel that an applicant just doesn't have it, despite his passing the minimum standards. Then the buck must be passed to the pilot himself, if he flies for himself, or to the men who hire him if he flies for others.

## THE CRITIQUE

Let us see what happened to Pilot A, the Private Pilot applicant who lacked our mysterious something. He was satisfactory maneuverwise, but it seemed to me that he didn't think ahead, or if he was thinking ahead he wasn't doing it fast enough. A man can make the right decision too late: if a motorist driving at 60 miles per hour decides he had better stop when he is only 10 feet from the railroad crossing, he has made the right decision but he will more than likely be dead in a few seconds.

Making the right decision too late has its drawbacks.

Grading an ability to make decisions is tough. Anyone can grade a spot landing, which either is or isn't. But how to grade Pilot A? Although he took too much time to make up his mind when a problem confronted him, he got his ticket anyway. One day, some time later, he was taking off on a calm day from a field too small for the plane. He had landed easily into a headwind and now was trying to take off without the wind. He got airborne, tried to climb too steeply, spun in, and killed himself. He also killed his passenger.

They both, no doubt, would have lived longer if the inspector had said, "No tickee, no launlee," or words to that effect. But this is not the whole remedy. The law says he must have a certificate if he meets minimum standards, and besides there is always another examiner who may not see the fault and will issue a certificate. Pilot A's death might have been prevented (1) by his not driving mechanized vehicles—an improbability; (2) by knowing his fault, say, of slow thinking and working hard to correct it; (3) by waiting for a strong headwind to assist take-off; and (4) by training himself to think quickly enough to have cut the throttle during take-off, thereby taking a smash instead of a crash.

Let's see what happened to Pilot X, the smooth ATR pilot. He obviously knew his plane; it seemed to be a part of him, he flew it so smoothly. But in the middle of the flight test he was given an "emergency" procedure in which congested conditions were simulated by a call from the examiner over the interphone, advising that the applicant's clearance had been cancelled and substituting a new one. This is hardly an unfair procedure, inasmuch as it happens frequently in actual IFR (Instrument Flight Rule) conditions.

Pilot X copied his revised clearance so well that he flew into another area. He forgot where he was, where he was going, and very nearly forgot what he was doing. It was good to know that all we had to do was pull down the blinds and see Catalina Island underneath us. The only thing we knew for sure was that we did not want to be on instruments in actual IFR conditions with Pilot X.

Pilot Y, the rough pilot, was much different from his companion. He had received the problem first and had no forewarning of the maneuvers, so the change in clearance must have surprised him. Of this he gave no indication: while he was polite, he didn't seem to care much for smooth flying or whether the check pilot liked him or not. But he gave the impression that he was thinking every minute and also thinking about the next minute. While copying his revised clearance he kicked the plane, in an almost literal sense, from his given heading to the desired heading, then held in the holding pattern for precisely the number of minutes he was supposed to hold. He flew over to his new position and held until he was cleared for a let down to a new airport, all without sweating a drop.

Kicking a plane around is not essential; thinking is. He barely met the minimum requirements for smoothness but his thinking was superb. Later on, when he became smoother (and almost anyone can learn to twist a wheel smoothly with practice and a critical instructor), he was to become my idea of somebody with whom flying was not only safe, but a pleasure.

Finally, what about Pilot Z, the chap who nearly flew us into a mountain by tuning in the wrong station? Certainly, after making such a mistake once, he wouldn't do it again. But it's like a box of matches: one doesn't know for sure if every match will light until he's tried them all. This method has inherent disadvantages. Would Pilot Z have to be tested in each possible emergency? Would he ever learn to remember to check his essentials without another pilot hovering over him like a guardian angel? He eventually got his license, but it would be safe to bet that if he is alive today, it is because he has *not* flown many instrument missions.

Does this mean that we condemn everyone who has made a mistake? Not at all. The best pilot, true enough, is a man with no faults, but we are still searching for him. The next best pilot has faults, to be sure, but he has Quality X and he has learned to guard against his faults. Guarding against one's tendency to err will be discussed at greater length in Chapter 22.

One of the better pilots told this story. "I was dive bombing, as a pilot based on an aircraft carrier, when I completed a run to find that I had (1) forgotten carburetor heat, (2) dived through a cloud, and (3) dived too low, snapping the stick back for the pull-out. Any of these errors committed separately would have been bad enough, but the three together were unforgivable. What I told myself cannot be repeated here, but it was so emphatic that I learned to think ahead all the time, and by not repeating those mistakes I thereby avoided others."

It would seem there *is* something a person can do to attain that indefinable attribute that the experts have, the ability to think and to think ahead. Any candidate for the hereafter can make a decision to slow down when he is only 10 feet from the train; experts decide *ahead* of time. Anyone can fly with the bad habit of procrastination, a slowness in making decisions, a forgiving disposition, and . . . well, a thousand other faults, but he never flies long enough to become an expert. An expert thinks, thinks ahead, and analyzes his faults. Then he corrects and guards against those faults.

If the greatest attribute a pilot can have is Quality X—the ability to think, to plan ahead, and to avoid doping off—then Pilot A (the Private Pilot) should have realized his shortcoming after his check flight. He would have guarded against his fault of not making prompt decisions by continually practicing making decisions, by forcing himself to act quickly, by taking rechecks, and by thinking ahead. Pilot X (the smooth ATR pilot) might have learned to think by recognizing his fault of hazy thinking and by concentrating on the correction of it instead of practicing smooth flying.

How can anyone tell whether he has Quality X or not? First of all, it is assumed that he already has a pilot certificate and that he knows how to move the controls for happy-landing flights. Second, one need not go to a check pilot, since check pilots can only sit in the airplane and observe maneuvers by which they can estimate pilot *technique*. If the maneuvers are performed satisfactorily, any applicant is entitled to his ticket. Should the applicant not be up to standard on the examination item "judgment," he still gets his ticket because it is hard to prove that a decision was below standard. Thus, no matter what apprehensions the check pilot may have about the applicant's lack of Quality X, the flight test is considered passing.

In other words, it is you who knows how you are doing. Did you tune in the wrong station? Did you become flustered by a change in clearance and fly out of your area? Did you try to take off from a short field under adverse conditions? Did you forget that the compass doesn't point north and lose yourself? *You* know about it, so get busy and "chew yourself out" for it, using the stiffest vocabulary at your command, as the dive-bombing pilot did.

Then get to work on your fault—both of them if you have two—and eliminate them. You can fly like a professional even though you have only a Private Pilot's ticket. Remember that any time you are not thinking, planning, or looking ahead of the plane, you are being taken for a ride, which is known in the trade as "having one's head up and locked."

There was once a group of experienced pilots who were taking the three-hour, cross-country instrument course described in Chapter 24. It was amazing to find that they had hardly a single minute available for reminiscing. They were busy holding a heading, checking in over check points, knowing the nearest field for emergencies, estimating fuel consumption, check points, keeping the log, estimating time over the next fix, check points, new radio locators to tune in, bearings on the ADF, and check points—all combined with steering the airplane right side up, and the latter was the least of it.

The finest ability a good pilot possesses is the ability to think, and to do it accurately, precisely, and quickly. That doesn't mean thinking *after* something happens; it means doing it before. True, some things cannot be foreseen, but the pilot who has made thousands of decisions beforehand is prepared, and he is accustomed to making decisions so accurately and so quickly that when the time comes he is not dumbfounded.

He has tested himself just as a check pilot would do, and he has corrected himself; he has given himself frequent flight tests, just as we'll do in Chapter 23. On a cross-country flight, do you know what you'd do in an emergency that demanded an immediate landing? Do you know which way to turn to the nearest field in case of a deferred emergency? Or what to do if you ran into headwinds that demanded an instant decision as to whether to turn back, land at the nearest field, or to continue? What do you do when you find yourself on an approach that is borderline: almost too high or the maybe-I-can-make-it kind? How you answer these questions, and others, will give you a fairly good clue as to whether you have Quality X or not.

Thus a pilot can be expert even if he has logged only fifty hours, but very few pilots are experts. Experts learned to fly by practice and hard work; while they were thinking and planning ahead they also acquired certain techniques of flying that permit them to fly with ease and at ease.

For example, there are a few easy rules which can be used in the first maneuver you ever made, the take-off. Then there are others which may be used in connection with flaps, glides, precision approaches, the compass, your map, flying the Omnirange, and the ILS.

If you wish to learn some special techniques as you develop Quality X and eventually fly *As the Pro Flies*, read about the Flying Bumper, who is waiting beside the runway for take-off clearance. He's flying a plane that has an $S_2$ speed of—but we're getting ahead of ourselves. Let's see if he knows how to take it off.

# 3: TAKE IT OFF

IT is unwarranted if anyone infers, from the title of this chapter, that we are no longer talking about airplanes. But if the subject does not seem to reflect creditably upon us, neither do the "bumps" and "grinds" which occur during many take-offs, and one can almost hear some pitiable instructor moaning, "Take it off! Take it off!"

Consider The Case of the Flying Bumper. He was one of those "safe" pilots who always took off with plenty of speed because he wanted a safety factor, such as 5 knots for his children and 5 more for expectations. He'd read about other pilots who had stalled off the ground and spun in, a maneuver which is frowned upon in most flying circles. So between the time he applied throttle and the moment his wheels left the ground the Flying Bumper did enough bumps and grinds to have earned him a starring role in any burlesque in the country. After taking it off he would fly swiftly in a slow climb, blissfully ignorant of the fact that he'd increased the hazards, beaten his landing gear within an inch of its life, and worn enough rubber from the tires to provide him with pencil erasers the rest of his life.

If you don't believe this, walk into any hangar and say aloud, "Take-offs are more complicated than landings." Then watch the hangar doors come down and listen to the hangar flying start up. Any pilot within range will swear he's always had trouble with landings, whereas, after learning to keep his starting run straight (some time before solo), his take-offs were as smooth as a custard pie in July.

This prevalent belief indicates that the average pilot knows less about take-offs than he does about the tsetse fly. He can't believe that an airliner take-off really *is* more complicated than a landing, or that there are more factors to consider prior to take-off than there

19

are before landing, or that under certain conditions it is possible to land but hazardous to take off.

So the average lightplane pilot regards take-offs with nonchalance. He was never required to do much more than keep his plane rolling straight and to get it off the ground. On the other hand, safe landings were a prerequisite before solo. After solo he ran into a discouraging plateau of hard landings, high landings, skidding landings, or subterranean landings. Landings, in fact, always are a problem.

Not only the average pilot but the general public thinks so. Watch the faces of airline passengers as they tense up for the landing. The pilot may have taken them through cumulo-nimbus, omitted compulsory check points, flown below minimum altitudes, drifted off course, and missed his approach. But if the landing is so gentle that one would think the pilots were avoiding the cracking of two bad eggs in the cockpit, the flight was a success and the passengers' faces light up. For them, the flight was perfect because it's the landing that counts.

But they never give a second thought to the take-off. It can be a hot day at 5,000 feet, and there can be two runways, a short one into the wind or a long one crosswind. Which one would *you* want to use? What factors influence the decision to take off on one runway or the other? What change of technique is required in either case? Should one use flap? If so, how much? Will it do any good to hold the brakes, apply full power, and then release the brakes? Does it really do any good to hold the brakes in a lightplane? How can one get more horsepower from his engine at high-elevation take-offs? *And what about $S_1$ and $S_2$ speeds?*

Granted that more finesse and technique are required for a greased-on landing than for a smooth take-off, just what should we know about take-offs that will increase safety in flight? Finally, how can we use this information? It's the *application* of knowledge that hinders one's heirs from collecting on one's insurance policy.

## POINT T

The best way to develop good technique and to learn correct habits is to make each maneuver a precision affair. This is going to be our theme both here and in the succeeding chapters, because

once a pilot has learned precision flying he has most of the habits
he needs for safe flying.

So it is with take-offs. Let's inspect our plane, climb into the
cockpit, go through the Checkoff List, and taxi out. While we wait
for tower clearance we'll park at right angles to the runway in order to check for incoming traffic and runway obstacles. This is not
because we distrust tower operators; it's primarily because *you* are
the captain of the plane and are therefore responsible for its operation.

With magnetos checked and the final checkoffs completed, we receive take-off clearance and taxi out. Now is the time to become
aware of at least three important items. In order of occurrence they
are:

1. Point T
2. Stalling speed
    *a.* $S_1$–$S_2$ speed
    *b.* Climbing speed
3. Emergency

Point T does not represent the great unknown; it is a definite
place on the runway at which we must be in the air or we'll have
to discontinue our take-off. With a partial power failure, we'd be
in bad shape if we arrived at the end of the runway and were still
on it instead of above it.

The best way to judge how we're doing at Point T is by a glance
at the air speed. We'll see how this applies when we discuss $S_1$–$S_2$
speeds, but our concentration upon take-off technique must not
prevent us from thinking about what we're going to do should the
unexpected happen.

Now apply power gradually, smoothly, and fully. Use full take-
off power, not partial power. A few pilots believe they can prolong
engine life by using less than full power during take-off, but
engine manufacturers have proved that a slow take-off with partial
power is wasteful, inefficient, and hard on the engine. The reason
is that with partial power a take-off is longer and the engine wears
out faster because of prolonged high-rpm operation—although this
applies to engines that turn controllable-pitch propellers, which in
turn permit the engine to turn higher rpm's. In lightplanes, low-rpm
operation is not advised, because the saving is negligible, the gear
and tires are on the ground longer, and the plane is not as high—

and consequently as safe—as it should be at the end of the runway. With full power you get into the air sooner, and the rpm's may be reduced sooner.

Fast take-offs are easier to control, and are easier on the gear and tires. The less mileage one puts on his undercarriage the more he saves, a factor which possibly interests owners of planes more than renters.

We're gathering speed as we roll down the runway. You're feeling the stick gently: does it require much forward or back pressure? If it does, mentally note to mark your stabilizer correctly (a spot of white paint will do the trick) so that it is set slightly nose-heavy thereafter. No more than gentle pressure should be needed to keep the plane on the runway or to help her fly. When the stabilizer is set correctly we can sense the precise amount of pressure required in a precision take-off. Any more than this and you are a buddy of the Flying Bumper, who holds so much forward pressure that the tires are compressed (in a three-point plane) or the nose strut and wheel are compressed (in tricycle-type aircraft). Then come the bumps: the plane struggles to take off, bouncing off the ground, into the air, and back to the runway. Or, during stalled take-offs, the plane tries to fly, only to fall back to the runway.

We're gathering speed slowly, although we have full take-off power, easy forward pressure, and full rpm's. Something could be dragging us back, possibly the Flying Bumper's technique, known as the grinds. Grinds are wearing if not boring, and they are the result of selecting an incorrect reference spot ahead of the plane.

Pick out a spot far enough ahead of the nose so that you can instantly be aware of nose movement. It is far better to err by selecting a spot that is too far than by looking at a spot which is too close. A degree of swerve is readily apparent to a pilot who looks far ahead, but to him who looks down at the runway the nose can be turning back to the hangar before he is aware of it. Then come the grinds: hard application of rudder to bring the nose back, which literally grinds rubber from the tires, then opposite rudder to uncorrect the correction. This excessive use of rudder (called "fanning" the rudder) also puts the large, flat area of the rudder into the slipstream, an area which provides much drag and no lift. Drag slows the plane greatly, enough to prolong the take-off run. The same is true for excessive elevator pressure; forward stick (down elevator) adds drag in copious amounts.

Use immediate but *gentle* rudder pressure to bring the nose back to the aiming point. Use the toes, not the insteps, and press them briskly with ankle motion, tentatively feeling how much pressure is needed to turn the nose, thereby never using too much. Result: no grinds, faster acceleration, and higher air speed. Naturally, as the air speed increases, less ankle motion and movement of the rudder are needed, but more pressure is required. This technique of feeling the rudder uses movements so slight that it could hardly be termed "fanning" the rudder, which is primarily a term for indiscriminate, mechanical rudder waving. Wave good-by with your hands, if you must, not with the rudder.

Wave good-by with your hands, not with the rudder.

## A PRECISION TAKE–OFF

We're now halfway to take-off point, the air speed is increasing normally, and we wonder if it's time to take off. But wondering isn't enough: what we want is a *precision* take-off! If take-off speed is 65 mph, why be a Flying Bumper and get 75? Increased speed does not mean that safety is enhanced; it usually means that the pilot is holding so much control pressure that he has no "feel," or that he isn't watching his gauges.

The gauges—as his instruments are jocularly called—is a term used loosely. Actually, there's only one VFR take-off instrument. We Private Pilots should know this instrument, check it periodically, and trust it; "seat-of-the-pants" flying was fine years ago, but today we need precision and only an instrument can provide it. That instrument is the air-speed indicator; it's on the panel and all we need to do is watch it.

Perhaps the best way to get used to using the air-speed indicator during take-off is by practicing in a parked airplane, where one can simulate a take-off, look ahead, glance down at the gauges and back to an imaginary runway without fear of committing suicide. In actual take-offs, surprisingly enough, the airplane will not veer off toward a runway marker the first time you look at the air speed, although that first, split-second glance from the runway to the air speed makes you feel as if you're tempting Fate.

So you flick a glance at it. It reads 57 mph—almost at $S_1$ speed. This is no time to wonder what the indicated stalling speed is, because $S_1$–$S_2$ speeds are computed in terms of the stall. The sad fact is that many a pilot doesn't know his indicated stall speed, or that this speed is the basis for his take-offs, climbs, and glides! As Chapter 5 discloses, every good pilot practices stalls in order to sharpen his senses and to check the air speed. Air-speedometers get old and their tubes become obstructed, like the rest of us. This means that the indicated stall speed will vary during the years.

Let us imagine that you have previously checked the stall speed in various configurations (i.e., with power on, flaps up and down; power off, flaps up and down). Note the indicated stall speed with *power-off-flaps-up;* this is your "red" stall speed. Paint a narrow red line on your air-speed indicator to indicate the stall speed, as in Fig. 1, in order that you may see the relationship between the

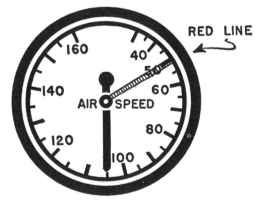

Fig. 1. Paint a red line (or use Scotch-lite tape) over the stall speed of your air-speed indicator.

needle and the stall speed at a glance. Now find the stall speed with *power-on-flaps-down*. This figure will be slower than the former one, so it need not be painted on the dial.

So when we glance at the air speed and see the needle on the red line over "50," we know that we're at the power-off stall speed, and the plane will probably fly. But to get off the ground now means that we'll be wobbling around at about 52 mph, just above the stall; a cut gun will drop us back with a landing hard enough to necessitate dental repairs. Also, to be in the air at near-stall speed means that we have a high angle of attack and an enormous amount of drag, which will reduce the rate of climb!

Just when do we want to get off the ground? The answer is that we want a precision take-off with rapid acceleration to get us airborne at the proper time, a take-off that is easy on the gear, saves tires, is safe, and is efficient. So far we have achieved this by using full power, by not fanning the rudder, and by not using excessive stick pressures. But as yet we don't know just when to get into the air.

## $S_1$–$S_2$ SPEED

The middle of a take-off is hardly the time to commence a discussion of $S_1$–$S_2$ speeds, but in books—as in movies—anything is possible. Just what are these speeds and how may they be applied to single-engine aircraft? How may they be applied to multi-engine aircraft? What value is knowledge of $S_1$–$S_2$ speeds to any pilot?

In Transport Category aircraft there are speeds known as $V$ (velocity)$_1$ and $V_2$, which are critical speeds. $V_1$ is the critical speed at which engine failure during take-off necessitates the take-off being discontinued and the airplane stopped in the remaining runway. This is because at $V_1$ speed and with less than full take-off power the plane cannot accelerate to take-off speed. For single-engine pilots it would seem that almost any speed would fit this description, and therefore that any application of this theory to single-engine lightplane operation is silly. But let's go on to consider $V_2$ speed.

$V_2$ speed is usually higher than $V_1$. Once $V_1$ is passed, the plane can be accelerated to $V_2$, take off, and climb. $V_2$ is almost the same as the best-angle-of-climb speed, which will be discussed in a moment. Thus, it is the speed at which one must take off whether or not one engine fails. In some twin-engine aircraft, $V_1$ and $V_2$ are the same speed; in single-engine aircraft, power failure definitely stops the take-off. The fact is that if we use these speeds we'll enhance flying safety.

Civil Air Regulations do not attempt to define $V_1$ or $V_2$ in terms of percentages. Nevertheless, an attempt to so define them is made here for the lightplane pilot who wishes to fly expertly, despite the fact that these speeds vary with loading and flap setting, and that for strict accuracy one must consult the manufacturer's flight handbook for exact speeds.

In computing $V_1$–$V_2$ speeds, consider a typical multi-engine airplane: At a certain loading and configuration it stalls at 72-74 mph, in which case the $V_1$ speed used was 86 mph, or 17½ per cent higher than stalling speed. The $V_2$ speed was 98 mph, or 29 per cent more than the stall. If we consider these figures as characteristic of most airplanes we may use them in flying our lightplane.

Let us call these lightplane speeds Speed One and Speed Two ($S_1$–$S_2$) and use the approximate percentages in our computations:

$$S_1 \text{ speed} = \text{stall speed} + 15 \text{ per cent}$$
$$S_2 \text{ speed} = \text{stall speed} + 30 \text{ per cent}$$

Thus, in a lightplane that stalls at 50 mph, $S_1$ is 57.5 mph and $S_2$ is 65 mph. The stall speed is obtained by the methods described in Chapter 5, with power off and flaps up, because this configuration has a stall speed higher than that with power on and flaps extended, which in turn makes our $S_1$–$S_2$ speeds slightly faster and more conservative.

We are now rolling down the runway toward Point T, our predetermined position on the runway at which we must have attained $S_1$ speed or discontinue the take-off. As we approach Point T we glance at the indicator: it reads 57 mph, so we continue to roll toward our take-off point. The value of such knowledge may be illustrated by the example of a pilot who was alert but who disliked Checkoff Lists. By the time he arrived at Point T, his plane was rolling at less than $S_1$ speed and the acceleration was noticeably slow. Had he continued the take-off he'd have met St. Peter socially at the end of the runway. Instead, he cut his throttle, taxied back, and located the trouble (a bad Checkoff List, naturally: he had his prop in high pitch).

$S_1$ is important to remember because it's also very close to the Minimum Control Speed (known as $V_{mc}$) used in flight tests. At this critical speed, control of the plane is difficult and climb is impossible without first lowering the nose to decrease drag and then accelerating to $S_2$ speed. Because lowering the nose incurs loss of altitude, we don't want to be off the ground at $S_1$ speed!

To be off the ground and literally staggering in the air at low speed would make us very vulnerable should we have engine failure in either single- or multi-engine planes, and any pilot so caught would have to display considerable dexterity to prevent a hard landing.

Remember, the high angle of attack needed to become airborne at $S_1$ speed would induce so much drag that by the time we did lower the nose and attain $S_2$ speed we'd be far down the runway and we might not be able to climb over those obstacles ahead. We want to stay on the runway, accelerate to $S_2$, and climb at the maximum *angle* of climb in order to avoid being embarrassed by those tall trees ahead that we'd just as lief be over as under.

## MAXIMUM ANGLE AND RATE OF CLIMB SPEEDS

We continue to roll during our precision take-off: at $S_2$ speed we apply gentle back pressure and get off the runway. Does this complete the take-off? Not at all. Now we have the tires and gear off the ground, but we are not at the best *rate*-of-climb speed. Or perhaps we want the best *angle*-of-climb speed; which one shall we use?

Press the nose down slightly and continue to accelerate to one or the other, depending upon the obstacles ahead. In any airplane, altitude is more valuable during take-off than excess air speed, so ordinarily we'd use the best *rate*-of-climb speed. Consult Fig. 3 on page 37. The best rate of climb is indicated on the graph, and it is about 10 per cent higher than $S_2$; thus, for our plane which stalls at 50 mph, the best rate-of-climb speed is approximately 70 mph.

Greater accuracy may be determined with the manufacturer's flight manual or handbook, which will give the speeds recommended for the wing of your airplane. Or the best climb speed may be determined experimentally by timing yourself with a stop watch and noting altimeter changes for several minutes of climb at various air speeds. The last method is the best because it allows for air-speed indicator errors. The first method (stall speed plus 40 per cent) is approximate, the second method (the handbook) gives *true* air speeds, whereas the third method gives the indicated air speed for best rate of climb by actual test.

But suppose there are obstacles at the end of the runway. In this case we want to use the best *angle*-of-climb speed because, although we don't climb as fast, a greater angle of climb enables us to be higher at the end of the runway despite the fact it takes us longer to get there. Glance at Fig. 3 again. The best angle of climb is shown on the graph at the point of tangency of the climb slope to the curve, and is slightly slower than the best rate-of-climb speed. For our lightplane that stalls at 50 mph, we'd climb at 67 mph. Once we've cleared the obstacles, we lower the nose, accelerate, obtain best *rate*-of-climb speed (70 mph), and get upstairs into that wild blue yonder.

We're off the ground and climbing, but the take-off isn't completed. What about the landing gear? The flaps? The power setting? And what about that take-off emergency? Some pilots climb out of the airport dragging their gear behind them, in the somewhat forlorn hope that the gear will be of use to them in the event of engine failure. The usefulness of the wheels vanished the moment the plane left the ground—unless we took off from one of those fabulous and hard-to-find 2-mile runways. After leaving the runway of an average airport, we are committed to take off, and the gear adds nothing but drag, and drag reduces the ability of the plane to climb.

Therefore, at the moment we establish our climb, *raise the gear.* But not at $S_2$ speed, because during our acceleration to climb speed a gust or a miscalculation of altitude may put us back on the runway. If the wheels aren't there we'll damage the prop. Raise the gear at climb speed, and feel the plane leap ahead as the drag diminishes.

The first power reduction comes next. Adjust the throttle to climbing manifold pressure and then adjust propeller pitch to climbing rpm's; in a plane equipped with a fixed-pitch prop, ease the throttle back. You're climbing steadily, using the position of the nose on the horizon as a check point that provides a constant, climbing air speed. *Hold it there,* because maximum climb occurs at that position only.

But we're still taking off. We have only 100 or 200 feet over the end of the runway; at our speed and altitude we cannot turn back in the event of an engine failure. We know that modern engines are remarkably free from sudden failure, which is very unconsoling as one disentangles himself from a once-gay airplane and reflects that *his* accident is the first since last Michaelmas and that if he'd thought about it he could just as well have gone that-a-way. So look out both sides and select the best spot for an emergency landing. This unwelcome event may never happen to you, but you'll land in a better field by being prepared.

He should have gone that-a-way.

## BRAKES, CROSSWINDS, AND HORSEPOWER

It's a hot day in a modest state located east of New Mexico and north of Old Mexico. They say it gets hot enough in summer to fry eggs on the runway, and whether this is proved or not, it does sound as if the runway were rather warm. It is. At this particular airport the altimeter reads 6,000 feet, although we're still on the ground. How long is the runway?

There are rumors to the effect that the runway is not as long as it looks, and on second thought we decide not to take off. There are a few vermilion-hued sites of interest across the border that would be safer, because our runway is about half as long as it looks!

Look at the Koch Chart in Fig. 2. This chart was formerly found on the back of aeronautical charts and is reproduced here for easy reference. Note the slanting line between the 6,000-foot elevation on the right and the 100-degree temperature on the left: it intersects the percentage scales at well over 200. Adding this amount means we'll need more than three times the length of runway at our elevation than we need at sea level.

This is because less-dense air—less dense because of heat and high elevation—lowers the efficiency of both engine and propeller, and we have fewer horses at our command. We take off slower and climb at a more shallow angle, and this means our take-off must be put off.

The safest procedure, if you don't have three times as much runway as you needed at sea level, is to wait until conditions are more favorable, like those at dawn when the air is cooler and denser, or at a time when there is a wind blowing—say about 20 mph. Take-offs into a 20-mph breeze are easy because the effective runway is greater: it has been increased by the distance from the point of roll to the point where the air speed reads 20 mph true (indicated air speed corrected for instrument error). What makes us still happier is that the *angle of climb* into a wind is steeper, although the *rate* of climb is unchanged. For example, in a wind velocity equal to air speed, the *angle* of climb would be straight up, although you don't go up any faster than before. Such angle of climb would permit one to clear skyscrapers with ample margin.

But suppose we have a lazy, zephyr-like breeze. Why not hold the brakes, apply full power, and release the brakes? This wouldn't help, because with a fixed-pitch propeller the advantage is slight. A propeller actually stalls in still air; the blades are similar to an airplane wing, which also is stalled in still air. Propellers do not develop full power until the relative airflow (which depends upon air speed and rpm's) reaches the speed for which the propeller was designed.

Then what about the flaps? As we'll see in the next chapter, flaps increase lift more than drag, up to approximately one-quarter flap, and will therefore lower the take-off speed and decrease the take-off run. They do not increase the *angle* of climb, which is always

## THE KOCH CHART FOR
## ALTITUDE AND TEMPERATURE EFFECTS

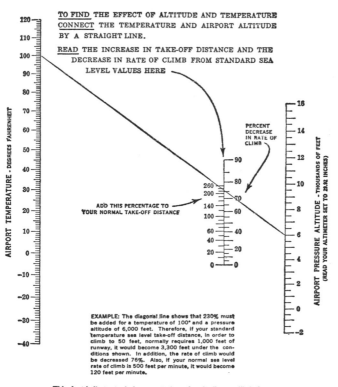

TO FIND THE EFFECT OF ALTITUDE AND TEMPERATURE CONNECT THE TEMPERATURE AND AIRPORT ALTITUDE BY A STRAIGHT LINE.

READ THE INCREASE IN TAKE-OFF DISTANCE AND THE DECREASE IN RATE OF CLIMB FROM STANDARD SEA LEVEL VALUES HERE

PERCENT DECREASE IN RATE OF CLIMB

ADD THIS PERCENTAGE TO YOUR NORMAL TAKE-OFF DISTANCE

AIRPORT TEMPERATURE - DEGREES FAHRENHEIT

AIRPORT PRESSURE ALTITUDE - THOUSANDS OF FEET (READ YOUR ALTIMETER SET TO 29.92 INCHES)

EXAMPLE: The diagonal line shows that 230% must be added for a temperature of 100° and a pressure altitude of 6,000 feet. Therefore, if your standard temperature sea level take-off distance, in order to climb to 50 feet, normally requires 1,000 feet of runway, it would become 3,300 feet under the conditions shown. In addition, the rate of climb would be decreased 76%. Also, if your normal sea level rate of climb is 500 feet per minute, it would become 120 feet per minute.

This chart indicates typical representative values for "personal" airplanes. For exact values consult your airplane flight manual.
The chart may be conservative for airplanes with supercharged engines.
Also remember that long grass, sand, mud or deep snow can easily double your take-off distance.

Fig. 2. The Koch Chart. At 6,000 feet, 100°F., you'll need 230 per cent *more* runway. Example: if you need 1,000 feet of runway at sea level, 3,300 feet will be needed. The rate of climb is 76 per cent less. Example: if rate of climb at sea level is 500 feet per minute, it becomes 120 fpm.

best with zero flaps, so the flaps may be raised one degree for each mile of air speed in excess of $S_2$ speed. The time to raise the flaps is discussed at greater length in Chapter 4.

Now suppose there are two runways at our high-altitude airport, and we are confronted with the decision of which one to use—the short runway into the wind or the longer runway crosswind. Let us imagine that the long runway lies more than 45 degrees to the wind, but the short one is right in the groove. Which shall we use?

Whenever wind is more than 45 degrees to a runway it becomes a crosswind, which is no help whatsoever; crosswind take-offs require more skill, such as using forward stick pressure to prevent the plane from skidding sideways during the run and damaging the landing gear. The grinds in crosswind take-offs are a necessity, not a pleasure.

The point is that the shorter runway is *effectively* longer because it lies into the wind. As mentioned above, hundreds of feet are required for the plane to accelerate to 20 mph, but as far as the plane is concerned the wings are flying at 20 mph when it is standing still in a 20-mile breeze. Therefore, the shorter runway may be the one to use. Airline pilots have tables for computing the best runway, but we Private Pilots must rely upon judgment, on-the-spot computations, and a large safety margin.

When we finally decide that all factors are favorable for take-off, we run up the engine, check the mags, and note that the rpm's are much less than they were at sea level. But before we cut the switches remember this: lower horsepower results from at least three factors—higher temperature and high elevation, both of which are accompanied by less-dense air, and the resultant rich mixture. Many pilots are convinced that because the Checkoff List says "Mixture rich for take-off" they are reading the Eleventh Commandment.

But the mixture is rich at high altitude, and the engine will develop more horsepower with a correct mixture. The stratagem of leaning the mixture will furnish many more horses to engine output; actually, many engines respond to a judicious leaning of the mixture control at altitudes as low as 4,000 feet.

This does not mean to take off or fly with a lean mixture: lean the mixture control until a rise in rpm's is obtained; if the rpm's rise, lean it out further until a drop in rpm's is obtained. This setting is excessively lean and it does indicate where the mixture control should *not* be set. Richen the mixture until the rpm's increase and then richen it considerably. (In flight, at cruise power, one would richen it only slightly to obtain the correct lean-mixture setting.) The engine will now develop full power without any risk of detonation or burned valves.

Now, ready for take-off, with mags checked, clearance from the tower if any, and having made our own visual check of the runways, let's use the knowledge we have assimilated. We use full recommended power, no more than one-quarter flaps, gentle stick and rudder, and flick an occasional glance at the airometer. The indicated take-off speed is the same as at sea level, so we do not pull the plane off at $S_1$ speed but continue on to $S_2$. At $S_2$ we get off the ground promptly, lower the nose, accelerate to climbing speed, and climb!

Then, with the gear coming up and the power reduced, we climb in a widening turn that takes us over the border, which from our altitude doesn't even look cherry pink. Nevertheless, we feel virtuous for having avoided it—but maybe we won't be able to take off next trip. We can always hope.

The co-pilot nudges us awake by pointing to the flaps. Are we high enough, or fast enough? Should we "milk" them up a degree at a time or shoot the works? This is a subject one shouldn't be flippant about, so let's devote a whole chapter to it.

# 4: DON'T BE FLIPPANT WITH FLAPS

IT'S two o'clock somewhere in the high elevations of the southwest, and the temperature is in the 90s. The heat boils upward in visible waves from the macadam runway as we start our take-off. Those tall trees at the other end of the runway shimmer in the heat like dancing girls from the *Folies Bergère*, but we don't wish to be introduced. Such things are beneath us, or should be, in a moment or two.

**The trees at the end of the runway shimmer like dancing girls.**

Halfway down the runway it's obvious that this take-off doesn't feel right. Either the plane is sluggish or the runway is too short; maybe the trees are too tall. As we get closer they stop shimmering, giving the impression that they don't like us. This is a decidedly mutual feeling, but it is too late to stop and it begins to appear that our flight will be a short one.

There isn't time to ask anyone what flaps are for, but if there were, the reply would probably contain one of those half-truths: "They are used in landings"—which would be something like saying that the landing gear is an attachment which is retracted after take-off. Flaps, like the landing gear, can be just as important in

34

the take-off as in the landing, as we now observe. Perhaps we should have studied the effect of temperature and altitude on take-off performance and have known more about the use of flaps.

But with those trees getting closer, being flippant about our flaps doesn't help. What we wish to know, and know quickly, is what to do with them? What setting is best? Should we use quarter, half, or full flap? And suppose that we do clear those trees: how much flap do we remove, some of the flap setting or all of it? Should we "milk" them up a degree at a time? What happens if the flaps are raised suddenly during a climb or a glide? Finally, what about landings? How should they be used during no-wind, high-wind, and crosswind landings?

Flaps, as everyone knows, are a device invented out of necessity. Pilots wanted slower landing speeds for their faster, cleaner aircraft, which touched down at higher speed than did planes with large wing area. But when the designers decreased wing area in order to decrease drag and attain higher cruising speeds, the new design provided less lift. This raised the stall speed and, of course, the landing speed.

Obviously, landing speeds couldn't be lowered by adding drag, because if only drag were added the plane would still stall—and land—at the same speed it did without drag. A device which contributes only drag—such as the parachute which is used after landing a military bomber—would simply require that more power or a steeper glide be used during the descent. The drag would help slow the plane after it landed but it couldn't lower the landing speed. What pilots really wanted was a device which would add more *lift*, thereby permitting a plane to land at a lower speed. Landing a plane at a lower speed is another way of saying that the stalling speed is lower.

Flaps did the trick because they provided both lift and drag. After flaps were added to the trailing edge of the wing, it was found that moving them downward from zero degrees (flush with the wing) provided a great amount of lift at about one-quarter (9°–16°) flap, and a huge amount of drag at full flap (45°). That is to say, the ratio of lift to drag (L/D) varied with the flap setting. This means that different techniques for flap operation are mandatory during take-offs, approaches, and landings.

Private Pilots are now flying planes equipped with flaps. Some planes have flaps that can be set at any desired angle, while others have flaps which can be set in only three positions: zero, one-quarter, or full. The principles of flap operation are the same for all planes, but the exact amount of flap to use is something best obtained from the manufacturer's flight manual which accompanies a particular airplane. For example, a certain design of plane requires one-quarter flap to be used during Maneuvering Speed,* in order that the plane may fly more stably. The reason for this is that lowering flaps to about 9°–16° (one-quarter setting) increases lift considerably with only a moderate amount of drag, whereas at higher flap settings the amount of drag is much higher in proportion to the lift.

On your next flight, find out what happens to plane performance by flying at less than $S_2$ speed and then lowering full flaps. Try to hold your altitude. Lift, of course, has increased, but drag has skyrocketed like inflation, and the engine labors mightily to pull the airplane across the sky. Next, apply full power and attempt to climb.

Any pilot who performs this experiment soon learns the reason why he should never repeat it during an approach or at low altitude. While waiting for the plane to climb he can sit lightly, squeeze, push on the rudders, and hope. After that fails he may rub his rabbit's foot, but that maneuver didn't help the rabbit and it won't help the pilot, because his airplane is flying at critical speed with excess drag. It will neither climb nor gain speed until the drag is reduced and there is more power available. Every horse is being used to overcome drag and none is left for lift.

The only way to reduce drag is to raise the flaps or lower the nose, and either or these maneuvers results in a sudden loss of altitude. The reason for this is that raising the flaps reduces lift, or lowering the nose (decreasing the angle of attack) results in less lift. Any loss of lift at critical configuration means that lift is less than the weight of the plane, resulting in loss of altitude. Therefore, in order to climb, it is first necessary to decrease drag by raising the flaps, which in turn diminishes lift and stalls the plane. Next, to recover from the stall, we put the nose down, but this also diminishes lift and we lose more altitude. In short, in order to climb

* Maneuvering Speed, Over-the-fence Speed, and Minimum Speed are explained in Chapter 5.

it is first necessary to lower the nose *and* raise the flaps, in order to reduce the drag which occurs at the high angle of attack and high flap setting. Any pilot who makes this test may be thankful he has a few thousand feet of air beneath him instead of a few thousand bristling trees.

Now back to our plane, which is rushing down the runway for a rendezvous with the trees. We reach down and do what we should have done prior to take-off: lower the flaps to one-quarter. Immediately they provide the additional lift that lowers the stalling speed and the take-off speed, enabling us to clear the trees. At least, we hope that we'll climb above them, but flap settings are critical because the rate of climb is less with flaps. We could still enter the forest ahead of us unexpectedly.

Glance at Fig. 3, on this page, which is the climb curve for a typical airplane at various speeds and flap settings. With zero flaps we have our greatest angle of climb, which is the line drawn from the origin (zero mph–zero rate of climb) to the point of tangency of the 0 degree flap curve. The angle is exaggerated because both coordinates are not at the same scale, but the exaggeration produces clarity. The greatest *angle* of climb occurs with no flaps, at a speed almost equal to $S_2$ speed and less than the best *rate*-of-climb speed.

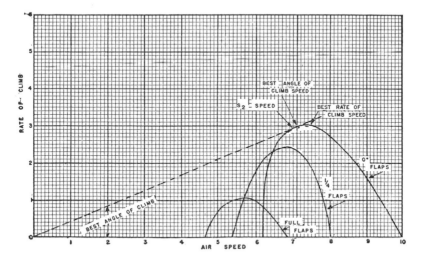

Fig. 3. Climb curves for a typical airplane at different speeds and flap settings.

Notice, too, that the rate of climb falls off rapidly at speeds either slower or faster than the best rate-of-climb speed.

Next, observe how low is the rate of climb with full flaps, and that $S_2$ and best climb speed are also lower. If this is so, why use flaps during take-off? The reason is that the plane leaves the ground sooner, it begins to climb sooner, and can clear obstacles better. It is entirely possible that by using zero flaps or by lowering the flaps too late during take-off, we'll not climb above the trees! And as for using full flaps, we might zoom over the trees, at which point we'd be in bad shape because we'd have to lose altitude before we could climb.

So, as we roar down the runway, rapidly evaluating the situation, we decide to lower one-quarter flaps immediately and resolve that when flaps are needed hereafter, we'll use them prior to take-off.

## RAISING THE FLAPS: QUICKLY OR SLOWLY?

But we've got one-quarter flaps that must be raised. This is a good time to clear up the old wives' tale which says we must always raise flaps slowly. There is a convenient rule for raising flaps. It is simply this:

*Raise flaps 1 degree for every mile in excess of $S_2$ speed.*

For example, if our plane stalls at 50 mph, don't raise the flaps at $S_1$ speed, which as we know is stall speed plus 15 per cent or 58 mph; wait until $S_2$ speed (stall speed plus 30 per cent or 65 mph) is reached. At 63–65 mph raise the flaps 2 degrees, at 67 mph 4 degrees, and so on, until at 75 mph all flap will have been removed. At 75 mph (stalling speed plus 50 per cent) it is mandatory that the flaps be raised because flaps are not designed or stressed for the loads imposed at higher speeds reached later.

This means that we may raise the flaps suddenly and be safe, providing that we have air speed. True, flaps must be raised a degree at a time with $S_2$ speed, a technique referred to as "milking" the flaps up. But at speeds in excess of $S_2$ (such as the Maneuvering Speed of 80 mph discussed in Chapter 5) there is so much lift available that the flaps can be raised immediately without fear of stalling or losing altitude. The pilot need only raise the nose slightly to provide the lift he lost when the flaps came up.

For instance, suppose you are holding your position in a holding pattern while waiting your turn to make an instrument approach at a busy airport. This means that you are flying at Maneuvering Speed, a safe, controllable, and economical speed which is about 60 per cent higher than stall speed, and that you are using a quarter flap to stabilize the airplane. The use of flaps depends upon the plane, however, and in a certain popular twin-engined craft, which is not too directionally stable at cruising speeds, the use of flaps at Maneuvering Speed does not increase stability; on the other hand, in some transport-category airplanes, one-quarter flaps adds much to the ease of slow flight, and if one is flying on instruments he has a marked desire for stability.

As we hold position in the holding pattern, Approach Control radios instructions to fly to the alternate airport. Do we milk the flaps? We do not. We want to be up and away promptly, so we "dump" the flaps, apply power, and hardly realize that we've raised the nose slightly, thereby providing lift to replace the lift we lost when the flaps went up. The rule of *always* raising the flaps slowly may be good policy for the novice, but expert pilots know their planes and fly accordingly.

## LANDING—WITH OR WITHOUT FLAP?

We're in the air, we've got the flaps up, and before long our imaginary flight will be at its destination. If we're on instruments we'll probably have to hold in a holding pattern and wait our turn to land. Shall we use flaps as we hold? What about flaps during the landing? What must we know about flap operation that will make it possible for us to make a missed approach? Or suppose that a strong wind is blowing across the runway: how much flap shall we use for the landing?

Glance at Fig. 4, which is a typical curve of the power required at various flap settings for any airplane. When no flaps are used, there is plenty of power left over for climbing, provided we climb at a certain speed. This speed is slightly faster than $S_2$ speed; at speeds less than $S_2$, the power required goes up rapidly. Next, look at the curve for quarter-flaps. Here we're using most of the power just to overcome drag, with very little left over to enable us to climb. Finally, look at the curve for full flaps and the sad story it tells: $S_2$ speed is lower, the best rate-of-climb speed is lower, and *we're using almost all of the power available to overcome drag!* With either decrease or increase of air speed we use all the power available.

This proves to us that drag costs money, and that with *any* degree of flap setting the power must be increased if we want to maintain the same speed we had without flaps. Therefore, we use flaps in the holding pattern only if their use increases the stability of the plane. Pilots who aren't flying on a government subsidy don't

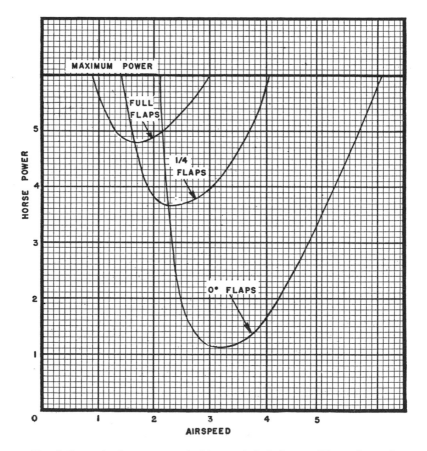

Fig. 4. Curves showing power required in a typical airplane at different flap settings.

churn for an hour with both gear and flaps down if this procedure can be avoided.

When we're cleared to land, we use one-quarter flaps during the approach in order to make the precision landing described in Chapter 6. We are careful not to decrease the air speed below $S_2$ at any time, because at less than this speed every bit of power will be needed merely to fly the plane! And we never lower full flaps until we cross the "fence," or airport boundary, at which time landing is a certainty.

Suppose that you do lower full flaps, but you have not permitted the speed to decrease below $S_2$. Then use full power and milk the flaps up one degree for every mile per hour in excess of $S_2$; this means that you can't climb immediately but will have to continue across the airport until the air speed increases. For this reason we never lower full flaps on the approach unless we need the drag provided by full flaps, which in turn enables us to descend at a steeper angle. Adding full flaps can prevent overshooting, but it is far better to reduce power during the approach than to be caught with your flaps down.

But wind velocities aren't always moderate and they aren't always "in the groove," as winds "down the runway" are called. Suppose we have to land in high, gusty winds. That's what happened to Pilot Z, who once landed his plane during such conditions with his flaps down. After the wheels were on the runway he relaxed, never realizing that a plane is not landed until the switches are cut. Because he still had air speed and because full flaps lowered the

He made a dis-gusting landing.

take-off speed, a small gust of wind was all that he needed to begin flying again. The additional lift was enough to raise him 10 feet from the runway, and at that point he ran out of gust, a condition aptly described as dis-gusted. He would have dropped back on the runway, had not an alert co-pilot opened the throttles and saved both the day and the landing gear.

A handy rule for flap operation in high winds or gusty winds is this: in wind velocities that are higher than half the stalling speed, decrease the flap setting proportionately. Example: wind velocity 20 mph, stall speed 50 mph, flap setting 9 degrees or less. Many pilots prefer to use zero flap when wind velocity is half the stall speed; after all, a plane landing at 50 mph in a 25-mph wind touches the runway at 25 mph. Why use flap?

The only constant characteristic of wind is its inconstancy, and sooner or later the wind will not be down the groove but blowing from one side. In crosswinds we certainly want minimum landing speed, high stability, and the least chance of having our windward wing lifted; we also want as much power available as possible. Therefore, one-quarter flap, certainly not full flap, will give us the best landing configuration.

As soon as the wheels are on the ground, "dump" the flaps. This term is descriptive but not accurate, because pilots have been heard using it to mean "lower" the flaps. Let us then *raise* the flaps in gusty or crosswinds as soon as the wheels touch down. To wait until it's time to taxi doesn't help slow the plane very much, and flaps do constitute a hazard in gusts. Besides, it is surprising how much a small pebble costs when it goes through a flap.

## QUESTIONS AND ANSWERS DEPARTMENT

1. If the plane isn't going to clear obstacles, why not increase the flap setting to more than one-quarter? The answer is that one may increase the setting, provided he has the air speed to climb. However, because the rate of climb and the angle of climb are reduced at higher flap settings because of added drag, and because so much of the runway has been used by the time the pilot thinks of adding more flap, he will probably not clear the obstacles. A better solution is to think of the flaps *before* taking off and to set them accordingly.

2. If both the rate of climb and the angle of climb are reduced

by flaps, why use them? The answer is that the use of flaps reduces $S_1$, $S_2$, stalling, and take-off speeds. In Fig. 3, which shows typical curves for any airplane, the rate of climb for zero flaps is three units per minute, whereas with a quarter or more flaps it is less. The angle of climb is a factor of the rate of climb divided by the air speed, and may be seen from the dotted line. (The exact angle is not shown because the rate of climb is in fpm, while speed is in mph.) These dotted lines run from zero to a point of tangency of the curve and show that the greatest *angle* of climb for any given setting is obtained at a speed slightly less than that for the best *rate* of climb. Which, freely translated, means that if the pilot takes off with a shorter run he can fly over obstacles easier, despite the fact that he is climbing more slowly and at a shallower angle.

3. Why can't one climb at slow speed with full flaps? Again the answer lies in Fig. 4, which shows typical power available and power-required curves for any airplane. The power available is a straight line going across the top of the page—6 units of power. Notice that the use of any flap requires more power, speed for speed, than no flaps. If the pilot takes off with quarter-flaps and does not get $S_2$ speed, all the king's horses won't enable the airplane to climb, because every horse is being used just to make the plane fly. The point at which the flap curve crosses the power-available line is the point where there are no horses left over, at either minimum or maximum speeds, so the airplane can't climb.

4. If one-quarter flaps, when needed, make the take-off safer why won't half or full flaps be even more safe? The answer is that more flaps will provide a quicker take-off but that both the angle and rate of climb will be less. Inasmuch as the actual climb commences when $S_2$ speed is reached, those trees could be protruding into the climb path which, as said before, has a smaller angle than would be the case had the pilot used less flap.

5. Why not get into the air as soon as possible and start climbing? In no instance is this good procedure. Stay on the ground at $S_1$ speed, get into the air precisely at $S_2$ speed, then accelerate to best climbing speed, which is slightly higher than $S_2$ speed.

6. What happens if the flaps are raised immediately after $S_2$ speed is reached? This situation is one in which the flaps *must* be raised gradually. Unless the pilot has accelerated to well above $S_2$, he can-

not climb after raising the flaps and he may also stall. Don't forget that there are as many $S_2$ speeds as there are flap settings, and that $S_2$ with a quarter-flap at normal loads will be very close to stalling speed with flaps up. Raising the flaps at $S_2$ will result in a total loss of climb and will place the airplane in a position from which the loss of additional air speed will stall the wing. If it should become necessary to raise the flaps quickly, *accelerate first* and then raise the flaps one degree for every mph over the $S_2$ speed without flaps.

7. Why can't one use more flaps during the glide in order to rise above the boundary obstacles he'd otherwise hit? This question presupposes that the pilot is making a forced landing without power available, in which case the answer is that some pilots have tried it, but the technique requires split-second precision. When flaps are added during the glide, the sudden increase of lift will balloon the plane over the obstacles, but the added drag requires that the nose be put down as soon as the obstacles are passed. (Nothing but an updraft will "stretch" a glide, because the plane lands shorter and slower with flaps.) The landing technique is tricky, and unless the pilot is quite alert he is liable to drop the plane in hard after he zooms over the obstacle.

8. Is the flap setting as critical in lightplanes as in airliners? No. Airline pilots have tables which show the amount of flap to use for certain runways at given wind velocities. If no flaps were used, the take-off run would be so long that obstacles might not be cleared, especially if an engine failed at $V_2$ speed. If too much flap were used, the plane would leave the ground sooner but the rate of climb and the angle of climb would be reduced. Should an engine fail with excessive flaps, the plane might not clear obstacles. Even at large airports, airliners use flaps to facilitate take-offs and to save rubber, which in airline operation is no small matter.

Although flap setting is not as critical for lightplanes as it is for airliners, the knowledge of how to use flaps is one of those finer points that the amateur pilot often doesn't have, but which the expert pilot has at his fingertips. He also knows how fast to glide during the approach, and that means he is flying at a maneuverable speed, a speed from which his missed approach procedure is easy. What is this Maneuvering Speed?

Let's see what Chapter 5 has to say about it.

# 5: ONE–TWO–THREE–GLIDE

PILOT Q was on final approach, "gear-down and cleared to land." His new plane had performed beautifully; it was fast, clean, and responded quickly to the controls. It also had a high stalling speed, so Pilot Q made his approach with plenty of speed. What if he did soar over the fence tail-high? He was flying fast enough to be in no danger of stalling or dropping in. He felt kindly toward his new plane, which glistened in the sun with the magnificent splendor of a big bird that didn't wish to land. This comparison is quite apropos—neither did the plane.

Even the weather seemed wonderful. The sun was shining, the sky was blue, and the wind sock was limp. With a limp sock—and no wind—the plane would touch down at a ground speed equal to the stalling speed; it wouldn't land, to be quite accurate, *until* it had stalling speed. When it soared across the fence, Pilot Q cut his throttle and eased back on the stick, only to zoom gracefully ten feet in the air and then back to the runway in a series of tantalizing, teasing near-misses. No power on earth could force that plane to land until it was ready to. This characteristic of planes is another reason why they are referred to in the feminine gender.

By the time he was halfway down the runway, Pilot Q had a soliloquy: To land, or not to land, that was the question. Inasmuch as he didn't seem to know just when the plane might be willing to land, a more practical question was whether to go around and lose face or to pay a future repair bill?

But Pilot Q was smart enough to go around, as all smart pilots do when in doubt, wondering what he had done wrong. Perhaps he hadn't remembered his checkout instructions. What had the check pilot told him—was it 80 mph in the glide and 70 mph over the fence? In these days of 2-mile runways, Pilot Q believed that it

didn't make much difference if he used one speed or another, but on
this occasion the runway didn't extend 2 miles. He knew, too, that
flying is so safe and so simple that an airplane isn't going to
get a pilot into trouble if he knows the barest rudiments of safe
flying. But a variation of 10 mph is often the margin between a dub
and an expert, and it does makes a lot of difference in the floating
characteristics of our aerodynamically clean airplanes.

For Pilot Q, the difference was enough to make it impossible to
land in a short field despite the fact that he was using flaps. He
didn't know that there is a definite gliding speed to use, or that there

Nothing can make her land until she's ready to.

is a simple rule for finding the correct glide speed of any airplane.
One-two-three—*glide!* could mean a new dance-step instead of the
three basic speeds an expert pilot uses during an approach.

In short, if one wishes to glide accurately he must know *how fast
to glide*. To be sure, we Private Pilots don't have instruments that are
within airline tolerances, and often the indicated speeds are so inaccurate that we don't trust them. We aren't expected, either, to fly
with our eyes glued on the airspeed indicator because we're also expected to feel what the airplane is doing. Again, the air-speedometer
often indicates different speeds in planes of the same make for reasons
of instrument error, poor calibration, dirt or water in the Pitot tubes,

or plane old age. How much should we trust that instrument, the awkward-named "air-speed indicator?"

There is a handy rule which makes it quite easy for average pilots to learn how fast to fly during approaches. It doesn't require an indicator that is accurately calibrated, either—just one that is in good working condition. Obviously one can't rely upon an erratic instrument, but once we ascertain that the air-speedometer is reliable, we should use it.

"But," Pilot Q might object, "how do I find out how my air-speed indicator works? I know it's not accurate because my plane is supposed to stall at 50 mph, whereas the indicated speed in a stall is 55 mph!"

That is exactly the way to find out—stall your plane. The stall speed is the most important to know, because other speeds are computed in terms of the stall. Before we test the instrument at stall speeds, remember that it rarely has a straight-line calibration curve, and that stall speed is the only speed you're calibrating. For example, you may find that the plane stalls at an indicated speed that is 10 mph faster than your handbook says stalling speed should be. This does not mean that you should add 10 mph to every indicated air speed. It is possible that the indicated air speed will be 10 miles fast at 50 mph, exactly correct at 90 mph, and several miles slow at 120 mph. In order to calibrate an instrument over the entire range, it would be necessary to lower a precision indicator or "bomb" below the airplane, fly at various speeds, and plot a calibration curve; this method is both expensive and difficult.

But stalling the plane is easy. Begin by climbing to a "safe" altitude, closing the throttle, and entering a shallow glide. Watch your indicator for slow, steady movement: if it doesn't jump or act erratically it is probably satisfactory for stall-speed indications.

Begin by easing the nose up to a three-point attitude and holding the nose there until the plane stalls. *Don't enter the stall abruptly.* Feel the stall warning as speed diminishes through the burble point, and keep the stick or wheel coming back. At the instant the elevator hits the "stop," note the air speed. Let's say that the indicator is accurate and reads 50 mph: this is where the red line, shown in Fig. 1, should be painted on the indicator. Repeat the test three times to confirm the accuracy and consistency of the instrument, then jot the figure down for future reference and for the red line you're going to paint.

You now know what the instrument reads or *indicates* when the plane is stalled. If it reads 50 mph at 3,000 feet when the wing stalls, it will read 50 mph at 3 feet when the wing stalls, because there are the same number of slugs of air passing over the wings as are finding their way into the air-speed Pitot tube. The speed of 50 mph is the one to use in the computations we're going to make for glide speeds.

Climb back to your safe altitude and run a few more tests in other configurations, that is, tests with power on, gear down, and flaps at one quarter. Because most pilots make approaches with this configuration, and because most take-offs are made with the gear down, one should know this stall speed. Use a configuration of full, cruising, and approach power: observe that the stall speed is considerably less with power and flaps than it was when the stall was executed in a "clean" configuration. Make a notation of these speeds because you're going to use and need them in work described in later chapters. To be sure, the figures will change slightly with weight (loading), and the true air speed will vary with both altitude and temperature. But the reading obtained at present loading and power settings will be your guide to what you must use later, and if you carry the same load at 10,000 feet as you do now, the indicator will indicate the same stall speed as it does now.

Thus, your "clean" stall speed is on the safe side of the stall. The same may be said for multi-engine pilots, who cannot fully stall their planes because manufacturers of large aircraft discourage full stalls. For these pilots, a stall to the burble point will be satisfactory because the indicated stalling speed at the burble point is only a few mph higher than it is for the full stall, and it's safe flying we're interested in, not 1-mile-per-hour accuracy. If the speeds are slightly on the fast side, they won't nullify the computations we're about to make.

## EFFECT OF LOAD ON STALL SPEED

Suppose that our plane is lightly loaded. How much difference will we find in the stalling speed when the plane is loaded to capacity with fuel, passengers, and baggage? Usually such loads don't affect lightplanes as much as they affect airliners, in which fuel and passengers constitute a larger proportion of the weight. Airliners are compelled to dump fuel before landing if the gross weight exceeds limits. But adding weight, be it passengers or ice, raises the stalling speed of any plane.

Suppose we add 540 pounds to a lightplane. What should we know about the effect of such weight on stalling speed? Take our lightplane that stalls at 50 mph indicated, and which weighed 1,800 pounds the first time we stalled it. The gross weight becomes 2,340 pounds, and the load factor is:

$$\frac{(\text{New weight})}{(\text{Old weight})} = \frac{2{,}340}{1{,}800} = 1.3$$

$$\text{Stall speed}_1 \times \sqrt{\text{load factor}} = \text{stall speed}_2$$

$$50 \text{ mph} \times \sqrt{1.3} = 57 \text{ mph, the new stall speed}$$

This is enough difference to make a pilot feel uncomfortable if he comes over the fence at slow speed. It is the reason for making approaches faster during icing conditions, as discussed in Chapter 12, and it explains why one must never consider an easy rule as the very last word. Rules are guides to safe flying, not commandments.

But there are easy rules, nevertheless, that we should know about glides. How can we determine, easily and quickly, safe speeds for the traffic pattern, our approach, and the final glide?

## HOW FAST TO GLIDE

Many pilots find any arithmetical computation so boring that they won't be bothered with it, asking, "Why not use a normal glide and be done with it?" But just what is a "normal" glide? There are so many definitions of the so-called normal glide that no two pilots agree as to what it is, and the term is used to describe widely different speeds that vary from the best-distance glide to the accuracy- or spot-landing glide.

*There is no single speed that can be used for different kinds of glides!* The reason is that plane performance varies at each speed, but despite this we need to be familiar with at least three: Maneuvering Speed, Over-the-fence Speed, and a Minimum Speed that we heartily respect. These speeds can be found with the aid of a rule so easy that it can be used in strange airplanes without pencil and paper. It is accurate for lightplanes, as it is reasonably close to computed speeds. The calculation can be made in flight, as soon as one has stalled his plane as described above, and accurate enough to make precision flying possible for us Private Pilots.

The three basic speeds that every pilot should know are:

*1. Maneuvering Speed.* This is the speed we'll use in traffic patterns, in holding patterns, and during approaches and let-downs. "Maneuvering" is the term often used to describe the speed at which abrupt movement of controls will not cause structural failure, but because the term is so descriptive we'll use it to describe the lowest speed at which we have maximum safety and controllability. It has been called the "downwind" speed used in airport traffic patterns, and it approximates very closely the so-called "normal glide" speed. It is the speed slightly beyond the "hump" of the curve plotted in Fig. 3 and therefore not the most efficient speed. Consequently, an airplane does not glide as far as it does at a certain slower speed to be described below.

But Maneuvering Speed is convenient for holdings and approaches because it's a conservatively safe speed, at which turns may be made and at which pilot error is not followed by a drastic conclusion. It is *not* the best speed to use for maximum-distance glides or the best rate of climb.

The rule is simple:

*Multiply the stalling speed by 60 per cent and add the product to the stalling speed.*

For example, if our lightplane stalls at 50 mph, we find that .60 × 50 = 30, which added to 50 gives us a Maneuvering Speed of 80 mph. Or, use 6 as the multiplier and omit 0 (6 × 5 = 30,) and you have an easy rule that can be used during flight, the time when easy computation is most needed. This is a very approximate rule, but it is as accurate as the average pilot, who cannot hold a glide within 1 or 2 mph. This speed is actually a bit conservative, or fast, and we may therefore use a slightly slower speed if we wish. We can use the same figure with power off or power on.

In actual practice, the airline pilots add another speed here, called the Approach Speed, but the Private Pilot needs only a single Maneuvering Speed. Using this until he's almost at the fence or boundary of the airport, he's acquired a more precise technique, as well as a safer one. The Maneuvering Speed as defined here may be slightly fast, but we know it is not so fast that we cannot slow it down to our next speed, which is:

2. *Over-the-fence Speed.* This is just what the term indicates— speed used when the plane passes over the airport boundary—although this presupposes that the boundary is a good distance from the runway, and that we intend to land exactly on the end of the runway. Over-the-fence Speed is actually attained far enough from touchdown so that we have a minimum speed during the last few hundred yards of the approach. The act of obtaining Over-the-fence Speed has often been referred to as "breaking the glide," which is not an accurate or correct term. Some pilots, mostly beginners, use this speed in making or "shooting" precision landings, but it is not one to be used for accuracy. On graphs it is at the very peak of the lift curve, which means it is the maximum distance glide.

Here's the rule:

*Multiply the stall speed by 40 per cent and add the product to the stall speed.*

For example, our lightplane stalls at 50 mph; we find that 50 mph × .40 is 20, which added to 50 gives us 70 mph. Here we have a speed that won't permit us to float very far and yet won't drop us in for a hard landing. It's quite conservative, so much on the fast side that some pilots may say it is for beginners only. But it is precisely what it is called, the safe, accurate speed to use over the fence. Because it is admittedly a bit fast, it may be reduced a few miles per hour, as will be described in the chapter on precision landings.

3. *Never-subceed Speed.* For the pilot who may be interested in flying at the very lowest speed compatible with safety—the speed below which he is liable to stall, land hard, or be vulnerable to sudden gusts of wind—this speed should suffice.

"Subceed" is not to be found in any dictionary; the antonym for "exceed" is nonexistent, and "subceed" is as good a word as any for what is meant by our minimum speed, the speed that a particular airplane must always be flown higher than. The worse that sounds, the truer it becomes: *Never fly slower than this speed.*

It is the speed required to be demonstrated in flight tests and which is called "Minimum Control Speed," referred to technically as $V_{mc}$. It is important because one must be able to recognize this speed instantly and know how to recover from it with the least possible loss of altitude. Some pilots call it by a less flattering term, because flight maneuvers attempted at this speed often are followed by undesirable results. We prefer to call it by a more ominous term: "Never-subceed" Speed.

Finding the figure for the Never-subceed Speed is easy:

*Multiply the stalling speed by 20 per cent and add the product to the stalling speed.*

In our lightplane which stalls at 50 mph, we find that .20 $\times$ 50 = 10, and that 50 + 10 = 60 mph. This is the speed we must always *exceed,* the only exception being the use of it after an engine failure, in making a spot landing. There is positively no "floating" effect at this velocity, and it therefore insures landing accuracy. How to use it is described in Chapter 6.

It has also been used by expert pilots in shooting spot landings for prizes, a contest which has practically disappeared. The winner of the contest was often the pilot who landed within a few inches of the spot, and the reason old-timers used this speed was that the sinking speed was high and the floating effect nil, making it possible to land wherever they chose to land. In fact, the floating effect was so nil that sometimes nil could be used to describe the airplane after the maneuver had been tried by less competent pilots.

It is, in short, for the practiced, veteran pilot who can hold minimum speeds accurately, who knows he can't turn at this speed and that he must react during the landing with split-second precision. It is not to be used in gusts, high winds, crosswinds, or take-offs; such a speed at full flaps would be disastrous because it is approximately $S_1$ speed, as readers of Chapter 3 will remember.

## HOW TO USE THEM

Once you know what one-two-three—*glide!* means, use the three speeds in every approach. "Ah," someone says, "but what about me? My plane stalls at 50 mph true but my air-speed indicator reads 65!" If you encounter errors like this, have the indicator repaired, clean out the Pitot tubes, see that they are located correctly, and recalibrate the instrument for stall speed. There is no method by which a precision approach can be made other than the method of knowing the three speeds, and it is far better to have an instrument correct at stalling speed than at cruising speed. Cruising speed may be estimated or computed by flying over a measured mile at cruising power and checking the speed. This speed will be your true calibrated cruising speed at that power setting.

But the stall speed and the computations are essential for all low-altitude flying, and every approach should be a precision approach, just as though someone had painted a large X on the runway. Let's see if X marks the spot you just landed on or just missed, in the next chapter.

*Note:* Transport Category aircraft use 1.3 (Stalling Speed times 1.3) for Over-the-Fence Speed. This is considered slightly slow for the Private Pilot, hence 1.4 is recommended in the text. A rule of thumb is that for each 5 knots of speed in excess of 1.3, the airplane is the equivalent of 100 feet higher at the fence position.

# 6: X MARKS THE SPOT

PILOT G was a remarkably good pilot. He knew how to stay on his course, keep the ball centered during turns, and he could be over a check point within 30 seconds of his ETA. He was alert, observant, and his reactions were fast. He should have had an enviable reputation as a competent pilot.

This was not the case. Pilot G had never bothered to make a precision approach, and his engine intermittently roared and popped as he added throttle or removed it on the approach leg. His sloppy approaches, always followed by an oil-can (three-in-one) landing, amused the crowd and terrified his passengers. His bad landings were his reputation.

He had a reputation for making oil-can (three-in-one) landings.

As was observed in Chapter 3, a pilot can break every rule known to flying and yet have an excellent reputation, because it's a greased-on landing that makes the passengers nod with satisfaction, and because brother pilots don't know how other pilots fly unless they fly with each other. Therefore, good landings mean much to everyone.

But smooth landings are easier to achieve if one knows how to make a precision approach. Perhaps it was no fault of Pilot G that he did not make his approaches as if a large X marked the spot where he was to land his plane, or for not attempting a technique he had never heard of. A landing, in the opinion of Pilot G, was merely a maneuver made at the termination of a flight; landings could be made at Point X, Y, or Z. What difference did it make *where* the plane landed?

It seems ironic to old-timers that today, when the true spot landing has become almost obsolete, precision landings are more important than ever before. For example, a certain jet bomber, which is so clean and so fast that a few mph in excess of approach speed cause it to land "long," must use a precision approach. Any speed less than approach speed brings the wing close to stalling, and any speed higher than approach speed causes excess momentum.

"So what?" asks Pilot G. "I'm not a jet bomber pilot, and the runways I use are long enough for my overshoots. Besides, it's actual flying that counts. And as far as my landings are concerned, I merely have a little trouble finding the ground, but that can be eliminated by landing practice—I hope." The answer is that Pilot G did not have either the correct approach to the field or the right approach to the problem. Good landings are easier when they follow a controlled, precision approach, because with controlled speeds there are fewer errors to correct or remedial techniques to consider. If the pilot knows he's going to land where he wants to and when he wants to, he can devote more of his attention to the actual landing.

This makes a precision approach a necessity, and precision approaches involve speeds. Which of the three speeds discussed in Chapter 5 shall we use?

## WHICH SPEED TO USE?

Suppose that we unwillingly participate in the declining statistics of engine failures, that one-time bugaboo of pilots. To be sure, engines are so reliable that pilots seldom practice power-off approaches, but engines do fail (even on airliners), and any pilot who doesn't know what to do is certainly no expert.

Added to this, spot-landing technique is similar to that used for precision approaches, which in turn make for better landings.

Finally, there are a few easy rules which make precision flying easier. An expert pilot doesn't fly solely by thumb rules, but he finds that rules—like thumbs—are mighty handy.

So here we are at 3,000 feet in one of those uncomfortable silences. The first problem is how to get somewhere. This requires that we immediately assume the correct angle of glide (air speed), or we'll be in trouble before we get anywhere.

"How to get somewhere" means correct, accurate air speed. Most pilots agree that success in the emergency or "spot" landing depends upon two factors, air speed and pattern. Of these, correct air speed is the most important part of the problem because it regulates the angle of glide and, therefore, how far one can glide.

We want a speed which will conserve altitude and enable us to glide as far as possible. After we have glided to a position above Point X, we need another glide, a nonfloat, rapid-sinking glide from which we can land on X without excess float. What are these speeds? The answer tumbles out glibly from almost any pilot, "The normal glide." But what is the "normal glide"? Again the reply sounds as if by rote. "The normal glide is one which takes an airplane the farthest distance in still air." This is not too enlightening, because we still don't know exactly what air speed gives us the so-called "normal glide."

As readers of the previous chapters have noted, there are three speeds to use: Maneuvering Speed, Over-the-fence Speed, and the "Never-subceed" (or absolute minimum) Speed. They are 60, 40, and 20 per cent higher, respectively, than the stall speed. One of them is approximately the maximum-distance gliding speed.

If any skeptical pilot will consult a lift curve, he will find that the maximum distance a plane can glide occurs at the smallest gliding angle (i.e., the shallowest angle measured from zero, or horizontal), and that this angle occurs at a certain speed on the lift curve. When the nose is pushed down to a steeper angle, less horizontal distance is covered. If the nose is pulled up, the plane loses speed and descends faster than it does at the correct speed. The correct speed, and the best angle, are found on the curve at a point where the speed is about 40 per cent higher than stall speed, our Over-the-fence Speed. In the case of a lightplane stalling at 50 mph, this speed would be a maximum of 70 mph.

The first thing to do, therefore, is to put the nose into the familiar position which we know will obtain Over-the-fence Speed—70 mph. The celerity with which we assume this angle depends upon whether we're cruising or climbing; from cruise speed we act slowly, from a climb we must act quickly. We know we needn't push the nose down as far as is needed to obtain Maneuvering Speed, which is close to the average description of "normal glide," because the curve proved that if we push the nose down that far and glide at 80 mph, we glide less distance. The reason for this is that drag increases as the square of the speed, and consequently we'll glide 7 per cent shorter by gliding faster. We also know that by not putting the nose down far enough, and thereby using Minimum Speed of 60 mph, we will likewise increase drag. This is because the angle of attack is greater at 60 mph than it is at 70 mph. We'll glide 9 per cent shorter by gliding too slowly.

If Over-the-fence Speed is so good for spot landings, why not use it during normal approaches? The answer is that in normal approaches we use power and do not need to glide 7 per cent farther; that at Over-the-fence Speed we do not have a margin of safety, and the penalty for making steep turns or failing to hold the air speed accurately is more drastic at the slower speed; that we must maneuver easily and gently at Over-the-fence Speed because stalling speed increases as the square root of the load factor—a very good reason why many pilots stall during gliding turns at too-slow speeds. But Over-the-fence Speed is best for long-distance glides, and it does not have a built-in floating effect that causes the plane to balloon when the stick is pulled back. The rate of descent is rapid and constant, and provides the pilot with knowledge of where he's going to land.

## SELECTING THE FIELD

If the first business at hand is how to get there, the next problem is where to go. Only experience will tell a pilot how to select a level, large, clear area for the landing, which must be within gliding distance. It should provide space into the wind and should be near habitation, roads, and assistance. This is like asking for pie à la mode with a cherry on top; whether the field does or does not meet our requirements, we'll take what's available and rejoice if it's suitable. Most certainly, we won't pass up a poor spot near at hand for a distant field that looks better. We can glide almost 5 miles from 3,000 feet, but we can't *maneuver* during the descent. Also, we don't know exactly how far we can glide because, although the altimeter reads 3,000 feet, we may not be that far from the ground. Furthermore, we never know if we can reach a far field, since we never know exactly how strong the wind is blowing. What we want is a sure thing: a field near at hand which we can reach and still have a minimum of 800 feet of estimated altitude, not 800 feet indicated at a field having an elevation of 600 feet.

Once in position over the field, we're ready to maneuver, which is called flying a "pattern." The word "pattern" is nothing more than a word: we'll fly *any* pattern that will enable us to get into the field safely. Patterns, if used incorrectly, are like the successful operation that killed the patient: no pattern is good unless it helps us gain the field. In an actual emergency we'll use any safe method; in flight tests a pattern may prove we know what we're doing, but for us the patient comes first.

In practicing this maneuver, remember that while practice is excellent, good pilots avoid flying too low at those green pastures which benefit the soul and are hard on airplanes. *Never* descend lower than 150 feet, because if it isn't obvious at that altitude whether the simulated emergency has been handled successfully or not, nothing is proved by going lower. Pilots with limited experience are inclined to descend lower than is prudent in order to prove that they could have made the field, all the while gliding more slowly in an effort to stretch the glide. At the last moment, and with a cold engine, they try to climb out of the pasture, and at that point the emergency becomes real.

## THE FINAL APPROACH

We've selected our field and are over it at an altitude we estimate to be less than 1,000 feet and more than 800 feet. Arrival at Point X now depends upon our choice of air speed and, to a lesser degree, upon pattern. Pattern, or how we maneuver, is something used to dissipate altitude in order that we may arrive at a position over the fence at minimum altitude. At that point we must also have minimum speed in order to land, so air speed, and holding it accurately, turn out to be 70 to 80 per cent of the solution of the problem. To be sure, judgment is the over-all factor, but good judgment is essential to all phases of flying. We must judge our pattern correctly, but this is impossible without a correct, constant air speed. Without knowledge of how a varying air speed affects accuracy landings, we'll find ourselves at Point Z instead of Point X.

What speed shall we use for final approach? If we select Maneuvering Speed, we'll have a glide from which it will be impossible to land without "floating" a few hundred yards. True, we'll have adequate safety during steep turns, gusts, and down-drafts, but this advantage is lost because of our confusion in not knowing where Maneuvering Speed will take us. At this speed we gain altitude rapidly when the nose is raised, so much so that we erroneously believe we're first overshooting and then undershooting.

The maximum-glide, or Over-the-fence Speed will take us farther, but some of the floating effect is still there. The plane is simply not ready to land at this speed, and the rate of descent (sinking speed) is not as constant as we'd like it to be. It is excellent for the amateur pilot who cannot maintain an accurate speed, and it is not close enough to stalling to preclude steep turns should they be necessary.

Finally, if we select the "Never-subceed" Speed we'll be at the absolute limit of adequate control, a speed at which any error of technique, or a sudden down-draft, will put the flight into a statistical report. Minimum speed will give us a high, constant rate of descent, but at the risk of safety—we'll not be able to turn steeply or to "play the glide," which is important in spot landings.

What we want is something between Over-the-fence Speed and the minimum glide, a speed that is slightly less than Over-the-fence. For a lightplane that stalls at 50 mph (flaps up), we'll use a glide speed of about 65 mph for an actual emergency landing. The benefits of this speed and how it enables us to play the glide will be seen shortly.

From our altitude of 1,000 feet, we know we can land somewhere in the field, but we wish to land at the near end. We shall therefore have to descend to a position downwind from the near end and be there at an altitude which is more than sufficient to permit a glide into the field.

*Disregard conventional patterns.* "Key positions" and patterns are good for flight tests, not for necks. To preserve our necks, we'll always stay close to the field so that a turn at any time will get us into the field. It is far better to maneuver back and forth in S turns at the windward boundary and make the field, than to successfully hit a key position and miss the field. Don't forget, though, that we're gliding at a speed slower than Over-the-fence Speed, so S turns must be handled with care. In a steep turn, altitude is lost quickly and the stalling speed is higher. There is less margin for error at this glide speed than there is at higher speeds. During one of the S turns, fly a base leg perpendicular to the approach leg. The advantage of a base leg is that it helps us to estimate wind velocities as we drift off the leg; if we have to "crab" in order to maintain position on a base leg, we realize that we must turn to final approach sooner than if we had held position without crabbing.

As we descend lower and closer, determine if the field is suitable for a gear-down landing. Plowed fields invariably are not suitable; turf fields usually are. If you're in doubt, leave the gear up. Repairing a broken prop is an easier job than fixing your head. To land gear-down in plowed or muddy fields will insure your going up on the nose and possibly over on your back.

*Don't use the flaps yet.* Flaps can always be lowered to prevent overshooting, but at our slow speed they can't be raised without immediate loss of altitude and, possibly, control of the plane. Besides, we have a better method for maneuvering ourselves into the field, as will be seen shortly.

Now we're at 400 feet estimated, and entering the crucial stage of the maneuver. By visualizing where the nose would be if we turned toward the field, we can determine if our position is correct. If at any time a turn is made toward the field, the nose should appear to be in the center of the field. Suppose you do turn toward the field on final approach and notice that the nose remains on center. This visual projection of the glide is a clue as to where the glide is taking you. And, with this nonfloat glide, the center is approximately where you'll land!

But the nose usually moves, which means that we won't land in the center. Our position is, moreover, slightly high, because we wish to avoid undershooting. Fortunately, we have no impracticable rules such as plague us during flight tests. We may add flaps, or S turn, or slip (although slipping a plane with flaps isn't desirable). We may also—and this is important—"*play*" *our glide.*

Playing the glide is important because we don't wish to use flaps until we are positive of making the field. Keep watching the nose. If it apparently moves forward, we are overshooting, whereas if it moves downward from the center, we are undershooting. We play the glide according to nose movement. If the nose moves upward, we raise the nose slightly, which means that we sink more rapidly because we are tending to glide at minimum speed, and thereby land shorter. If the nose moves downward from center, we lower the nose and glide faster, obtaining our maximum-distance glide, the Over-the-fence Speed, and land farther. In general, 10 per cent variation in speed is permissible. For example, if stalling speed is 50 mph, we can play the glide ±5 mph.

It can now be understood why it is mandatory that we hold the glide speed at a definite figure. It is the only control of accuracy we have. We *must* have a constant sinking rate without any ballooning effect, and this is safely attained only at a speed slightly less than the Over-the-fence Speed. But holding an accurate speed doesn't mean we must watch the air-speed indicator constantly; rather, we use it as a guide. We have too many other things to occupy our attention, so we must fly by listening, seeing, and feeling, with occasional glances at the air speed.

As we glide closer to the field we see that we've avoided that horrible denouement, the undershoot. For this, there is no remedy. Fortunately, we have taken precautions to overshoot and we now have our remaining ace, the flaps. Begin by using them gently, a little at a time: lower a quarter-flap first and see what happens. The immediate effect is an apparent increase in gliding range, but soon the speed falls off and the nose must be pushed down to over-come the added drag. Thus, we land shorter than we would have without the flap, we land slower, the stalling speed is less, and we descend at a steeper angle.

As soon as it's apparent that we're going to land far, lower the remaining flaps and watch the nose. We're going to land right on Point X with this method, and land quickly, with little flare-out needed. All that remains after most landings in pastures is to truck the plane back to the repair shop and to pay the bills, which doesn't hurt half as much as it might if the pilot hadn't known his glides.

A last word about flaps. Flaps may be used to "hop" over an obstacle because they provide immediate lift, but the plane goes no farther, because we never get anything for nothing. What happens is that we must descend at a steeper angle after passing the obstacle, and we land shorter with flaps than without flaps because of the added drag. Moreover, the pilot must be prepared to use quick technique in flaring out after he flies over the obstacle. It is impossible to stretch a glide—we can only play it as described above.

Remember, the glide-speed thumb rule is a guide only. A percentage figure won't fly the airplane for you, although the principle holds good for all planes. The rules may be taught to students, but the actual speeds used must be modified according to the skill of the pilot and the stability of the airplane. And under no circumstances should spot-landing practice be conducted in other than a designated airport if the pilot intends to descend lower than 150 feet. Do your low altitude work at a field where the results of poor judgment and a cold engine will be mitigated by a nice long runway. Instructors are handy, too, to help smooth out the rough spots and to avoid the tendency to concentrate on one thing at a time.

## BETTER LANDINGS WITH PRECISION APPROACHES

There is an old wheeze about an anxious mother who reluctantly permitted her son to take flying instruction. Her parting advice was, "Fly low and slow, son." This advice is the kind one might expect in a mother-in-law story. As a matter of fact, this *is* the advice the Navy gives their aircraft-carrier pilots, the difference being that the carrier pilots know just *how* low and slow to fly in order to land their planes on the bobbing carrier deck.

Knowing just how fast to fly is the secret of any precision, low-altitude flight, not only for spot landings but for power-on approaches. But what we need now is not the slow speed used in the emergency landing, but a speed that makes our approach constant, very accurate, quite safe, and so easy that it can be learned by all Private Pilots. After reaching the airport boundary we want a speed that will permit us to land at a desired spot without floating halfway across the field.

What is the speed to use for this power-on, precision approach? What does it do for the pilot? Take Pilot G, for example, who knew the speed to use on his downwind leg, how to vary flap settings during the approach, and how to reduce power in order to fly over the boundary at his Over-the-fence Speed, thereby touching down on Point X with the finesse of a power-off spot landing. Result: an enviable reputation as a skillful pilot.

Pilot G began his precision approach in the traffic pattern at the prescribed altitude; although the altitude varies at different airports, the variations between altitudes recommended at different airports do not affect the essential maneuver. Suppose that we are flying the approach ourselves and have entered the downwind leg, we go through our Checkoff List for landing, obtain clearance to land, and are all set except for the gear and flaps which are "to go," or to be handled later.

The downwind leg is the place for our first power reduction. Change to a power setting that will obtain Maneuvering Speed, 60 per cent higher than normal stalling speed. Do this long before reaching the crosswind, or base leg, in order that everything may be well under control, and we can become used to the feel and sound of the reduced speed. Now there is nothing else on our minds but making the approach and landing. We have plenty of control because Maneuvering Speed enables us to make turns or to maneuver with safety. True, this speed is accompanied by float after the flare-out, but this is a power approach, not a forced landing, and we'll change speed after the final power reduction. We like Maneuvering Speed because it is fast enough to compensate for any change in stall speed caused by variation in gross weight, such as the amount of fuel, passengers, baggage, or ice we happen to be carrying. Not only is this speed safe and convenient; it's precise, and will enable us to make a precision approach if we hold a *constant* speed. Any variation of speed makes an accurate approach almost impossible.

As we proceed down the leg, some pilots may become apprehensive about the landing gear—"itchy" is a more common and descriptive term. There are two views about the gear. Method one is to clean up the landing check list and to lower the wheels at once, in order that X won't mark the spot where the fuselage disfigured the runway. This method demands we use a second power reduction in order to descend. The other view, method two, maintains that it is easier to wait until we arrive at the point of second power reduction, then lower gear and flaps instead of reducing power, thereby adding enough drag to cause a descent.

Method two is very good procedure in ILS and GCA approaches, and will be used in Chapters 16 to 19. It is good because little or no change in power is necessary to put the plane into the average 2½° glide angle used in approaching runways. However, if one is apprehensive about the possibility of making that expensive and embarrassing maneuver—the wheel-up landing—get the gear down on the downwind leg and use additional throttle as required to drag the gear through the air.

So here we are, smart and comfortable, on the downwind leg, waiting until we arrive at the position from which to turn from downwind to base leg. At airports with wide traffic patterns, or for straight-in approaches, the principle described next is the same. We estimate where the nose would be if we had commenced our approach. If the nose would be on Point X, the time has come to turn to base leg; if we are in a straight-in approach, we may consider ourselves to be on a base leg.

This is the place to make the second power reduction. If we are using method one (gear-flaps already down), we reduce power to approach speed. *Learn this setting.* If you have only a tachometer, know the rpm's for a 250-fpm descent; if you have a manifold pressure gauge, know the Hg (hydragyrum or mercury) setting that will obtain the desired angle of power-glide and rate of descent required. Reduce power to this setting and resolve to change the setting as little as possible until the time comes for the final power reduction.

If we are using method two, we achieve the effect of a reduction in power by lowering gear and one-quarter flaps. The added drag enables us to descend without any juggling of power setting, and for this reason method two is better for the instrument pilot. Passengers like it too, because the plane descends without any disturbing power change.

Now comes the interesting part of the precision approach. With either method, we are in position on base leg or straight-in approach from which we can land precisely on Point X. The nose should be covering Point X, and if the nose stays put we are all set. But what if the winds exceed estimates? What if we turned too late or have no wind? How can we tell which condition exists, and what can we do about it?

As we learned during spot landings, the position of the nose is our clue. The line of glide, projected from the nose to the airport, indicates the spot at which we'll have zero altitude at Maneuvering Speed. This means we'll float slightly beyond Point X, provided that the nose is apparently glued to the spot and the air speed remains constant. The beautiful feature of this technique is that we are automatically compensating for wind, we don't have to juggle the throttle, and no further changes need be made from here on in.

This ideal condition seldom exists. Suppose that the nose creeps ahead, indicating that our angle of descent is too shallow, a circumstance which can be caused by too little wind, too much power, or too little flap. We're too close and too high. Need we reduce throttle? If the throttle setting is correct and has been determined from settings used during previous approaches, *don't reduce power!* Instead, add a little flap; as the nose rises, the air speed falls off, and you lower the nose to regain constant air speed. This is when the nose returns to Point X and in most cases stays there.

But suppose the nose creeps downward, indicating that the angle of descent is too steep, caused by increased wind, too little power, or too much flap. Presuming that the power setting is correct, do we necessarily have to add power? We do not, for the reason given in Chapter 4. When a plane is flying at Maneuvering Speed, reduction in flap setting is neither hazardous nor poor technique. The old wives' tale about not raising flaps under any circumstances, or always "milking" them up, applies only when one has a slow air speed, such as the Minimum or Over-the-fence Speed. At Maneuvering Speed we may remove flaps either completely or a few degrees at a time; by raising them we lose some lift and considerable drag. The loss of lift is regained by raising the nose slightly, but raising the nose does not decrease the air speed because we have much less drag with the flaps up. This means we glide *farther*. In practicing this technique, pilots won't be aware of the necessity of raising the nose because at Maneuvering Speed and with a quarter-flap the change is slight and the action is almost reflex. As the nose comes up, it should regain Point X and hold. If it does not, there is nothing left for the pilot to do except to add power.

But if we must change the power setting, it can be done gradually, because power changes with this method are small. Even with planes having only three-position flaps (zero, quarter, full), the reduction can be so smooth that the passengers will not notice any change. The perfect approach—no matter what kind of flaps one has—is the approach with the fewest changes. With variable flaps, the perfect approach is one in which the throttle is untouched from the first reduction to the final reduction. The maneuver is smooth, enjoyable, gratifying, and impressive—so easy that the unperturbed pilot makes smoother, better landings. The passengers believe that their pilot is a twenty-plane Ace.

Here comes the fence, our imaginary position a few hundred yards from the end of the runway. As we approach the fence, begin to ease the power off so that we'll have Over-the-fence Speed at that point. Now we know that the plane will land on Point X, because at this speed we have little floating effect. As we pass the fence, we lower full flap and thereby land exactly on Point X. At this speed, with full flap, we're committed to the landing, because we will soon be flying at less than $S_2$ speed as we flare out for the landing. Leave a few rpm's on during the flare-out to provide better control, and allow the wheels to touch gently by looking far ahead and "feeling" the ground with gentle, imperceptible movements of the elevators. Any type of landing can be used for this approach, but the wheel landing is especially good when used with a precision approach because it's easier to make (see Chapter 9) and the passengers like it.

Listen to the "shh-squeak" sound of a greased-on landing, and when the wheels touch, remove the last few rpm's, raise the flaps, and complete the roll-off. No other pleasure in flying gives more satisfaction than a perfect approach followed by a nicely lubricated landing—unless it's those looks of pleased surprise on the passengers' faces.

# 7 : CHANGING YOUR BAD ALTITUDE

PILOT J was nervous as we sat waiting for taxi instructions prior to take-off. So was I. Pilot J was about to fly his Instrument Rating test, and because this rating is the highest that can be placed on a Private Pilot's Certificate, he had a right to be nervous. So did I.

It wasn't that Pilot J didn't have the right attitude. He wanted to pass the test, he'd practiced diligently for it, and he knew he'd have to do his turns, climbs, and lost procedures correctly in order to prove that he was competent to fly solely by reference to instruments.

He'd have to prove also that he could think while he flew the gauges, copied flight clearances, computed headings, and reacted to revised instructions. That's easy for an experienced pilot, but it's hard the first time. That's why Pilot J was nervous.

The reason why I was nervous was not because of Pilot J's *attitude* but because of his *altitude*. To be sure, we were still on the ground, so we had the altitude we should have—ground level at the airport, which in our case happened to be 100 feet above sea level. To be sure, I wanted Pilot J to do his best and to pass the test, but the thought persisted: what if this were for real, with an ILS minimum of 200 foot ceiling at our destination? What would happen if Pilot J took off with his bad altitude?

When the control tower operator had given us permission to taxi out for take-off, he'd also given the altimeter setting: 30.00. Pilot J had reached over to set his altimeter accordingly, and cranked in a setting of 30.00 with the adjustment knob. It was then that the termites in my kinaesthetic muscles started to twitch. Although the elevation of the airport was 100 feet, the altimeter read 200 feet! We were theoretically in the air!

The correct method of changing his bad altitude should be

obvious to an experienced instrument pilot, but Pilot J didn't so much as glance at the new setting. Neither do 75 per cent of other applicants for ratings. Why? Probably because they haven't been told that the aging process applies to man-made gadgets as much as it does to the makers of the gadgets, and that altimeters, like everything else, must be corrected, adjusted, and overhauled from time to time.

But altimeters are seldom sent in for overhaul. If they can be used when the setting is inaccurate, *what* was wrong? Certainly the trouble was not in the tower, where at least two accurate altimeters are required in case one goes bad, and I was reasonably sure that the airport was still at 100 feet. I looked over at Pilot J, who was ready for take-off and didn't want a check pilot making conversation. Pilot J was copying his clearance for a simulated instrument flight.

What should he have done about his altimeter setting? Is this error, if uncorrected, serious enough to warrant disqualification of the applicant? What might happen if he failed to correct his setting? What if it had read minus 100 feet? What should he have known in order to correct it?

These are some of the questions Pilot J did *not* know how to answer, but inasmuch as most flight examiners and inspectors try to put any applicant at ease, and because most applicants are nervous to begin with, I tried hinting. Hinting is not the best method to use in resetting an altimeter.

"What's the field elevation here?" I asked him.

"One hundred feet," said Pilot J, wondering how an inspector could be so stupid.

"Your altimeter reads 200 feet."

"Yeah," agreed Pilot J, amazed that I didn't know why it read 200 feet. "The tower gave me 30 inches as my setting. I just set my altimeter."

"But the field elevation is *100* feet."

"But I've got my altimeter set at what he gave me," insisted Pilot J, with that tone of voice a person uses when he knows he is being razzed or kidded.

That ended the argument.

"Okay. Take off when ready," I said.

So we took off and flew the test, and by the time Pilot J was ready for his 400-and-1 shot (an approach under simulated conditions of 400-foot ceiling and 1 mile visibility) he—but we're getting ahead of the story. Take-off time is not the time for flight instruction, and Pilot J, like many Private Pilots, did not realize that an altimeter is simply an aneroid barometer, a barometer which does not contain liquid. It contains a sealed, metal sphere with a diaphragm which contracts or expands according to the atmospheric pressure. It is connected to a needle that is made to revolve around a dial calibrated in feet, so that the number of feet is really an indi-

Fig. 5. What's wrong with this picture? If the field elevation is 100 feet, and if the altimeter setting is 30.0, what must the pilot do prior to taking off on an instrument flight? For solution, see page 72.

cation of atmospheric pressure, not the actual number of feet between the altimeter and the sea. The wet barometer, unlike the aneroid barometer, contains a column of mercury about 2½ feet high (about 30 inches), which varies in height with the atmospheric pressure. It would not be practicable for aerial use.

The figure of 30.00 inches is not precise for sea level. The more accurate figure of 29.92 inches for "normal" sea level was obtained some years ago from barometric readings taken at 40 degrees latitude, from which the *average* pressure at sea level was found to be 29.92 inches of mercury. Next, a rate-of-change table was worked out, in which an average temperature at sea level of 15 degrees centigrade (59° F) was used, assuming an average decrease in temperature of 2° C (3½° F) per thousand feet. When this hypothetical condition obtains, we have what is called "standard atmosphere."

With these tables it was easy to build an aneroid barometer having a needle which indicated feet instead of pressure. The drawback is that "standard atmosphere" exists only in someone's imagination, and actual atmospheric pressures vary from hour to hour. For example, set your altimeter to field elevation when you leave the plane; the following day, or possibly the next hour, the altimeter may read either higher or lower than field elevation. That's where the correction knob came into Pilot J's flight test. He could re-set the altimeter needle to field elevation by turning the knob.

By setting it to the altimeter setting given him by the tower, Pilot J should have read his airport elevation directly from the altimeter. Ordinarily, if the altimeter is so set it *will* read field elevation, and, conversely, if the field elevation is set correctly by the pilot, the instrument reads altimeter setting. This also means that if an accurate instrument were set and taken to sea level, it would read "0" altitude. The readings taken from the altimeter are called *indicated* readings.

Indicated altitudes are used for low approaches, because a low approach is made with a recently received setting, and because the error in the instrument is not great enough to call for a *calibration* altitude. Indicated altitudes are used for traffic separation along airways, because other pilots are also using indicated altitudes obtained in conjunction with settings received via radio while they are over check points.

Pilot J didn't know that one of the best places to check his altimeter is on the ground, prior to take-off, after the tower gave him his altimeter setting. When he turned the knob to set the altimeter, it read 200 feet instead of 100.

What difference did this error make on the instrument flight check? By the time Pilot J climbed to an indicated 3,000 feet and leveled off, he was fairly well relaxed—at 2,900 feet. This wouldn't make much difference on a cross-country flight or in flying an assigned altitude on the airways. Nor would it have much bearing on the high-altitude flight-test maneuvers, such as orientation or timed turns. It wouldn't make much difference on *any* part of the flight test, because Pilot J had full visibility and a check pilot with him. But what would have happened had he been alone, on an actual instrument flight with 400-1 weather conditions?

A 400-1 shot isn't the hardest thing in the world. There are also 200-½ shots. For a Private Pilot, a 400-1 shot is hard enough, and he is usually denied the privilege of landing under worse weather conditions because of his limited equipment. But when the weather is given as "ceiling 400 feet," it doesn't mean that the clouds are exactly at 400 feet, as if someone had cut them off with a razor at that altitude. Very few pilots expect the clouds to end at precisely 400 feet or the ground to be perfectly visible when the altimeter reads 400 feet above airport elevation.

In conditions like this, called variable ceilings, what happens if the pilot dips down an extra 50 feet (as most instrument pilots do) in hope of seeing the ground? Here we are on a flight test, with the blind-flying hood in place, descending to 400 feet according to our altimeter. We should now be able to see the ground and perhaps the runway, with the approach lights beckoning with a welcome gleam. If we can't see the ground, we duck down a little bit lower.

So did Pilot J, who was permitted to descend to what he thought was 350 feet above the ground. He thought he was at 350 feet because his altimeter said so; hadn't he set it before take-off? At this moment the blinds were removed. He was only 250 feet from the ground, and because he wasn't quite lined up with the runway he had to turn steeply to align himself.

The seriousness of his error may be illustrated by an accident which occurred under similar conditions. In attempting to turn at low altitude after breaking contact, the pilot dug his wing into the ground and crashed, killing several passengers. Investigation proved that the altimeter was "faulty."

When Pilot J's altimeter read 350 feet, he was actually flying at 250 feet, which was not only below the altitude for normal, safe approaches but was in violation of Civil Air Regulation minimums. His position didn't look comfortable and it felt worse. It would have been barely satisfactory with full visibility, and if we had been on instruments, our approach would have been rightly termed hazardous. Nevertheless, he made his turn, landed the plane, and checked the altimeter. It read 200 feet, exactly as he'd set it, but according to the instrument we should still have been in the air on final approach!

## HOW TO SET THE ALTIMETER CORRECTLY

What had happened to the instrument was that linkage, diaphragm stretching, and age had caused it to read incorrectly. When Pilot J adjusted his altimeter to the setting given him by the tower, the setting was correct but the needle registered 200 feet altitude. His best bet was to have had the altimeter repaired and calibrated prior to the flight test; airline altimeters are checked frequently, and airliners always have two altimeters for cross-checking.

But if Pilot J, like many other pilots, did have an instrument with inaccurate settings, the inaccuracy should have been noted at the time his setting was made. Then the instrument could have been reset to indicate the field elevation, which in this case was 100 feet. The barometric scale on the dial, instead of indicating 30.00 inches as given by the tower, would be reduced to about 29.90 inches, as shown here.

Fig. 6. If field elevation is 100 feet, set the altimeter to 100 feet. If the altimeter setting had been given as 30.0 and you now read 29.9 from your altimeter, the instrument error is —0.1, which must be subtracted from any future setting obtained from the tower or during flight.

A glance at Fig. 7 shows that pressure varies about an inch with each thousand feet elevation, or about one-tenth with every hundred feet. Because the scale in the barometric pressure indicator on the dial of the altimeter is in 20 hundredths, Pilot J could have reset his altimeter correctly for each 20 feet of error.

| Atmospheric pressure in inches Hg | Altitude indicated (barometric scale set at 29.92 feet) |
|:---:|:---:|
| INCHES | FEET |
| 31.02 | 1,000 |
| 29.92 | S.L. |
| 28.82 | 1,000 |
| 27.82 | 2,000 |
| 26.81 | 3,000 |
| 25.84 | 4,000 |
| 24.89 | 5,000 |
| 20.58 | 10,000 |

Fig. 7. Atmospheric pressure varies about 1 inch for each 1,000 feet of altitude.

When Pilot J turned his adjustment knob to move the needle from 200 feet to 100 feet, in order that the altimeter might show airport elevation correctly, he should have noted that the altimeter setting had become 29.90 instead of 30.00 inches. Thereafter, when altimeter settings were received via radio, one-tenth would have to be subtracted from the setting during take-offs, landings, or in flight. Example: tower gives altimeter setting as 30.15. Required: new setting. Solution: subtract one-tenth from 30.15 and set altimeter to 30.05. The altimeter may have been indicating 5,150 feet when the information was received, and if it had been reset to 30.05 it would have read 5,050 feet—a 100-foot difference.

This explanation did not satisfy Pilot J entirely. "That's fine," he agreed, in the age-old policy of agreeing with the inspector, "but suppose I'd been given my setting before take-off, and my altimeter had read '0' altitude on the field. I'd have been 100 feet *safer* during my low approach! What's wrong with that?"

If Pilot J had set his altimeter according to those specifications he might never have gotten down at all. That is not to say he'd still be up there. It means that had the ceiling measured 400 feet, Pilot J would have descended to what he believed was 400-feet altitude. With his altimeter reading a plus or "safer" altitude, he would have been at 500 feet, an altitude well above ceiling, and from which he could not see the ground. Of, if he had "cheated" by descending another 50 feet, just to make sure, he still would not have broken contact because he would have been at 450 feet. Then there would have been no alternative except to fly to his alternate airport, which is required to have at least 1,000 feet of ceiling.

Dilemmas like this can be avoided by using accurate instruments. But what if every pilot cannot afford a recalibration, or if the error is not enough to warrant repair? The method used by expert pilots is excellent. They form the habit of setting their altimeter to field elevation for all flights. Then, when the altimeter setting is received from the tower, they can instantly read the calibration error for that altitude. In old instruments there can also be a different error for other altitudes, and for this reason planes that are used for instrument work *must* have accurate altimeters. For Pilot J, who flew primarily from his own field, one solution is to mark the instrument with white ink, or paste a paper to it, showing the amount of error. In the first example, in which the altimeter read lower than actual height, we'd place a minus one-tenth ($-0.1$) on the dial; thereafter, we'd subtract one-tenth from any setting given to us. In the second instance, in which we read less than true altitude, we'd place plus one-tenth ($+0.1$); thereafter, when airport towers or airway radios give the altimeter setting we'll set our altimeter according to their instructions, then correct it by the plus-or-minus notation.

There are other uses for altimeter settings, and other ways to use settings for safe flying. For example, in night landings, when accuracy is more important than it is during the day, an incorrect altimeter setting can cause overshooting or undershooting. Don't forget that 100 feet of altimeter error can cause 1,000 feet of horizontal error. To have an extra hundred feet over the edge of the field is not as bad as having zero feet before one gets there, but either situation is embarrassing. The pilot who checks his altimeter calibration can get into the traffic pattern at the correct altitude and make more accurate approaches.

What about the cross-country pilot who flies into a colder area? Cold weather is more hazardous than warm weather, as far as altimeters are concerned, because cold air is denser and there is a greater change of pressure for each 1,000 feet ascended. If the readings are taken at face value, the pilot may find himself flying too low over rough country, because the indicated altitude may be higher than the true altitude by as much as 10 per cent. For example, if you were flying at an indicated 10,000 feet and the temperature was $-30°$ C, the true altitude would be 9,000 feet.

Flying into a low-pressure area is also dangerous if you can't obtain an altimeter setting. Remember that your indicated altitude can be 100 feet too high for every $\frac{1}{10}$ inch of lowering pressure. If the barometer falls an inch during your flight and you don't receive changes by radio, you could actually be scraping the tree branches despite the fact your altimeter readings were giving a false sense of faith, hope, and security.

Finally, what about *pressure altitudes* and *density altitudes?* The Private Pilot need not be concerned about them. They are used to determine air speed and engine performance; engine-operation curves are based upon pressure altitude because the latter is easily obtained during flight. To find pressure altitude, merely turn your altimeter setting to 29.92 (we suppose that this time it's a calibrated instrument, but if you have to add or subtract a correction figure, do it) and read pressure altitude from the altimeter. It usually won't be much different from indicated altitude, but Private Pilots who insist upon accuracy can use it in computing true speeds. It merely means that you now have an altitude reading based upon standard atmosphere, which is what your air-speed indicator is designed for.

As for Pilot J, he eventually became a top-notch pilot, with an excellent attitude and good altitudes, but as far as the flight check is concerned we'll let you be the flight examiner and decide.

What do *you* think? Would *you* have given him an instrument ticket? Or, put less bluntly, would you like to ride behind a pilot during instrument flight if the pilot had a bad altitude?

# 8: QUIT STALLING

READ what the Civil Aeronautics Board has to say in its numerous bound volumes of reports on pilot accidents. These make interesting reading, but they have never been best sellers. This is no fault of the C.A.B., but in order to aid a worthy cause and to stimulate interest, here are some excerpts.

". . . When the aircraft was at an altitude of approximately 200 feet, the engine lost power. The pilot selected a plowed field and approached it in a shallow gliding-turn. He undershot the field and the aircraft stalled at about 75 feet, falling to the ground and striking on its landing gear at an angle of about 40 degrees. . . ." Flip a few pages and pick another item at random. ". . . In attempting a right turn at about 500 feet, the aircraft stalled and fell into a right spin. Partial recovery was effected at 150 feet, but the aircraft continued to settle until it struck the ground in a near-level flying position and was demolished. . . ."

At this point one is tempted to discontinue such mirthless reading. It certainly isn't a good way to start the day, although the incidents are suitable for ending the day. Hoping that the reading will became more cheerful, let us turn the pages and read on. ". . . Immediately after take-off, the pilot made a 180-degree turn and flew back over the field, at which point the engine cut out. In trying to turn at low altitude in order to land in the field, he stalled and entered a left spin, completing about half a turn before striking the ground, almost vertically, on the nose. . . ."

The last three words undoubtedly refer to the nose of the plane, which makes the subject so serious that we ask, "Isn't there a way to quit stalling and commence flying?" There is, indeed, and we'll start with the *four senses* used by good pilots. Take Pilot M, who needed all of them. He is taking off downwind, so his ground speed is faster than usual, which leads him to believe he isn't climbing steeply enough. He can *see* that the nose is higher than it should be, he can *feel* the rapidly softening stick pressure, and he can *hear* the declining pitch of sound as the slipstream becomes slower and the engine labors mightily. Also rebelling is the deep-feel of his stomach muscles, but the best sense of a good flier—that something called common sense—was on its day off, and he didn't receive the messages from the first three senses, "Quit stalling and begin flying."

He thought he wasn't climbing fast enough.

Years ago, instructors told their students that the only way to avoid stalls was to observe the first three rules of flying, all three of which were to "keep flying speed." But pilots continued to stall. Next, they were told that their senses must be as sharp as the razor's edge; they were taught "Slow Flight" or "Minimum Control Speed" and encouraged to feel the stall, but stall accidents continued.

The reason for these accidents was pilot error, because modern airplanes are not going to whip off into a stall the moment one takes his hands from the wheel to light a cigarette or makes a wry face at the stewardess' coffee. Planes do not fall out of control from sheer whimsy, as any flight instructor can vouchsafe after trying to demonstrate a clean spin entry. But planes do enter partial spins, and although recovery can be effected just by releasing the controls, this method doesn't work at low altitude.

If our planes don't stall unless they are forced to, there must be a way to keep pilots from stalling! Isn't there a training precedure for this? Yes! Isn't there an aid that will tell the pilot how to avoid stalling? Yes. Will these methods work by themselves? Not always, because they must be used together. A device can help any pilot to avoid stalls by warning him he is stalling, and the device works so well that it may be relied upon when the power is on or off. It works whether the plane is fully loaded or at minimum weight, with acceleration changes during take-offs or in landings. But adding more power or putting the stick forward is the pilot's duty, and only he can do that.

Therefore, the four senses are still needed in order that we may react promptly, but given normal sense perception and a gadget we shall conquer the inadvertent stall. The senses will increase our expectations of longevity, enable us to fly better, and permit better take-offs, climbs, turns, maneuvers, and landings. The effect of sharpening the senses is to improve general flying, not merely to help eliminate stalls.

Let's describe the four senses and methods to sharpen them before describing the instrument used to avoid stalls.

The senses we need in flying are:
1. Visual sense—the eye
2. Hearing sense—the ear
3. Kinesthesia, or muscle sense
   a. touch (the fingers)
   b. deep-muscle sense (in the stomach area)
4. Common sense. This is important but it isn't entirely germane to stalls. It applies to flying in general.

## VISUAL SENSE

Vision—the first, most important sense—can be used to improve coordination. Watch the nose and the rate at which it turns during skidding or slipping turns: the nose moves around the horizon faster in a skid, more slowly in a slip. Because a plane turns at a certain rate for a given speed and angle of bank, you can become accustomed to seeing the rate of turn at a given bank. Install an inexpensive ball-bank indicator (Fig. 19), establish a turn, and see if the ball is centered. Once it is centered, use the nose to coordinate rudder with ailerons in the turn; notice how the rate of turn diminishes during turn recovery when the ball is centered. One can coordinate the controls much better by watching the plane than by watching the ball.

Whenever we fly our lightplane, either high wing or low wing, in conditions of low visibility when the horizon is obscured, the time has come when we'd rather be on instruments. But there is no such thing as being half on instruments, because a pilot becomes confused from flying by instruments one moment and by reference to terrestrial features the next. Inasmuch as these half-and-half measures are extremely poor technique, we'll continue to fly by visual reference to the ground.

But VFR requires us to use each of the four senses, and of these the most important is the eye. Ever since we first learned to fly, the eyes have given most of the clues as to how we are doing. But with the nose obscured, we must observe the wing, which we can use in maintaining level flight, climbs, and steep turns by gauging the angle of attack.

Look out at the apparent chord line that is formed by an imaginary line from the leading edge of the wing to the trailing edge. This is not exactly the chord line, but we may call it that for all practical purposes. This line appears to be nearly horizontal in level flight, as we look at the angle it makes with the ground. Impossible as it may seem, one can visualize a slope that is horizontal or vertical to the ground and mentally compare the angle these slopes make with the chord line. Find out for yourself by checking this angle in level flight, climbs, and glides.

For example, in level flight the angle can be estimated despite the fact that the wing tip may be above the horizon, as is the case in high-wing planes. As you raise the nose and climb, watch the chord line. In a climb, the angle between the chord line and the ground is greater than it is in level flight. When you have the correct climbing attitude you can hold the climb almost as constant as you can with the nose used as a reference point. The chord line is one of the most important reference points a non-instrument pilot can use during low visibility.

In some respects it is better than the nose, because the angle doesn't vary with the size of 'chute, cushion, or seat-level you

THE APPARENT CHORD LINE

Fig. 8. The chord line looks like this in a climb.

happen to be using; it doesn't vary as the result of haze or smoke; it is possible to fly level as long as there is ground visible below you. In half-mile visibility a climbing turn can be made by visual reference to the chord line even though the nose is pointed at nimbo-stratus.

The use of the chord line in steep turns is not only handy but amazing. Put the plane into a steep bank (more than 45°) and watch only the chord line, after having checked the area for other planes. Do *not* use the nose for a reference point—don't so much as look at it during the complete 360° turn. Now, using the chord line, you can see how it decreases as you lose altitude or increases as you gain altitude. In fact, you can execute steep turns better by using the chord line instead of the nose for a check point, and you'll find that you maintain altitude within plus or minus 10 feet!

## HEARING SENSE

Hearing may be the least important of our flying senses, but it's not to be disregarded. Go back to level flight, climbs, or turns and watch the chord line. When the chord line angle decreases, the plane is descending and engine rpm's increase. So does the sound of the airflow. This method may not work so well in a four-engine airliner but it's fine for lightplanes. Listen to the sounds of the engine, the airflow, and the vibrations that accompany each speed, because they tell a story of flight attitudes. Yet many pilots seem to fly as though they need a hearing aid, and disregard the sounds that are warning them. To disregard these warnings often enough is to invite the C.A.B. to write a report about us.

Hearing, like any other sense, must be used frequently in order to sharpen it. One may think he hears all the time, but he automatically shuts out sounds and becomes oblivious to them. A good pilot trains himself to recognize the changes in sounds during climbs, glides, or turns, as well as to recognize that hardworking sound of an engine going up-hill. But just hearing them won't help if the pilot doesn't react as quickly as Pavlov's dog; reaction to sense perceptions must be instantaneous. This doesn't mean that one must hear commonplace noises; some pilots have trained themselves not to hear routine engine sounds but to hear variations in them. The variation that makes them jump highest is the lack of noise, but any variation does bring an immediate reaction.

## KINESTHESIA, OR SENSE OF FEEL

Admittedly, seat-of-the-pants flying is not as necessary or as popular as it once was, because today we have instruments to tell us what is happening during flight. But in VFR flight the sense of feel is something we can hardly do without. We must *feel* the amount of pressure required on the controls during take-offs, turns, and landings. Mechanically pushing the stick forward during take-off will certainly bring those bumps and grinds discussed in Chapter 3.

*Feel* of the controls is attained by grasping the stick with the fingertips, not as one seizes a baseball bat, and by pressing the rudders with the balls of the feet instead of the insteps. Thus instead of leg motion we press one rudder at a time by slightly raising one ankle while pressing the other. This often helps those pilots who press with both feet and consequently can't tell how much rudder pressure is being used.

*Feel* the pressures required. For example, in take-offs, climbs, or steep turns you can feel the stick or rudder pressures that are needed to keep the plane straight or the ball centered. In turns, as the bank is increased, more back pressure, opposite aileron pressure, and right rudder pressure are needed. Remember both the feeling and the amount of pressure, and the next time you're in a climb or steep turn you'll recall two things: that pressure is needed and that a softening stick is a cue that the plane is being flown near the stall. Then it's time to quit stalling and start flying again.

Feel the elevators during landings. Ease the plane down to the runway with small, imperceptible back pressures; realize how easy it is to feel the "softness" of the elevators as speed diminishes and the plane is ready to land. This doesn't mean that we're flying the controls instead of the airplane, because we're emphasizing control pressures and not control movements.

There is much difference between pressures used in fast glides and slow glides. This brings up the subject of *deep-muscle sense*, the muscles which signal acceleration or deceleration. These are the muscles which signal the unpleasant sensation one feels in an elevator that moves downward rapidly, or the heavy feeling of upward motion. The deep muscles in the abdominal area tell a pilot how many g's are present in a steep turn or during a pull-out. They also aid by warning of deceleration in slow glides and in the stall.

Stall your plane some fine day at about 3,000 feet by pulling the nose up to the horizon and holding it there. Stalls which are practiced swiftly don't help much because hardly anyone inadvertently stalls this way; if he is going to stall it's while preoccupied and in a slow glide close to the ground. Most spin fatalities result from the kind of stall that the pilot "didn't know he was entering." Bring the nose up slowly, keep bringing the stick back, and turn your sense-switch to full on.

See, hear, and feel this stall. Notice where the nose is, and the angle of the chord line; hear the laboring sound of the engine during a full-power, half-power, and power-off stall; listen to the airflow diminish, and the diminishing pitch of the slipstream; feel the stick and rudder pressures as the controls soften, and feel the burble point with your deep muscles as the plane loses lift.

When you've got your senses to the point where they notify you immediately and prompt reaction is possible, you've become a better pilot than you were.

## COMMON SENSE

Common sense is the Quality X of Chapter 2. It applies to all flying, but not all fliers possess it. It may be acquired—to a varying degree—by learning to evaluate one's sense perceptions, by making decisions promptly, and by acquiring a kind of confidence that is liberally seasoned with doubt. Chapter 22 takes up the subject of doubting and checking yourself.

There is little question that no pilot may be considered either safe or competent if he is lacking in common sense, because without it he cannot evaluate the other senses. The principles set forth in Chapters 2 and 22 should enable the average pilot to become an expert pilot, which is the sole aim of this book.

## STALL–WARNING INDICATORS

But suppose your senses aren't as sharp as you'd like them to be, and you still aren't fully confident of your ability to quit stalling. Isn't there something that can be added? Inasmuch as this is the age of instruments and we no longer are as dependent upon our senses as of yore, why isn't there a device to prevent stalls?

Take Pilot K, for example. We were scarcely off the ground when he eased the nose up precisely at climbing speed, just a bit faster than $S_2$. He climbed more steeply and more efficiently than most pilots, yet he wasn't watching his air speed with hawk-like attention.

The plane felt good, and my quick glance at the air speed verified that we were not only flying safely but at the maximum rate of climb! All the way up to altitude the speed stayed on the mark, a fine example of precision flying.

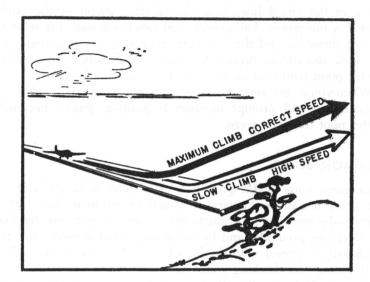

Fig. 9. How too fast an air speed affects the rate of climb.

"You must have had excellent instruction," I commented.

"Got a second pilot who's on the job night and day," he replied. "I can take off, climb, glide, and land at the correct speed, regardless of power or loading. I could throw away my air-speed indicator and still do it."

"Where's the second pilot?" I asked, looking around for hidden bodies.

He pointed to a dial on the panel that was about the size of a basic-panel gauge. On the dial was a vertical needle pointing to a curved line. The left side of the line was red and the word SLOW was printed there, while the right side of the line was green and was marked FAST.

"Watch this!" said Mr. K, a trifle smugly. He eased the throttle back and held the nose in a climb. The air-speed indicator sluggishly began to fall off, but the "second pilot" immediately moved to slow and a horn blew. Pilot K then applied power and briskly but smoothly put the nose down to avoid the stall; at this, the needle moved back to center (into the green area) and the horn stopped blowing. He then checked the area for traffic and rolled into a steep bank: the increased load factor now raised the stalling speed. The "second pilot" responded by moving toward slow, although the air-speed indicator told us we supposedly had a "safe" speed. When the bank was increased slightly, the horn blew and Pilot K eased out of the turn.

"It's just as dependable in glides, landings, or with a load of ice. Or in take-offs, or with twin-engine aircraft, or in single-engine operation. The only time I need that air-speedometer is during cross-country flights when I want to compute an ETA (Estimated Time of Arrival)."

It began to appear that the air-speed indicator might be obsolete. Why use it at all if it read "safe" during high-load conditions when the gadget was blowing its horn in Gabriel-like fashion?

Let it be known right now that the manufacturer of the SCI (Speed Control Indicator) makes no claim that the SCI replaces an air-speed indicator. Many pilots know it by the name Stall-warning Indicator, but what they don't know is that this remarkable co-pilot is the best aid to safe flight since the Wright Brothers defied gravity. Some gadgets blow a horn while others flash a light or cause the control column to move violently when the air speed and the stalling speed coincide.

The SCI does more than warn of a stalled attitude; it indicates accurately when a pilot has attained best climb or glide speed; it tells him *instantly* whenever he approaches a slow speed. It does this without air-speed–indicator lag and without air-speed–indicator errors. (Air-speed indicators don't actually lag; the momentum of the plane causes the air speed to diminish slowly, thereby causing an impression of lag.) The SCI is accurate under conditions of higher loadings and the resulting higher stall speed; once installed, it remains accurate because it operates by electricity and is not dependent upon Pitot tubes or other dirt-accumulating devices.

This gadget was enough to make one reconsider. As readers of Chapter 5 know, we've been strong for precision air speeds. Did the gadget contradict everything we've stressed? Were our thumb rules of 20 per cent for minimum, 40 per cent for Over-the-fence, and 60 per cent for Maneuvering Speed incorrect? If the Speed Control Indicator is a reliable aid in maintaining safe or efficient air speeds, why use an air-speed indicator? What are the short-comings of the SCI? Would I throw away my air-speed indicator or ignore it under Instrument Flight Rule conditions?

We'd hardly landed before the installation was being inspected. There were three component parts for our single-engine lightplane. The first was a device to measure lift, called a "lift transducer," which was simply a small, horizontal vane protruding less than an inch from the leading edge of the wing. The vane could move up or down with any change in angle of attack as the air rushed by during flight.

Within the wing and behind the vane itself were some small coils of wire. Whenever the vane moved upward with large angles of attack, the electrical properties of the coils varied. Whenever the vane moved downward, the electrical coefficient varied in the opposite direction. These impulses were sent to the second component.

This second component—called the "lift computer"—was located in the cockpit, at any convenient place that would make adjustment possible during flight. It had several adjustable knobs that we'll discuss in a moment. These adjustments were to compensate for acceleration, loading, and single-engine operation, thereby making the third component behave properly.

The third part—the dial of the SCI—was Pilot K's "second pilot." It was located in the basic-panel group because he needed it directly in front of him, and it was connected to the lift computer. Whenever the vane on the wing moved upward at large angles of attack, the needle moved into the red portion of the dial. If the needle got too far to the left, a contact was made which caused a horn to blow, a light to flash, or the stick to buffet. These necessary annoyances are optional—some pilots like all three. Whenever the vane on the wing moved to a position accompanying maximum climb, the lift computer sent this information to the SCI, and the needle moved to center. When the vane moved downward, because of the negative angle of attack during dives or cruising flight, the needle went to the right of the dial, at FAST.

After we'd examined the instrument, Pilot K again took off and climbed to altitude at maximum-lift speed. He put the gear and flaps down, reduced power, and obtained a glide at a normal rate of descent. Then he stalled the airplane slowly and without acceleration, noting the *indicated* air speed.

The instruction handbook furnished with the SCI directed that we then increase the stall figure just obtained by 20 per cent (stalling speed $\times$ 1.2), and ease the nose down until the air speed indicated the 20 per cent figure. Then, by adjusting the lift computer, the needle of the SCI was brought to the SLOW position at the right edge of the red line.

Anyone who has read Chapter 5 will recall that this figure is exactly that given as our Minimum or "Never-subceed" Speed!

The second step in the handbook directed that Pilot K fly at 40 per cent above the stall speed (stalling speed $\times$ 1.40), and make another adjustment on the lift computer so that the needle reached the center of the dial, in the green portion. This is the figure recommended for Over-the-fence Speed and the maximum-distance glide to be used in forced landings! Finally, adjustments were made to compensate for acceleration, power, and flaps.

We were ready to make our approach and land, and this time Pilot K was prepared to stake his insurance on my ability to take the controls. The handbook instructed us to get on base leg at an air speed that placed the SCI needle at FAST. This speed, it was evident, was 50–60 per cent faster than stalling speed and, if anything, slightly slower than the 60 per cent speed used in our Maneuvering Speed.

Next, the instructions directed that as we turned on final approach we reduce power to obtain our desired rate of descent with the needle centered. We made the approach with a 2½° angle of glide, and obtained correct air speed by means of flaps or throttle, thereby flying at the best glide speed. After centering the needle, we checked our air speed: it was 40 per cent above the stall! This meant that we had an air speed with adequate safety margin, a nonfloat speed which would enable us to land exactly where we wished, without undershooting or overshooting. It also meant we were using the maximum-distance, maximum-lift glide, which can be held right to the ground or may be "broken" by reducing power, thereby enabling us to make the precision approach recommended in Chapter 6!

The approach and landing having pleased Pilot K, he authorized a take-off. We applied power, held the plane on the ground until the needle moved out of the red, nosed over until the needle was centered, and climbed. We were off the ground at $S_2$ speed and we began to climb precisely when we had maximum lift. As soon as we gained enough altitude we rolled into a steep turn; at 60 degrees of bank the load factor increased our stalling speed to 1.4 above

Fig. 10. The effect of gliding too slow, just right, or too fast.

normal, but because the SCI had been compensated for acceleration and load factor, the needle of the SCI moved into the red. We increased power, the air speed crept up to a figure which increased the lift enough to overcome the added g's, and the needle moved back into the green.

The needle would have indicated a high angle of attack had we been on an approach at dangerously slow speeds whether the increased load were ice, fuel, or passengers; commercial pilots must compute the best approach speed under varying conditions, but the SCI does this complicated job automatically.

Suppose that we had been flying a multi-engine aircraft and had had a take-off engine failure. Because the SCI is also adjusted for $S_2$ speed, single-engine operation, and acceleration (with or without flaps), the SCI immediately jumps into the red whenever the angle of attack exceeds safe operation. Compare this to air-speed indicator action. It takes time for the air speed to diminish, but the SCI shows angle of attack right now, and right now is when a pilot needs to know.

Does all this mean that we should throw out our air-speed indicators and forget about 20–40–60 per cent speeds? Not at all. For those Private Pilots who cannot afford more equipment, the thumb rules give them speeds that are conservatively safe. Flying, however, can be done better with an SCI; and for those pilots whose reaction time is delayed, or whose senses are not as keen as they were, the warning horn or stick buffets are, quite literally, life savers.

There must be something the matter with this remarkable instrument, so let's see what faults we can find.

1. "The SCI must be set in flight." If an unskilled Private Pilot sets his SCI by an air-speed indicator having an inaccurate calibration curve, or if he mistakenly sets it at 1.2 for a climb instead of 1.4, he'll be flying too slowly when the SCI needle is centered. This is pilot error, rather than instrument error. Even an altimeter can be set incorrectly. The SCI is accurate providing it is set accurately in the first place.

2. "Should the SCI fail—and any instrument can fail—the pilot may have forgotten the air speeds to use." On the other hand, SCI users claim the opposite is true. If a pilot uses the SCI in conjunction with the air-speed indicator, he can learn more about his indicator by observing how air speed varies under different conditions.

3. "The pilot must still fly the plane, not the gauges." This argument is weak because the best automatic pilots also can't think. Someone must be there to do a man's job, preferably a man.

4. "The approach speed of 40 per cent higher than stalling speed must be maintained very accurately because it is a bit slow for the beginner, inasmuch as it allows no margin for error." Chapter 6 recommends 60 per cent for the approach speed. What's wrong?

The objection must be conceded. An approach speed of 40 per cent higher than stall speed *is* too low for beginners. But the SCI may be set in flight so that stalling speed plus 60 per cent (stall speed × 1.60) causes the needle to be centered. Talking speeds is not too accurate; we should be talking about *angle of attack*. But if we don't have an SCI we don't have an angle-of-attack indicator, so we are forced to discuss glides or climbs in terms of air speed. The trouble with air speeds is that one can stall at speeds which are twice as high as the normal stall speed—80 to 100 mph. A steep turn, a sudden pullout, or crop-dusting with excess weight, are all accompanied by a higher stall speed. The fine thing about the SCI is that it indicates STALL at the exact moment the angle of attack increases to the stalling point.

5. "The SCI doesn't show air speed, and the pilot can't tell how much more or how much less speed he needs to meet the conditions for his maneuver." This is not strictly true, because the SCI may be set so that relative readings inform the pilot how much needle motion is required to change the attitude of the plane and, consequently, both air speed and angle of attack.

6. "Won't the SCI cause the pilot to become an instrument watcher at the expense of alertness?" This depends upon the pilot, not the instrument. Exercising the neck by turning it to look around during VFR flight is a must, regardless of how many or what kind of instruments one has on the plane's panel.

What the SCI does is to enable us to use our thumb rules to better advantage. We won't throw out the air-speedometer just yet, but we'd be smart to use the SCI, which computes the best glide instantly and accurately.

At least, with an SCI aboard, we can be sure that we've quit stalling, and are flying with precision and accuracy.

# 9: STALL LANDINGS OR WHEEL LANDINGS?

PILOT N was coming in for a landing. The wind was strong and gusty, blowing down the runway one moment and at an angle to it the next. Pilot N wasn't as familiar with tail-wheel airplanes as he should have been because he usually flew nose-wheel aircraft. He believed that tail-wheel airplanes must always be landed fully stalled, in a three-point position. This was his first misconception.

Pilot N next erred in his selection of approach speed. Having read most of the previous chapter before turning out the light, he dreamed he was stalling and awoke next morning with a New Year's-type resolution to the effect that he, too, was going to quit stalling. He carefully selected Maneuvering Speed for the approach, changed to Over-the-fence Speed at the proper point, and descended to the runway at low speed, with flaps down, for a full-stall landing.

These approach speeds are usually satisfactory, but they weren't suitable for existing wind conditions. Just as the plane got into landing attitude, the wind became gustier, the controls grew mushy, and the diminished air speed furnished less lift, causing Pilot N to drop 10 feet from his altitude and 5 years from his life.

What happened, as dazed movie heroes put it? What speed should be used in gusty wind? What type landing would have been better, a full-stall or a wheel landing? When is a full-stall landing better than a wheel landing? Which is easier to make? And why did he momentarily stall if he was using our much emphasized Over-the-fence Speed, which is 40 per cent higher than stall speed?

In these days of nose-wheel airplanes, the answers to these questions *must* be known by every well-rounded pilot, particularly by those who fly both nose-wheel and tail-wheel aircraft.

Let's see what happened to Pilot N, whose molars were jarred by the impact of his landing, which might have been anything from 10 inches to 10 feet. Gusts are sudden, brief blasts of wind; a freshening gust is called positive, while a diminishing gust is called negative. A positive gust will cause a plane to acquire more lift and will raise the plane as many feet as there is excess lift provided by the gust. A negative gust will subtract several pounds of lift, dropping the plane until stable, constant wind is encountered

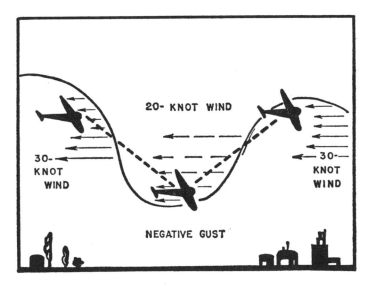

**Fig. 11. How gusts affect a plane.**

or until enough lift is provided from higher angle of attack or more air speed.

But at high angles of attack, such as those used in full-stall landings, a plane is very susceptible to gusts. When Pilot N dropped, his plane was momentarily stalled. Had he been using an approach with more speed and less angle of attack, a negative gust would not have stalled the plane. Also, with increased wind velocities, it is neither necessary nor desirable to fly at Over-the-fence Speed because landing speeds are lower, making precision landings much easier.

The full-stall landing, with its slow touch-down speed and higher angle of attack, was not the landing to use. The full-stall (also called three-point) landing is for special cases, such as ditching at sea or landing in very small fields. After speed is reduced at the fence position, the pilot continually eases the nose up until the ground is reached, at which time the plane is in a tail-down, three-point attitude with a high angle of attack. This technique calls for much alertness and finesse. Any error in judging height above the runway, in knowing the floating characteristics of the plane, or in holding an accurate approach speed will result in dropping in, floating, or being suddenly picked up by a gust of wind that may lift the plane back into the air and as suddenly let go of it. There are times when the full-stall landing is preferred to a wheel landing, but not when there are gusts, and not when one wants a consistently gentle, accurate landing.

Let's see how hard each type of landing can strike the ground. The maximum rate of descent of a stalled plane can be that of a freely falling body, but tests made by a national aeronautical organization prove that planes do not drop from a stall like a freely falling body. However, let us say the maximum rate at which a plane may fall from a stall is that of such a body, and then see how hard one may strike the ground from a given height.

The formula for rate of descent in feet-per-second is $V_2 = 2gD$, where $V$ is the rate of descent, $g$ is gravity, and $D$ is the distance dropped in fps. An object dropped from 2 feet strikes the ground at:

$$\sqrt{2 \times 32.2 \times 2}, \text{ or } 11.3 \text{ fps, or } 680 \text{ fpm}$$

This is another way of saying a full-stall landing dropped from 2 feet would be approximately as disagreeable as a wheel landing that was made from an approach of 680 feet per minute down, flying into the runway without breaking the glide. As few pilots make landings that are this bad, examine the figures for a landing from 2 inches, which is gentle enough for anyone.

A full-stall landing from 2 inches (.167 feet) feels like this:

$$V^2 = 2 \times 32.2 \times .167$$
$$V = 3.3 \text{ fps, or } 200 \text{ fpm (approx.)}$$

This is to say that the smooth, easy stall landing from 2 inches *could* strike the runway with about the same impact as a plane striking from a glide of 200 feet per minute down.

Theory, however, must be modified by tests. Do the figures just given agree with actual landings? In order to obtain figures for landing forces, instruments for registering acceleration of $g$'s were installed in many different makes of aircraft. (One $g$, or one gravity, is acting at all times; 2 $g$'s would be twice normal.) The maximum number of $g$'s registered during stall landings was that of a 1½-foot drop, or about 600 fpm down. But—and this is most interesting—it was impossible to compute how hard a plane strikes the ground from 3, 12, or 24 inches because there are too many factors to be considered, such as landing-gear design, shock absorbers, wing load, etc. In the tests, sinking speed varied not only with each plane but in each landing! A plane could strike hard from 2 inches, or it might "grease" itself on the runway.

A stalled airplane is not, therefore, a freely falling body; we can only conclude that a stall landing may be made at 1g (the perfect landing) or it may not. This is not too conclusive. Even more bewildering is the introduction of a few more variables like winds, gusts, and pilot techniques. Recall the case of Pilot M, who used full flaps on the same approach. Pilot M had completed his landing and was congratulating himself, when a sharp gust literally lifted the plane off the ground. Only by immediate application of full throttle did he save the day—and his airplane. After becoming airborne, he made a second landing, used less flap, raised the flap on touchdown, and remained on the ground.

Stall landings are consistently less consistent, but there is a place for them, such as ditching at sea, where minimum touchdown speeds are mandatory, or in small fields where the landing must be made immediately following a steep glide. But for smoother landings all the time, in gusty, turbulent air, or in winds of high velocity, there is a better way to land.

## WHEEL LANDINGS

Consider the experiments made with the same planes, which were wheel-landed. When the planes were landed on the wheels, the *maximum* downward velocity (that is, the hardest landing) was found to be 1.7g's. This is only 0.7g more than a perfect, normal-weight landing of 1g. (Compare this with the maximum of 4g's during stall-landing tests!) What is more important, wheel landings were consistent, they were gentle, and landing forces could be computed. For example, an aircraft that descends at the rate of 200 fpm strikes the ground with the same force as a freely falling body dropped from 2 inches. Thus, pilots who didn't try to ease the wheels on the runway could land, on the average, more gently than pilots who used full-stall landings.

There are, to be sure, rearward forces that must be considered in both the full-stall and the wheel landing. Landing a plane is accompanied by a rearward moment caused by the force needed to spin the wheels, a moment proportionate to the size of the wheels and the ground speed. In a large plane, this moment is enough to worry plane designers, as The Case of the Military Bomber illustrates. Tests during wheel landings showed that although a maximum of only 1.6g's was placed on the gear vertically, the huge force required to spin the gigantic wheels caused a rearward moment that snapped the tail like a whip, causing it to fail. The force was greater during wheel landings because the ground speed was higher than the speed during stall landings.

But these forces which act upon the tail of our lightplane are not as great as those on a bomber, because ground speeds are slower and the wheels are lighter. We need not worry about the forces in stall or wheel landings in lightplanes because landing speeds are never in excess of Over-the-fence Speed (in no wind) or Maneuvering Speed minus the wind (in strong winds). For our airplane, that would be 70 mph minus zero, or 80 mph minus 20, 25, 30, or whatever the wind velocity happened to be. This means that only the downward force need be considered in lightplane landings.

"That's all very good," says someone who is unconvinced, "but suppose I wanted to land short! I'd have to make a stall landing!"

Not so! Admittedly, the stall landing is the only landing to use for ditching, in plowed fields, or in small fields that must be approached with steep angles of descent. In each of these cases the power-approach, full-stall landing is best because contact with the ground is made at slower speed. With a power approach that is just above stalling speed, a pilot can stop flying the moment he cuts the power, but such flying requires much skill and excellent technique. Yet stall landings are not necessarily shorter.

*Speed for speed, in the approach to an airport runway, the wheel landing is shorter.* This is a breathtaking statement, but it was proved some years ago when a national airline conducted landing tests in which movies were made of the full-stall and wheel landing. Landings were made fully stalled, on the wheels, with brakes, and without brakes. To make the test completely reliable, all approaches were made by the same pilots, over the same point, at the same altitude, and the same air speed.

In each case—as was to be expected—the runway distance from the approach position to final stopping point was almost exactly the same for each landing when brakes were not used, a total of

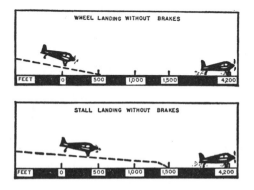

Fig. 12. Landing distance—no brakes.

4,200 feet. Next, each pilot was permitted to use his brakes. Approach speeds and altitudes were the same as before, but full-stall landings consumed 400 feet more runway than did wheel landings. The reason for this is that during stall landings the plane floated over 1,500 feet of runway before the wheels touched, whereas wheel landings were made by pushing the plane on the runway, at which time the brakes were used. Brakes and rubber are expensive, but if one must land short, the wheel landing is the best way to do it. It is assumed, of course, that any pilot who uses brakes at high roll-off speeds knows both his and the plane's limitations, because in a few planes this technique is impossible. Brakes must be used with care, but it's still true that for most planes the wheel landing is shorter, as Fig. 13 portrays. We'll admit that it isn't so much the landing itself that is shorter, but rather the fact that one can be using his brakes on the same stretch of runway that the stall-landing plane floated over while waiting for touchdown.

Now watch Pilot N make his new approach under gusty conditions. He selects a faster glide over the fence merely by continuing to use his Maneuvering Speed, which, as we know, is a bit on the fast side, yet his landing speed will not be excessive because of the gusty, 25-knot wind which reduces ground speed to about 50–55 knots. To be sure, he is going to have flying speed for quite a while after leveling off a few inches from the runway, but this

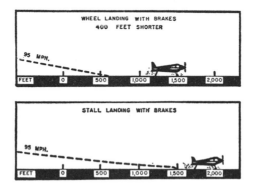

Fig. 13. Landing distance—maximum brakes.

won't bother him because he'll push the wheels onto the runway as soon as possible.

He's using no flaps whatsoever, because in high winds—and a wind of 25 knots is a high wind—his landing speed is already reduced considerably, and he doesn't need any flaps. Also, flaps would increase lift so much that even by the time he stopped rolling, he'd be practically airborne. In winds of less velocity he perhaps would use flaps, but he'd be ready to raise the flaps as soon as his wheels touched, in order to remove any danger of becoming airborne should a sharp gust strike the wings.

Pilot N goes over the fence and down to the runway, tail high, and lands on the wheels with the least angle of attack possible. Now there is no possibility of ballooning back into the air, because his angle of attack is less and he's using forward stick pressure, and this in turn enables him to use brakes effectively. As he tentatively applies brakes and the wheels bear more of the weight, he is alert to feel any tendency to nose over (in tail-wheel planes), or he uses the elevators judiciously (in nose-wheel planes). Tail-wheel planes are more vulnerable, because they can nose over with excessive use of brakes, or they can begin flying again after the tail goes down during the roll-off.

When the tail goes down, Pilot N is in the same uncomfortable position he experienced when he stall-landed, but this time it's different. He's had time to attain a straight roll-off; he's had full control of ailerons and rudder, and time to feel the wind conditions before the wing stalled. It is much easier to let the wing stall when the wheels are already on the ground than to stall them beforehand.

In the last analysis, it isn't a question of which type of landing is better but which is the one to use. A pilot might as well execute his will as go into the water tail high; he might as well plan on eating mud pies if he lands in a muddy field wheels first, because he's going to be plenty muddy after the plane flips over on its back. These are times when power-on, nose-high, full-stall landings are a must.

But for our long, macadam runways, or during variable, gusty winds, or when we're loaded with ice, or for passenger comfort, here's how to win the Pilot-for-Today Award:

1. Get your approach stabilized, using Maneuvering Speed as described in previous chapters.

2. After the glide is established, check to see if the nose holds position on Point X as it did in no wind. If it descends and if you have to add much power, the wind is stronger than usual; and if the bumps are hard, you have gusts.

3. Make your final power reduction so that you have Over-the-fence Speed in advance of reaching the boundary. (*Don't* change to Over-the-fence Speed if there are strong gusts or if wind velocity is more than half the stall speed.)

4. Lower full flaps at the boundary. (*Don't* lower any flaps if you have gusty winds in excess of half the stall speed.)

5. Leave on a little power until you reach Point X. You may "break the glide" slightly or hold your approach down to the runway; you may "burn it on" by landing at a faster speed, or you may land with the tail slightly low. Either method is acceptable, but

high speeds burn rubber and rubber costs money. Whether you push the wheels down or allow them to "kiss" the macadam, contact will be made with the downward velocity of a free fall from less than 2 inches.

6. As soon as you can (when the wheels touch is the best time), reach down and "dump" the flaps. Start using the brakes if the runway is short, otherwise let nature's friction slow you down. Friction is less costly than brake replacement. Be alert when you use brakes. A little practice will teach you just how much you can brake the plane without breaking it, and how quickly you may slow a tailwheel airplane without having the propeller take divots from the runway. If the nose does dip you've got plenty of elevator control, providing the tail is high, inasmuch as airflow keeps the tail up and airflow means control. In most nose-wheel aircraft, the brakes are no problem.

7. If a wing dips, don't hesitate to pick it up with ailerons, because that's what they're there for. To be sure, you'll add drag if the aileron is put down to pick up a down-sliding wing, but you've got plenty of brake or rudder control to offset the drag and stop any incipient turn.

There you have it. Whether you're a nose-wheel or a tail-wheel pilot, you should be acquainted with the advantages of either way to land. You may have an emergency one day in your nose-wheel plane and have to make a stall landing, or you may wish to attain a slower touchdown speed by partially stalling the plane in airliner fashion before the wheels kiss the runway. Should the day come when we no longer have tail-wheels, there'll still be a time when the stall landing is better. But in general the wheel landing is best for everyday flying in each kind of airplane; it's better, easier, faster, and shorter than the three-point landing, and that makes it four against three!

# 10: IT DOESN'T POINT NORTH

THERE was once a dear little lady on the Pacific Coast who had trouble with directions and who could turn left when the right way would have been easier. One day, she visited friends who lived on the corner of a five-sided block and who were a very spirited couple. Upon leaving her friends, the little lady turned right once instead of twice, expecting to find the main boulevard, but instead she nearly drove into the Pacific Ocean.

She installed a compass in her car.

That did it. The very next day she patronized a novelty store and bought a compass, installed it in her car, and was immensely relieved—for about one week. The reason she had a week's happiness was that she hadn't used the compass. It wasn't until she needed it one dark night, after revisiting the Pacific Ocean, that the awful truth dawned upon her—the dratted thing didn't point north!

This isn't news to any pilot but it was news to the dear little lady, who complained to her novelty dealer, only to be told by him that compasses must be compensated. After that was done, the compass pointed elsewhere than north in a uniform manner, always being incorrect by about 15 degrees. Sadly she gave the compass to Junior, who put it on his scooter as an ornament.

It might easily be considered an ornament in some airplanes. If anyone doesn't believe this, he can try solving the following problem. First, however, he must sit down and pretend to be flying in bad weather, with static roaring from the radio and the fuel gauge bouncing on EMPTY.

At this point he recognizes a landmark, finds it on the map, draws a line to the nearest field, and finds it to bear 200° true. The compass reads 32°. What will the compass read when he is on course? Which way shall he turn, right or left, to arrive on course? Remember, one must fly the airplane while he is solving the problem.

In the cockpit, this problem can be terrifying if one doesn't know an easy solution and is trying to solve compass problems quickly. All he needs is an easy rule, yet half of the applicants being tested for ratings don't know one. When asked the *true* heading during the flight test they fumble, hesitate, and usually give an incorrect answer, especially if the check pilot looks puzzled and says, "Are you sure?"

Many of these pilots have learned jingles that ought to be in Mother Goose Rhymes, jingles about ducks, virgins, dead men, and Chicago. When the pressure is on and we've got to find our way home, all we need is a phrase that works in the plane, and we don't care if "Ducks Can Make Vertical Turns," or "True Virgins Make Dull Company," if "Dead Men Vote Twice," or "East is Least West of Chicago."

Take the example of Pilot O, who took off one day for a flight to the desert. Had he known one simple rule he could have saved himself as well as the money spent searching for him. After his flight became overdue, the customary checks were made and for several days planes went out searching the area between his point of departure and his destination.

Then a smart pilot went to his map, drew a course 30° to the right of Pilot O's true course, computed the maximum distance that Pilot O could have flown during wind conditions as they existed the day his plane disappeared, and drew a circle on the map. That's where they found the plane, but Pilot O had become Pilot Zero.

Pilot O's mistake was not unique. He had drawn his true course on the map and correctly measured the bearing. But he had no simple rule, or perhaps the rule he knew was confusing, because he incorrectly applied annual variation, which is given on all aeronautical charts. In his locality the variation was 15°E., but instead of subtracting this amount he added it, eventually flying a heading that was 30° to the right of his desired course.

Yes, he could have caught the error if he had used his finger to pinpoint himself, as will be described in Chapter 11. Yes, he should have had radio aids, and yes, the mistake isn't usually disastrous. But the mistake he made does occur, in one form or another, so frequently that pilots should know an easy, simple, workable rule for reading the compass, which doesn't point north.

During flight tests I have asked many applicants to fly true north. This shouldn't be an impossible problem, but during a flight test—or when the pressure is on—they sweat to get the answer and not always do they find the correct one. What once was easy becomes impossible. They not only worry about variation and deviation but they forget whether to add or subtract them in going from compass to true.

It is nearly 3,000 years since the Chinese first found that a lodestone (a stone containing iron) was magnetized, and that if it were suspended freely by a string it would always settle in one position with one end of the iron pointing in the general direction of north. Since that time it has become the most important navigational instrument we have, despite the fact that it doesn't point north.

It points east of north, or west of north, depending upon one's location. If the location happens to be on a certain isogonic line (called the agonic line) and if there are no other large bodies of metal nearby, such as airplane engines, it *will* point north. But the agonic line zigs from northern Lake Michigan and zags off the coast of southern Florida; pilots who intend to fly up and down this line can disregard variation, but they'll still have deviation and their compasses still won't point north.

## AN EASY RULE FOR THE COMPASS

Now go back to our problem. We're flying 32° by the compass and we wish to fly 200° true. What we need is a rule that works in the cockpit, not one that was used in a classroom, because the cockpit is where the rule is needed most. We want to know (1) where we're going and (2) which is the direction of shortest turn to a desired heading.

Here is the easy rule that makes compass courses easy:

*Compass to true ... add east.*

That's all there is to it. It works, but it does have to be memorized; piloting is the pilot's business, and he does have to remember something. Now we look at the compass (32°) and recall that the map gave our local variation as 15°E; using the rule we obtain:

Compass (32°) to true ... add east (15°)

True = 47°

We're therefore flying a true heading of 47 degrees. But the airport is located on a bearing of 200 degrees; we wish to turn in the direction of the shortest turn, either right or left, to save time and gasoline. Which way shall we turn?

Whenever a pilot is given such problems, particularly on a flight test, he should visualize where he is. This can be accomplished best by using the compass "rose" in Fig. 14, which will be used in all of our instrument work in later chapters. It is called *Your World* and is an extremely valuable aid, especially during instrument

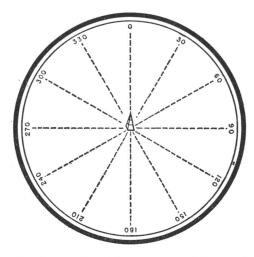

Fig. 14. *Your World.* Make a replica of this compass. It is indispensable for cockpit use in solving orientation problems. For example, the station is always in the center; therefore, if you are flying outbound on a heading of 200°, you are at the bottom left of *Your World.* To find the shortest distance to turn from 200 to 355, simply glance at the chart, and presto! you have the answer.

flight. Visualize yourself on the 47° radial flying out from the center; 200° is in the southwest quadrant, to the south and right of 47°; therefore we turn right in order to get on 200° quickly.

As you turn, compute the compass heading to steer a true heading of 200 degrees. The rule says *Compass to true . . . add east,* so 200 plus 15 is 215. This is more than we want. Try 185 plus 15, which equals 200 and which *is* the heading we want. Do *not* consider this reasoning as childish and attempt to learn a new rule. Know one rule well and you'll never go wrong.

But what about pilots who fly mostly on the *East Coast,* where the annual variation is *west?* The easy rule still works. Suppose we're flying from New York to Boston, where, according to the map, the variation is 15° *west.* Our rule comes to mind like an old friend, *Compass to true . . . add east;* it logically follows that we subtract west, so we realize that in order to fly 200° true we must steer 215°, because 215 less 15 is 200.

As we fly onward, wistfully hoping that the airport will show itself, we suddenly remember that there is no such thing as a perfectly calibrated compass. It is certain to deviate on at least one compass heading and, in order that the pilot may know the error, he has on the instrument panel a calibration or compass deviation card. This card has twelve readings which were obtained when the compass was calibrated, readings taken every 30 degrees. A glance at the card tells us,

| For . . . 180 | 210 | 240 . . . |
|---|---|---|
| Steer . . . 178 | 209 | 240 . . . |

Therefore, for 185 we'd steer 183, or instead of steering 215 we'd steer 214.

As it is difficult to fly a compass heading within a degree or so without a Gyro Compass, we might have found our airport had we not corrected for deviation, but the 15° of variation is another matter. Certainly we'd not have found it had we incorrectly applied variation and flown 30° from course, as Pilot O did in the flight that ended so unhappily.

## FOR EXAMS ONLY

But what about examinations? So far we've solved compass problems in the airplane, where they are extremely important, but before one is allowed to fly to distant points he must have a certificate, and that calls for a written exam. Also, when one plans a flight, he should write on his map both true and magnetic courses. It must be conceded that this complicates the problem; furthermore, examination questions ask for *magnetic* course, and for this we almost have to know a jingle.

But compass headings are seldom corrected for deviation until *after* we get into the airplane and consult the deviation card. One never sees a pilot with this card in his pocket. In every instance a pilot plans the flight by obtaining the true course from his map, allowing for variation and getting the magnetic course, correcting for wind to obtain the magnetic heading, and he then waits until he gets into the air before he reads the deviation card and steers a *compass heading.*

Nevertheless, exam questions require that we know how to use both deviation and variation, so let's learn a jingle that goes with our rule. Here are a few that have been used for years:

1. *True Virgins Make Dull Company* ... *Subtract East.*

This statement may be debated furiously by those who qualify, but it need not arouse ire because it simply is a supposedly easy way to remember that the jingle stands for *True* ... *Variation* ... *Deviation* ... *Compass.* It is good only in the classroom because it works only in going from map to compass.

2. *East is Least West of Chicago.* This means that variation is easterly on the West Coast, but it doesn't say whether to add or subtract it from true headings. It is confusing to everyone except those in Chicago, where the variation is about zero, even on windy days. It doesn't mention deviation of magnetic headings, and is therefore the least valuable of the jingles.

3. *Can Ducks Make Vertical Turns?* This one can be used in or out of duck season, and is just as good as Number 4 if we append *Add East* to it.

4. *Can Dead Men Vote Twice?* ... *Add East.* Politically, one might answer this query affirmatively in some areas; aeronautically it means *Compass* ... *Deviation* ... *Magnetic* ... *Variation* ... *True* ... *(Add East).* It's good because it's almost like *Compass to true* ... *add east.* Our basic rule is best for use in the airplane, where we need it, but the basic rule doesn't work for exams, because nothing is said about deviation or variation. But if we know

a basic rule, we can modify it, and we won't have any trouble remembering how the two rules fit together.

Consider our first examination question, which reads something like this:

"You are to fly from X to Y. Find the true course, the magnetic course, and the compass course. Compass deviation is 5° west."

We take a ruler and draw a razor-like line from X to Y, place a protractor on the line, and read the bearing exactly. Your answer for written exams must be accurate within a degree. Suppose that it reads 200 degrees. Next, we remember our easy rule and write it on scratch paper, like this:

That's all we need in the plane, but it helps to fill in the rest, which is needed for answering the examination question. Try to remember the jingle, and fill in the blanks, like this:

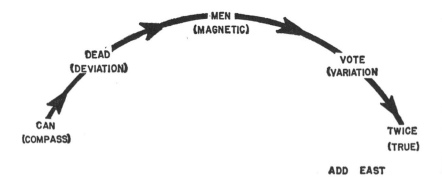

Now, if we add east going from left to right, we shall have to subtract east going the other way. Draw the lower half of the circle by writing in the words as they appear in the top half:

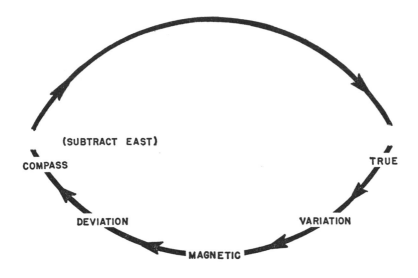

(SUBTRACT EAST)

COMPASS

TRUE

DEVIATION

VARIATION

MAGNETIC

Finally, if we subtract east, we'll logically add west, so write that in:

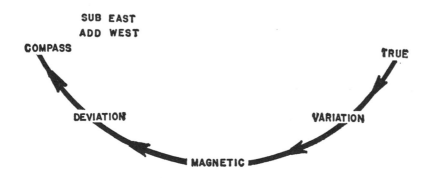

SUB EAST
ADD WEST

COMPASS

TRUE

DEVIATION

VARIATION

MAGNETIC

And there you have it, all developed from a useful rule needed in the cockpit, to a bit of less useful information that may well be forgotten after the examination. You'll never use it after the exam, and it need not clutter your brain. Now finish the examination problem. True course, 200°; variation (from map), 15°E; magnetic course is 200 minus 15, or 185°; deviation (from problem), 5°W; compass course is 185 plus 5, or 190°.

## FROM MAP TO COMPASS

Practically, that's nothing like what we do in the Ready Room. We wish to know what course to steer when we get into the airplane, so we draw our course line on our chart. Suppose that it is also 200°: we write "200 T" beside the line.

Now the easy rule helps; we don't burden ourselves with anything but *Compass to true . . . add east.*

Realize that in going from true to compass we do the opposite—subtract east. Therefore 200 minus 15 equals 185, so we write "185 M" beside the course line. After getting the wind from aerology and obtaining the magnetic *heading,* we get into the plane, check the compass deviation card, and are happy to find that it doesn't say whether the deviation is east or west. It simply says:

For    180
Steer    179

We therefore steer 184 instead of 185 to make good a compass *course* that will take us to our destination, and if we allow for wind we will correct the course a few degrees and steer a compass *heading,* but that is another story and has nothing to do with how a compass works.

The important thing to realize is that the compass does not point north; we must know how to take one look at the compass and instantly solve for true course. Can this be done in one step?

Certain navigational experts go so far as to say that unknown winds or variable winds will offset whatever small deviation there may be in the compass. But if we wish to be strictly accurate, we must allow for deviation. This can be done in a single computation during short flights in all sections of the country, or during long flights in the western states, where variation does not change as rapidly as it does in the east.

For instance, we're flying in the Middle West where the variation is 10°E, on a compass heading of 307. For approximate conversions from compass to true headings we glance at the compass, automatically saying, *Compass to true . . . add east,* and thereupon add the two figures: $307 + 10 = 317$ true.

For precise computations we'd first read the compass, 307, and *next,* the compass deviation card, which says:

| For | 300 | 330 |
|-----|-----|-----|
| Steer | 301 | 333 |

Thus, if we are already steering 301 we'd be making good 300, and similarly 307 becomes 306. Then we'd add the variation of 10° to get the total of 316°. In other words, we could have added 9° to 307° and obtained 316°, so from now on in this area we'll add 9° to the compass heading to obtain the precise true heading.

Finally, suppose that some eager inspector asks you to fly true north, which is a problem that confuses most Private Pilots. To do this quickly and thereby impress the inspector favorably (a four-star recommendation), start turning to a compass heading of zero. This promptness alone will fool any inspector. While you're turning, remember your rule *Compass to true . . . add east.* You know, or should know, the variation in your home area. Suppose that you live on the West Coast where annual variation is about 15°E. Turn slowly and figure out that if you fly zero (360, or north), then zero plus 15 equals 15, which is too much. You must then fly 345, because 345 plus 15 is 360; stop the turn at 345 and ask the inspector—innocently— if he also wants deviation included. This not only shows him you know what you're doing but it gives you another moment to figure out the deviation card. If the inspector says yes, a look at the card will tell you:

| For | 330 | 0 |
|-----|-----|-----|
| Steer | 333 | 2 |

It seems that 345 isn't listed, so we estimate 345 to be about 3°, and the card should read: For 345, steer 348. We turn to 348 and get a nod of approval. Inspectors like to test applicants who can think, and this might be the straw that turns the scales in your favor.

Knowing *one* rule and being able to use it can easily be the difference between success or failure. It's the first step in learning how to fly cross country. The next step is the map. Let's see how this subject can indeed be glamorous by reading the next chapter.

# 11: GLAMORIZING YOUR UGLY MAP

PILOT P was high over the North Carolina Appalachians, flying southward to Atlanta. It was summer, the country was beautiful, and the landscape below was a blur of foliage that obscured roads, railroads, rivers, and other landmarks. Conditions like this make piloting difficult for most pilots, but not for Pilot P. He was listening to a radio program while he flew a compass heading, a program of soothing melodies sponsored by sweet-smelling soap.

Pilot P was about to need the soap being advertised. Because of an unsuspected defect, the compass bowl cracked, sprinkling him generously with kerosene solution. Within a few minutes the bowl was dry, Pilot P was all wet, and the soap opera forgotten. Operational matters demanded his full attention. Where was he? Where was the nearest check point? Where was Atlanta?

Atlanta was exactly where it had always been, but Pilot P had his

Pilot P was about to need the soap being advertised.

doubts. He had heard that the Appalachians in summer are most difficult for contact navigation. With the compass inoperative, he'd have to pin-point himself from check point to check point, and he'd have to keep his finger on his number—number, in this case, meaning the map. He took the appropriate aeronautical chart from his map case and began to study it carefully, but the time to glamorize one's ugly map is *before* the dance. Pilot P wished that it was time for intermission and that he'd learned an easy rule to make map reading a joy.

With a pencil and protractor, he commenced the beauty treatment by drawing a line from his point of departure to Atlanta, almost due south. He measured the true course and marked what he hoped was his actual position. Then he held the map before him to see if any portion of it looked like the terrain below. It didn't. Pilot P was holding the map the way maps are made, with north at the top, which caused the terrain to be upside down. He could not turn the terrain but he could have turned his airplane. Instead, he turned his head, which was not too comfortable. He didn't turn the map around because that would result in the names of landmarks being upside down, and the important things on a map, as far as P was concerned, are the names!

His terrain was upside down.

A wing went down and the plane began to turn; it turned through 30° before Pilot P caught it. By that time he'd forgotten to remember the check point toward which he'd been steering when the compass broke. He was many degrees off course, he wasn't even on course, and of course he was consequently quite lost.

Let's leave Pilot P to his troubles. He'll eventually extricate himself and provide a happy ending, although he'll be a wiser pilot hereafter if he'll realize that an ugly map can be quite glamorous when it's handled properly.

Take your sectional aeronautical chart in hand before making your next cross-country flight and see what you read there. Less than 50 years ago a map like this, which can be obtained for 25 cents from Coast and Geodetic Survey, would have been a twentieth century marvel. Beautifully engraved, accurate to a pin-point, and detailed to include prominent cultural markings, it is a little-appreciated Private Pilot's navigator. Any Private Pilot with a modicum of brains and a little altitude can navigate from point to point despite the fact that his compass isn't working.

Look at your chart. It is a Lambert conformal projection, which means that it conforms to the earth's surface. Maps in geography books are usually Mercator charts, which are distorted. Compare any continent on a Mercator chart with the same continent as shown on a globe, and see how Mercator continents widen out at the top.

Your Lambert chart is made without this distortion. If sections are pieced together, like the maps one sees on the walls in Flight Shacks, one may see that lines of latitude and longitude actually curve, just as they do on a globe. This means that a straight line drawn from one point to another on the map is the shortest distance between them on the earth's surface, a great circle course.

Therefore the mileage and the route may be computed directly from the chart; mileage may be obtained by using either the nautical mileage scale or the latitude divisions (a nautical mile equals one minute of latitude, or one degree of latitude is 60 nautical miles).

## THE OTHER SIDE

Before drawing the line on your chart which will represent your proposed track, or true course, see if you know what the map is saying. There are two sides to a discussion, and there are two sides to a map. Turn it over and see what else is available for the sum expended. The equivalent of 14 pages of information is listed, from aeronautical symbols and topographical features to flight plans and search-rescue procedures.

1. *Aeronautical symbols.* It's no longer necessary to land at an

airport in order to be disappointed at not finding what you want there; it saves time to be disappointed en route. For example, the little blue box beside the airport says, Podunk . . . 18 L H 46, followed by the radio frequencies in use. The L H does not mean that Podunk has a left-hand traffic pattern. The symbols explain that L means minimum lighting facilities are offered, while H indicates hard-surfaced runways; 18 is the elevation in feet, and 46 is runway length in hundreds of feet. Check the symbols and see how radios, beacons, ranges, and Omniranges (VOR) are given.

2. *Topographical symbols.* These are the most important of all, because in flying cross country you want to be able to *read* your map. Notice that cities are represented by yellow splotches that vary in size according to the area, and that superhighways and roads are plainly marked. But the most important markings are the relief features, the hydrographic features, and the cultural landmarks.

The map is telling you a story, as though you were reading a book. Notice the blue that represents water, the green for land under 1,000 feet elevation, the cream, buff, and brown for higher elevations. Look at the contour lines signifying relief. The 1,000-foot contour line is what would be shore line if the sea were to rise 1,000 feet. Thus, they tell us what a mountain looks like: if the lines are close together, the mountain is steep; if the lines are circular with a sharp, inward sweep, they represent a round mountain with a valley. If the contour lines bulge outward toward the sides of the map they represent an arm jutting out from the hill or mountain. If there is a blue line in the inward-shaped contours, a stream flows down it. (But beware those dotted blue lines in desert areas; they are streams only when it rains, so don't look for water.)

Learn to recognize the symbols for peaks, bluffs, sand, and the swamps, streams, lakes, and washes. They'll help when you're flying cross country and pin-pointing the map, as we'll be doing shortly. Next, which will help to distinguish one town from another (they look alike from the air), are the cultural markings, which include oil tanks, oil fields, race tracks, open-air theaters, bridges, and railroads. Be careful of those "Iron Compass" railroads, because if a pilot uses the Iron Compass in navigating, the wrong railroad can take him off course and the conductor won't warn him of his error.

Suppose that visibility lowers to less than 3 miles, and you're outside a control area. The map shows how aircraft are separated at 500-foot intervals for different directions of flight. For example, in flying easterly headings, at altitudes from 3,000 to 17,000 feet, we'd fly at odd-thousand altitudes plus 500; westerly headings should be flown at even-thousands plus 500. These are not too hard to remember, but few pilots do. There is no need to—they're on the map. Should the visibility lower and become obstructed by clouds, your map gives the separation required between the airplane and those clouds under varying visibility minimums and during different flight clearances.

Should you be forced to change your flight plan en route, the map contains a flight plan form. This enables a pilot to give his flight plan in sequence, without six omissions which require six requests for completion by the Air Traffic Communication Station (ATCS). Finally, there is a list of the airports on the map, with their location, elevation, length of runways, and the facilities available; also shown are the Defense Zones and the Prohibited Areas one must avoid.

## TRUE COURSE

Pilot P, had he used his map both prior to flight and during flight, would have had as much relief as his map. He would have known that in summertime he should be more alert than usual to recognize check points in a mountainous, densely-foliaged area, and that there'd be fewer highways, railroads, roads, bridges, race tracks, dams, towers, steeples, electric transmission lines, and cultural features to help him navigate.

If he'd taken a ruler-protractor he would have drawn a course line such as we'll draw between our point of departure and the destination. This is the true *course*, and we must fly a *heading* that will cause our path, which is called the *track*, to coincide with the course. After drawing the line, we place the protractor half-way between our points, at the point where the course intersects a meridian of longitude, which is true north. Where the course line intersects the right side of the protractor is the angle, or true course. Write the number beside the line we've drawn and place an arrow beside it in the direction of our flight. The variation (see the isogonic line on the map) is 1° east, so subtract it from the true course and write the result (the magnetic course) beneath the true course, so that it looks like Fig. 15, on page 117.

We now have the *true* course (175) and the *magnetic* course (174) marked on the map and available for instant reference. Next we use a navigational computer and obtain the *magnetic heading* (magnetic course corrected for wind), recalling that we always obtain the *compass heading* after we get into the cockpit and read the deviation from the compass deviation card.

Using the appropriate scale on our ruler-protractor (we'll use nautical miles), lay the ruler on the course line and mark the course in 10-mile intervals, writing the cumulative mileage at each interval like this: 10—20—30, etc. Thus, at any time during the flight, we'll be able to make a progress check without any difficulty.

## SHARP AS A PIN POINT

Now, unlike Pilot P, we're going to be sharp, sharp as a pin point, and this is where cross-country flying is fun, much more fun than being doubly bored by flying lazily and listening to soap advertising. Because we're flying a southerly heading, which is most confusing to map readers, we'll have to be sharp, and the best sharpener is an easy rule, as will be described in a moment.

We get into the plane and check the deviation card. It reads, "For 180 steer 178"; the magnetic course was 174, the computer gave 170 as the magnetic heading, so we'll steer 168. We take off and get set on our predetermined heading. All the way up to altitude we're in familiar territory and can stay on course without too much effort. As soon as we level off at altitude and get cruising speed, we make a notation of the *exact* time on the chart, at the exact check point over which we note the time. This is called pin-pointing our position.

We look at our map. Because we're flying south, we are flying down the map, from top to bottom. The river we actually see below us is at our right, but on the map it's located to the left. That bridge we just passed is behind us, but on the map it seems to be above our position. The only things we can read accurately and easily are the names of the cities, rivers, or mountains, but names are not printed on the ground.

## HOW TO HOLD THE MAP

It's the shape or appearance of the terrain that we see on the ground, so *turn the map until the true course coincides with the track of flight.* Like Mahomet, who was compelled to go to the mountain, we shall have to turn the map if we cannot turn the terrain. Upon turning the map so that north on the map coincides with true north, the whole world falls into place like a jigsaw puzzle, and instead of looking at a confusing piece of paper, we now find that the paper tells us a story. The landscape falls into place as it should; the mountain yonder is on our right, just as the map says; that twisting river bends to the right instead of the left; that small town slipping beneath the wing is also behind our position on the map instead of being ahead of us.

Let the visual experts laugh and term this child's play. They may be right, but our problem is the man-sized job of navigating the airplane, and we can't be bothered with such caviling. Turning one's map is not only psychologically sound, it's practicable. Most of us are not so versatile that we can look at a map which is being held opposite to the terrain and say, "That point at the bottom-left on the map is actually ahead of us and to the right. That river, twisting downward on the map, can be plainly seen ahead of the plane, except that it's twisting forward. That town toward which we're flying is at the bottom of the map." (See Fig. 15).

It's easier to learn to read words from inverted or sideways positions than it is to revolve the entire map in the mind's eye. It's easier just to look at the map when one is to the left of course, see where he is, and know that a turn to the right in the plane is also a right turn on the map. In fact, our pin-point navigating is now so interesting that we nearly forget to navigate, so let's get back to our check point.

Suppose our ground speed is 120 knots; this means we're covering 10 nautical miles every five minutes. As the check points slip beneath us, keep an eye moving along the map and learn how fast you seem to progress on the map. If you have marked the map in 10-nautical-mile intervals, you can expect to find the next check point sliding past in a certain number of minutes. When it disappears beneath your seat as you look downward, note the exact time on the chart, again pin-pointing your position. Now take the computer, set it to the elapsed time and mileage between check points, and see if the ground speed is what you estimated it to be in the Ready Room. If it's the same, your prognosticated wind was correct, but in most cases the speed will vary. Make a second 10-mile check to verify the ground speed, and after that you should be able to establish an ETA (esti-

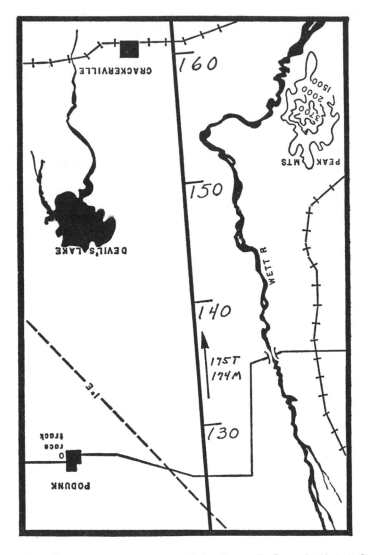

Fig. 15. Draw the course line on your map; write headings and mileages beside it. In flight, hold the map so that the course line is in the direction of flight, and north on the map points to true north. Although the printed information on the map may not be right side up, the map will look exactly like the terrain.

mated time of arrival) that's accurate within a minute or two, something to be proud of, something that will mark you as an expert instead of a dub.

You've now established your ground speed and the correct heading to maintain your *course* on the map and your *track* over the ground. Now when you estimate the time over the next fix you are ready for any change in wind direction or velocity that would cause you to become "lost" en route, or, more accurately, to cause your destination to become lost. Suppose that the next fix is not directly beneath you the next time you look down. What to do about it?

In the first place, looking directly downward is not good practice because it's too difficult. Fly a half-mile or so to the right or left of the course so that you can see both sides without effort. Sometimes there are landmarks on either side of a town that will be obscured by one side or other of the fuselage. Flying to one side of the track increases the visibility. Granted, there's always some portion of the ground below that the fuselage obscures, but one can see this less-important section of the course by looking ahead.

You look down at the terrain to find that although you've maintained an accurate heading, you're to the right of the course. This means an immediate course correction is indicated. Initial course corrections should be made with definite, large bites in order to quickly ascertain drift, although making many large corrections in a cross-country flight would be tiresome. Once a track is maintained, small corrections are made to keep the plane on the track.

But an initial course correction of 30° is advisable because (1) it carries the plane quickly back on course, (2) it's a convenient number to subtract from the compass heading, (3) a lesser figure might just be enough to correct for the change in wind. Then, when you're back on course, remove part of the bite (say, 20°), steer 10° into the wind, and see what effect the new heading has in holding the course.

"But," you say, "how do I know that I'm a mile or 10 miles to the right of course? I'm at 10,000 feet, and a mile doesn't seem to make much difference." The answer is that the terrain must be studied from different altitudes. Pick out a prominent point, find it on the map, and find the distance of the point from your position. Say to yourself, "That point is 12 miles away; I am at 10,000 feet." Then estimate the distance of other points, and before you know it, the expert on distances in the cockpit is you. Remember to turn the map until the true course coincides with the track of flight, because you not only can recognize check points from the similarity of the shape on the map to the shape of the terrain but also can tell the direction of the object. An object that bears 30° relative (that is, 30° from the nose of the plane) should also be 30° to the right of the course line we drew on the map, plus or minus the wind-correction angle.

Now make the position report to ATCS. It's not compulsory in VFR flight, but it's the smart thing to do. Give your report in IFR phraseology: "Podunk Radio, this is Nan 777 over Sadler's Wells 56 (the time in minutes is sufficient, as the operator supposedly knows it's one, two, or three o'clock) at nine thousand, five hundred, VFR destination Utopia. Over."

Keep your finger moving along with the plane, knowing ground speed and drift, descending in time to arrive over your destination at traffic-pattern altitude. You land, tie the plane down, and put your glamorous map into the map case with a feeling of affection. And a rather smug smile comes over your own map when you recall what a satisfactory flight it was, with an ETA that was right on the money.

Over Sadler's Wells.

# 12: THE REFRIGERATOR IN YOUR PLANE

THERE'S an engine in the sky with a couple of wings attached to it and a couple of men sitting behind it. This is not news, and no one bothers to look up. There are thousands of such events happening every day, planes that fly when the weather is clear and planes that fly when it isn't. This particular plane is flying in humid weather across a sky obscured by a layer of visible moisture which pilots call stratus or solid overcast. Suddenly the engine skips a beat, but even this doesn't cause anyone but us to become alarmed, for they are on the ground whereas *we* are sitting behind that engine.

When the engine skips a beat something inside of us skips two beats. Before looking for a place to land, we examine the cockpit, hoping that the trouble may be located within arm's reach. We fumble around in our sleek but comparatively low-powered plane and move the mixture control to a leaner setting, which does smooth the engine a little but not for long. Soon less air is admitted into the carburetor and the engine becomes as rough as it was before. We cannot go on indefinitely leaning the mixture, because engines do require fuel. What shall we do?

The armed services gave pilots the word on ice. They said that ice is an enemy more dangerous than an enemy plane! Yet some pilots don't seem to know that this enemy exists, mistakenly assuming that ice is a product which comes out of a refrigerator in cubes, or possibly thinking that the refrigerator in our plane does make ice cubes.

To not be aware of carburetor ice can be hazardous. Take the example of a pilot with whom I was dive bombing, way back when. We were dive bombing from 15,000 feet, and it was his turn to dive. The target was an old battleship which was making maximum knots for a cloud cover that might protect her. Pulling his throttle back and putting the prop into high pitch, my friend rolled over in order

**120**

to have at her, although that meant diving through a small portion of the clouds. I watched him dive, drop his water-filled bombs, level off, continue to glide, and finally land near the battleship with a mighty splash of water. After they had picked him up, minus his plane, he said that when he opened the throttle the engine back-fired and quit!

He landed near the battlewagon with a mighty splash.

Nowadays we Private Pilots are taught preventive measures, and we know that ice can form in the carburetor on a clear day when the temperature is in the 70s. Yet many pilots don't know how to tell when the refrigerator is making ice! How can we recognize it, and what should we do about it? Then there's the just-as-dangerous ice which forms when we have visible moisture, the kind that accumulates not in the carburetor but on the plane itself. When moisture is present in the form of freezing rain or snow it can become a weighty matter within minutes.

Fortunately ice that forms *in* the airplane, although it's most insidious because our refrigerator is up in the engine compartment where we can't see it, is also the easiest to counteract. By *in* the airplane we don't mean the cockpit, although that icy feeling that makes us frigid when the engine coughs is definitely in the cockpit.

## ICE *IN* THE AIRPLANE

So here we are at 5,000 feet, with stratus outside, ice in the carburetor, and icy feelings inside. We are not flying a deluxe job with a manifold temperature gauge, a fuel-air analyzer, a manifold pressure gauge, and a coffee percolator. We are sitting in a lightplane looking at a basic panel, and we must analyze the engine roughness in order that we may land at an airport instead of the nearest unpaved cow pasture.

What happens is that the evaporation of gasoline in the carburetor causes a temperature drop of as much as 60° F, and as air becomes colder it becomes denser, squeezing moisture out of the air. This moisture is deposited on the metering elements, where it freezes, causing an incorrect fuel-air ratio and resulting in a rich mixture, loss of power, and a rough engine. Or ice may form around the fuel jets, the throttle butterfly valve, or the adapter, causing a gradual dropping off of rpm's (or manifold pressure, with constant-speed props), exactly as if you'd closed the throttle and without any rough-engine symptoms. Soon the air speed decreases and your first inclination is to add power by opening the throttle.

This is so confusing that someone asks, "Why not fly with car-buretor heat on and avoid these dilemmas?" The answer is that using carburetor preheat reduces the power output of an engine. Some pilots do fly with carburetor heat at a minimum, but their plane has a carburetor temperature gauge and they maintain heat at a temperature of 35° to 40° F. But lightplanes do not ordinarily have such gauges, and to use heat results in loss of power; heated air is less dense than cold air, and with less air there are fewer horses available from the engine. Less air also means a richer mixture and a rough engine, and the possibility of attempting to obtain smoother operation by leaning out the mixture. Lean mixtures bring on overheating and possible detonation. Overheating and detonation may be discovered only by watching the head-temperature gauge; the undesirable results of detonation cannot, as in an automobile, be detected by a "ping"—overheating and roughness are the only apparent indications. The bill for repairing damaged heads or burned valves is another indication, but a bit late to be of much help.

The correct method is to use preheat as it is needed. Private Pilots have been repeatedly warned to use heat when the engine is idling at low speeds prior to take-off, and they have been cautioned to use heat before reducing throttle for a power-off glide. But the method of using heat while en route isn't so well known, and they don't seem to realize that heat must be used *before* icing conditions become serious, because carburetor heat comes from the exhaust manifold, and after ice has formed in the carburetor the engine develops less power. With less power there is less heat available to melt ice; more ice is formed and the vicious circle is sometimes completed with a forced landing. Then the pilot climbs out of the cockpit to see cups of water draining from the carburetor.

Why not eliminate the refrigerator in your plane by a few simple steps? Here they are, for *any* kind of weather.

1. Apply carburetor heat by using
   a. full heat
   b. intermittent heat
   c. a constant low setting or continued rechecking
2. Use mixture control as described below.
3. See and feel steps 1 and 2.

*1. Carburetor heat.* Let's suppose that we have a condition of reduced power, evidenced either by a rough engine or loss of rpm's and air speed. We don't so much as suspect carburetor ice, so we lean out the mixture and increase the throttle setting. This compensates for the rich mixture caused by the ice on the metering elements and all goes smoothly—for awhile. But in a short time (less than a minute, with severe icing conditions) the engine is rough again, and soon the mixture is in full lean position. This is definitely not the action to take first, as full lean is also the cut-off position.

We know that we're flying relatively low horsepower, which furnishes only a small amount of heat from the exhaust. Low-horsepower engines are also quite allergic to water, and because we have encountered icing conditions suddenly, as evidenced by our rough engine, we conclude that ice is forming in the carburetor too fast for comfort. We know we have sudden ice, that there is plenty of it, and that to use full heat continuously will melt the ice quickly, form excessive amounts of water, and literally drown the engine.

At the same time, we know that loss of power means that we'll have less carburetor heat, and we need all the heat we can get. We decide to take immediate action because we're almost entering the vicious circle described above. We apply *full* heat momentarily. Half heat, in our lightplane engine, is often as inadequate as none at all, whereas continous heat will melt the ice too fast. So we use full heat for a few seconds and then remove all but a portion, leaving enough so that no more ice will form. A gasoline engine actually thrives on a *little* water, as fighter pilots in World War II found out with water-injection carburetors, so the small amount of water entering the engine won't hurt it or cause engine failure.

Now we'll watch the tachometer for a rise in rpm's, and listen to the engine for decreasing roughness. As the ice melts we should experience more power, increased smoothness, and more rpm's. After we finally remove all the heat, the rpm's should give us normal power for the throttle setting we're using. At this point we momentarily apply heat for a final check; application of heat should reduce power, because hot air is less dense than cold air and the mixture is richer. This is the conclusive proof that normal conditions again exist in the carburetor.

What is our next move? To use heat? If so, how much? Can engine damage result from excessive carburetor heat? The answer is that in lightplanes such damage is not likely, but in any airplane we'll have poor efficiency, rough-engine operation, and higher fuel consumption. Therefore, to continually use unnecessary heat is poor technique, and we must find a better way.

For pilots who don't have a carburetor temperature gauge, there's only one good method: this is to use as little heat as possible and to check continually for ice during icing conditions by using more heat and by watching the instruments.

These instruments are the tachometer, the air-speed indicator, and the manifold pressure (Hg, or hydragyrum) gauge. If you don't have a manifold pressure gauge, the rpm's tell what power you're using and the air-speed indicator tells you whether you're getting the power that you should be getting. Set your throttle (or Hg's) for cruise. Expert pilots know the indicated cruising speed that results from a given power setting (rpm's and manifold pressure) at a given altitude. When the rpm's fall off (or the Hg decreases), we don't nervously jump to the conclusion that we've got a creeping throttle and that we must add power, thereby worsening the situation.

*Use heat*, and if the rpm's or the Hg increase, you've just removed some ice from your carburetor. The engine smooths out, the air speed increases to the normal speed for the power you're using, and you reduce heat to a low setting. If this setting keeps ice from forming, reduce the setting until you find the minimum necessary for cruise. In dry air, of course, no carburetor preheat whatsoever is the best setting.

2. *Use of mixture control.* Just to be difficult, let us suppose that

after removing the ice our engine still runs rough. Ordinarily, a modern carburetor does not require adjustment of the mixture at altitudes below 5,000 feet, but the impossible can happen, and when we apply step 2 (lean the mixture) our engine smooths out. Is there any harm in using the mixture control at low altitudes?

We know that an excessively lean mixture *can* damage an engine, because it raises the combustion temperature, burns the valves and —especially in engines of higher power—causes detonation. Which is better: to fly with a rough engine and a rich mixture, or a smooth engine and a normal mixture? What is a normal mixture? How can we analyze mixture troubles without head-temperature gauges or a fuel-air-ratio analyzer?

Flying with a rich mixture and a rough engine is not good technique; roughness is hard on pilots as much as engines. Regardless of your altitude, we want a normal, efficient mixture. If the carburetor is rich at low altitude it should be adjusted by a mechanic later, but right now we want the correct mixture, and obtaining this is easy whether or not we have analyzers.

A reliable method, which is guaranteed never to burn a valve, is to get set at cruising power at any desired altitude. Now lean the mixture slowly and watch the tachometer (even in planes with manifold pressure gauges and constant-speed propellers). If leaning the mixture causes an immediate drop in rpm's, the mixture is too lean and should be returned to normal. But if, as is more often the case, a *rise* in rpm's occurs, the mixture was too rich. Although this normally occurs at altitudes above 5,000 feet, remember that we're flying an engine, not an altitude.

Continue to lean out the mixture until a drop in rpm's is observed. This setting is too lean, and the mixture must be enriched until the rpm's return to the maximum rpm's we had when we adjusted the mixture. This is the setting for maximum efficiency, but to be on the safe side and have a cool mixture, we'll move the mixture control slightly toward rich. As we move it, *feel* and *hear* the engine. Our tachometer reads rpm's in hundreds, but our senses feel roughness in fractions; with a little practice one can become adept at finding the proper point at which to adjust the mixture for smooth operation. Thus the tachometer tells us how to set the mixture for efficiency, and our senses give the setting for smoothness.

As you adjust your carburetor, remember that every engine requires different techniques; some carburetors ice up quickly and require 40° of heat at all times. Others are ice-free, needing little heat and using fuel piggishly at this temperature. If you use steps 1 and 2, you'll become an expert who knows his plane and doesn't fly by a rule book, and who uses those easy rules to smooth out his rough flying.

To sum up:

1. Be alert for ice in any weather condition. When in doubt, use heat, but use the minimum amount of heat at all times.

2. When the engine runs rough, check for ice first, by using full heat intermittently. *Don't increase the throttle setting* to counteract carburetor ice.

3. After any possible ice is eliminated, adjust the mixture.

4. Adjust it by watching the gauges and using the senses. Common sense, as always, is a great help.

## ICE ON THE AIRPLANE

Ice *on* the airplane can quickly become such a weighty matter that the plane becomes too heavy to fly. Ice can form all over the airplane, on the prop, tail, fuselage, windshield, Pitot tube, or controls. But it's the shape of the ice on the wings, as much as the weight, that worries us.

In order to broaden the subject for the Private Pilot, let us consider that ice is any form of frozen moisture; thus we have frost, freezing rain, sleet, wet snow, hail, rime ice, and clear ice. Now that you know how many kinds there are, remember to avoid all of them, because lightplane pilots can't do much about ice except to avoid it.

But knowing something about ice is essential in order to know how to avoid it. For the experienced instrument pilot there are clues as to when to ascend to warmer air and how to descend through freezing strata, but to fly in this kind of weather requires a high degree of proficiency in instrument flying and equipment not installed in lightplanes. Let's remain on the ground in this kind of weather; knowing a little about ice tells us when we shouldn't take off.

*Frost.* Frost is actually frozen dew. It should be called frozen don't, because you don't dare take off with frosted wings. It looks harmless and benign, but one might as well try to take off with a flat board instead of a cambered wing. Frost is an excellent spoiler of lift, and the plane simply won't get off the runway. Luckily, it doesn't form during flight so there's no danger from frost there. It can't be removed with a broom, usually, and one must use warm air inside a hangar or warm rags if there is no hangar. Beware of using water, because it will surely freeze and cause trouble; a thin coating of ice on a wing is better than frost, but water gets into aileron hinges and controls, jamming them.

*Freezing rain.* This becomes the most dangerous ice that may form on the airplane during flight. It is an almost frozen rain that becomes solid ice when it strikes the plane; a coating of hard, clear ice (not rime ice, like that which coats refrigerator trays) forms all over the plane, adding to the weight and spoiling the lift. In a few minutes the wing becomes so spoiled that it stalls at a higher speed, the plane weighs more, the propeller furnishes less thrust, and the plane is forced to descend.

Instrument pilots know that they can avoid these conditions by climbing above the freezing rain. As they fly higher into the cloud level, the temperatures will be above freezing, and they fly at this level. Private Pilots, however, should not attempt to fly in freezing rain with any kind of rating.

Fig. 16. Climb into warmer levels to avoid freezing rain.

*Sleet.* Sleet is not a menace because it doesn't stick to the plane like freezing rain, the reason being that it is already frozen. Because it comes from almost-freezing temperatures, instrument pilots don't climb into the area where it originates, but continue to fly at their altitude. If they were to climb, they would find small particles of water at freezing temperatures that would quickly become part of the airplane.

Private Pilots are usually not flying in sleet, so it may be poor consolation to know that sleet is not a hazard.

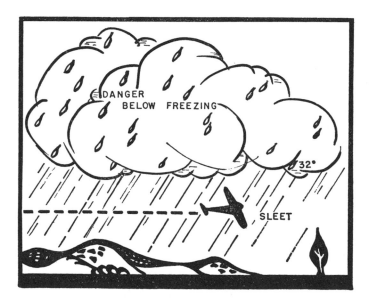

Fig. 17. When flying through sleet, do not attempt to climb out of it but proceed without changing altitude.

*Wet snow.* This will stick to the plane and form ice; it comes from levels that are well below freezing, so instrument pilots climb to this colder area, where the snow is frozen harder and will not adhere to the plane.

*Hail.* This is formed from frozen rain drops that increase in size after having gone up and down a few times in updrafts and downdrafts such as are found in cumulo-nimbus. Hail cannot adhere to the plane, but it can be hazardous because of the size of the hailstones and the speeds at which the plane strikes them. Change course to avoid damage to your plane in hailstorms.

What can we Private Pilots do about ice? Excepting frost, which can be removed prior to flight, there are only two remedies: de-icing equipment and evasive action. We don't have pulsating rubber boots

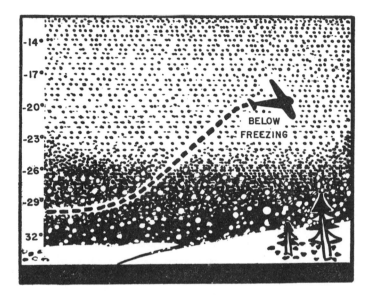

Fig. 18. In wet snow, climb to colder altitude
where snow will not adhere to the plane.

on the wings to dislodge ice, nor do we have alcohol for the windshield and propeller, so we must avoid icing areas.

This may best be done by visiting the weather bureau before take-off or by listening to half-hour weather sequences during flight, or by radioing for more detailed information. Find out what's ahead; realize that the first indication of ice should be followed by that life saver, the 180° turn.

Here's what's important to remember about ice on the airplane:
1. Avoid ice and icing areas. Pilots flying contact can't cope with

it, and the occasional instrument pilot is no match for instrument weather and ice too. The best advice is to turn around or land.

2. If you do get a load of ice, don't bank steeply. It is possible to be very near the stall in level flight because of the weight of accumulated ice, inasmuch as stalling speed increases with weight, as discussed in Chapter 5. In a 60° bank the gross weight of the plane is twice that of level flight.

3. If you have ice, make your approach at an air speed of at least Maneuvering Speed or higher—never less. Don't use Over-the-fence Speed. If the plane feels sloppy at any speed, use all the power and speed you need to maintain control.

4. Don't rely too much on the air-speed indicator. Instrument pilots have Pitot heat, but in a lightplane the Pitot tube will get iced up too. Although the air-speed readings are lower than true speed, fly by feel and stay well above stalling.

5. Do not use flaps. Flaps usually become so iced that they add no lift and lots of drag; the added drag might be more than the engine can pull. If you need the added lift, cautiously try one-quarter flap. If you get no lift from the flaps, raise them.

6. Land the plane on the wheels (for tail-wheel aircraft) and don't try to make a semi-stalled landing (for nose-wheel planes). With a load of ice, your plane is probably very near stalling, even at Maneuvering Speed or greater.

7. A retreat is the best form of attack against ice. As General Whatsis said, "He who flies and turns away will live to fly another day."

# 13: THAT MYSTERIOUS NEW PLANE

YOU watch her approach, and your eyes glisten. She has a reputation for being quite fast and difficult to handle, but one would never guess she was other than a perfect lady. Inside that graceful body is a powerhouse, and you long to find out for yourself how it feels to control all that speed and class, to be master of all that femininity.

Although you're eager to be introduced, you have a healthy respect for this new plane. Rumor has it she's tricky during landings and has to be watched closely; she stalls at a higher speed than does the plane you're used to, and she's so clean that there isn't much warning before the stall. Nevertheless you're fascinated, because the change from low power to higher power, or from single- to multi-engine is a thrill almost equal to the thrill of first solo.

You have deep respect for the mysterious new plane, not only because she's feminine but also because there are many "musts" to consider before you push a throttle in The New Plane. This doesn't mean that one must sit in the cockpit timidly, as we might sit had the airport jokester hidden a bear trap in the seat cushions. It means that we must use firmness, not timidity, in flying any airplane, and that our awe is based on respect tempered by knowledge.

What do you want to know before rolling down the runway on take-off? What should you know before making an approach for a landing? Certainly we know that the same flight technique and the usual control pressures cause the nose and wings to go up or down, but that isn't enough. It isn't enough, either, to talk to the man who flies one, although that does help. What we want to know are the facts which will enable us to fly her safely during first solo and professionally after 10 to 20 hours of familiarization. Let's go to work in a systematic manner to learn all we can about that mysterious new plane.

## MANUFACTURER'S AIRPLANE FLIGHT MANUAL, OR HANDBOOK

Whether we're flying a lightplane or a four-engine airliner, the first step in checking out is the handbook. As planes become faster and cleaner, they seem to become more complicated; handbooks that come with lightplanes aren't an inch thick, like those of an airliner, but the pilot who refuses to study his handbook prior to checking out is more than an inch thick. There are too many changes, too many different features, too many flying characteristics that differ from one plane to another.

Sit down in the cockpit fearlessly.

Take the example of Pilot Hurryup, who checked out in his newly-purchased plane after a fifteen-minute ride that consisted of a take-off and landing. He was en route home in his new plane when the sun went down, and he'd forgotten to find the location of the light switches. Luckily for him, he'd taken a flashlight with him and he found the switches. After the sun departed he became cold, so he reached down to turn on the cabin heat, which was situated conveniently close to the oil by-pass and had a handle exactly like that of the oil by-pass. You've guessed it: he pulled the by-pass instead of the cabin heat and heated his oil instead of his blood. Because he was well-oiled financially he could easily afford a new engine, but he might have had a forced landing. A landing in the mountainous terrain over which he flew could have made necessary a major overhaul of both plane and pilot.

*Fuel.* The handbook may have either more or less detail than is listed here, depending upon the size and horsepower of your plane, but there are certain items which all handbooks give, such as the octane rating of the fuel and the viscosity of the oil for your engine. Never forget that it's the pilot's responsibility to have his plane serviced correctly, not that of the gas-pump attendant. Find out about the fuel system, how to switch tanks, the hazards of running a tank dry, and how much oil to carry; in some engines too much oil can cause oil-reservoir rupture. Such minor things as air pressure are important, as Pilot E found out. He permitted an attendant to perform all necessary services, such as inflating the tail-wheel tire because "it looked low." Pilot E took off with ease, but his landing was accompanied by a burst of air from the tail wheel, and he became a ground-loop statistic. Ground loops aren't fatal accidents, but they're expensive and embarrassing.

*Controls.* The controls may seem to be unimportant because in today's aircraft we also have elevators, ailerons, and rudder. The controls are certainly conventional, but what about the tabs? Correct tab setting is important for take-off; in planes of high horsepower the nose can't be kept down during take-off if the tab is incorrectly set. We'll paint a white mark on the elevator tab to indicate take-off setting.

The landing gear may be retractable. If it is, locate both the gear and flap switches. Nowadays, most planes have distinguishable handles for gear and flaps, but handles can't think. In one airplane the gear and flap switches are not only similar, but adjacent. The sight of a plane landing, rolling to taxi speed, and settling to the ground like a nesting hen is amusing, but not to the pilot. Find out if the plane has an automatic device that prevents the wheels from being raised when the plane is on the ground; if it does not have such a device, memorize the location of the landing-gear switch so that you'll never try to raise the flaps by reaching for the landing-gear control. If the switch is wheel-shaped, mentally note that fact.

Retractable gear also have a manual control which can be used in the event of electrical failure. The hand crank may be tricky. In a certain make of airplane, the crank goes around like a dervish when it's released for manual operation, and if the pilot doesn't know how to use it, the revolving handle can break his arm. Electrically operated flaps should receive the same attention because, although one *can* land without his flaps, flap failure will occur nine times out of ten when they're needed most.

In addition to the flap handle or switch, flaps have limitations, and your handbook tells you what they are. Certainly, they add lift and more drag, but what are the limitations? Usually, flaps shouldn't be lowered at cruising speeds because they're designed for maneuvering-speed operation. Is there a cockpit indicator? What is the best setting for take-off, approach, and landing? In lightplanes that have only a three-position, manually-controlled flap there are, nevertheless, limitations and best-operation positions.

## TWIN–ENGINE OPERATION

Sooner or later the single-engine pilot feels the allure of multi-engine operation. The thrill of seeing two fans pulling him across the sky and of feeling the power of two engines is irresistible, but the thought of having two throttles to push, two tachometers, two oil pressures, temperatures, mixtures, and two of almost everything causes apprehension. Yet this new plane is controlled by a wheel, elevator, and rudder, just like any other airplane, and learning to watch the instruments, synchronize the propellers, and fly the plane is not much more difficult than using a single engine. What is it that we must learn?

The fundamental knowledge we must attain is that of *power* and *speed*. Modern, light (under 12,500 pounds), twin-engine aircraft have excellent performance and greater reliability than single-engine lightplanes, but many pilots believe that because they have two engines they are completely protected from forced landings, should one of the engines fail.

But without knowledge of how to operate the remaining engine, how to "clean up" the airplane and the engine, and how to use power and the best speeds of flight, all a pilot has after engine failure is a *delayed* forced landing, because the plane cannot climb on one improperly used engine flown at incorrect speeds.

All this information is best derived from a combination of the manufacturer's flight manual (or handbook) and experimentation. For complete safety in twin-engine airplane operation we must know two speeds:

1. *Minimum control speed* with one engine out. This speed may be higher than $S_2$ speed, or it may be close to it; consult your handbook for the recommendations for your particular airplane. Make a notation of this speed. It's important because below this speed you won't have control and you can't hold altitude or climb, even with full take-off (maximum) power from the good engine! After you are checked out and have flown several familiarization flights, we'll obtain the exact speed by actual experiment, as described below.

2. *Best climb speed* with one engine out. This is the airspeed at which we have the best rate of climb with one engine out; or, if the plane won't climb with only one engine, the speed at which we have the slowest descent. It may be very close to the engine-out Minimum Control Speed. Both of these speeds are different from two-engine speeds, and they must be learned.

Remember that altitude is more valuable than excess air speed, because when an engine fails we lose air speed faster than we do altitude. If this seems illogical, recall that we can always put the nose down from 200 feet at stalling speed, but we're in bad shape if we're at 50 feet with cruising speed. We must know the speeds to use in obtaining the best angle of climb and the best rate of climb with both engines operating.

Remember that climb (and sometimes level-flight cruise) is impossible with gear down or flaps extended, and that with one engine cut we must have a "clean" airplane (gear up, flaps up, prop in high pitch, and other details described below).

Remember to always use full (maximum except take-off) power immediately after engine failure. Form the habit of "fire-walling" *both* throttles after engine failure; experienced pilots believe that during flight at high altitude this is unnecessary, but the habit may sometime serve you well.

## THE CHECKOFF LIST

By this time, if the handbook is voluminous, you're completely confused. It's a cinch you can't take the handbook in one hand and fly with the other, so, as we read on, why not make a Checkoff List? Some manufacturers print a Checkoff List, others do not; the most complete and satisfactory list is made by the pilot himself. Some Checkoff Lists are inadequate, others contain superfluous items, but the best list contains minimum essentials for safe flight. Remember, the bigger the airplane and the more professional the operation of it, the more detailed and exacting is the Checkoff List.

**He took the handbook in one hand and flew with the other.**

As we read the handbook and learn about our plane, we begin the rough draft of our Checkoff List. After we revise it and type it in the smooth (sometime after ten hours of flying, when we know all the items we'd like to include), we'll mount it between plastic covers and place it in the cockpit within easy reach.

You'll want to include these items:

> starting
> warm up
> take-off
> cruise
> landing
> securing plane
> emergency

This may take two sides of an $8 \times 11$ sheet. If it does, you're probably flying multi-engine equipment and you're smart besides.

To be sure, a Checkoff List needn't be the size of the Treaty of Ghent, but it must contain everything you shouldn't forget.

Now, as you study the handbook, jot down items under the following headings and subheadings. The list below is representative, because each plane is different, but the list *is* complete. Add or delete items as you see fit, but be sure to make a list that will keep you out of trouble.

1. Starting

Check plane, pull prop through, get into cockpit.

Adjust seat.

Fasten safety belt.

Check freedom of motion of the controls (wheel and rudder).

Brakes set (or chocks in place).

If battery cart used: *master* switches *off*.

If no battery cart: *master* switches and generators *on*.

Master magneto switch *on*.

Mixtures rich.

Oil shutters *warm*.

Throttle(s) closed, then cracked slightly.

Carburetor heat *off*.

Props in *high* pitch.

Cowl flaps *open*.

Panel switches: position lights, landing lights, Pitot heat, oil dilution and radios *off*.

Check fuel supply in all tanks.

Fuel selector on fullest main.

Engine selector on *both*.

Vacuum selector on desired engine.

Cross feed *off*.

Wobble pump to desired pressure.

Prime engine(s) _____ shots.

Fire guard on engine.

Energize starter, turn engine through two revolutions, then magneto *on*.

(Note: In case of fire, keep engine turning, move mixture to lean, open throttle, use fire extinguisher.)

If no oil pressure in 30 seconds, cut switch.

At _____ pounds oil pressure, move props to *low* pitch.

Remove battery cart.

Move master battery and generator switches to *on*.

2. Warm Up

Warm up at _____ RPM (or less if oil pressure above _____ until take-off temperature attained).

Oil shutters closed (if temperature in green, leave open).

Oil by-pass *hot*. *Warning:* Do not take off with by-passes hot.

Avoid prolonged ground operation. Do not exceed cylinder head temperature of _____.

Adjust trim tabs for take-off, to markings indicated:

Elevator to white mark, or to _____ degrees.

Ailerons _____.

Rudder _____.

Exercise props (move to high pitch) twice during warm up.

Check mags at _____ inches Hg for RPM drop; visually check engine for vibration.

Check ammeters, voltmeter.

Check carburetor heat for temperature rise.

Check full power. *Do not* check mags at full power.

Check flaps for full travel.

When oil temperature _____ degrees, oil by-pass to *cold*.

Oil shutters to cold.

Check radios.

3. Take-off

Mixtures rich.

Oil shutters cold.

Carburetor heat cold.

Propeller pitch low.

Throttle tension tight.

Gas on desired main.

Primer closed (*off*).

Wing flaps as desired: maximum lift = _____ degrees.

Engine selector on *Both*.

Cross feed *off*.

Control tabs set.

Engine cowl flaps as required.

Engine instruments:

Oil temperature: ("in green" or _____ degrees).

Oil pressure _____.

Fuel pressure ———.
Head temperature ———.
Gyros uncaged.
Horizon uncaged.
Altimeter set.
Clock set.
Controls free and unlocked.
Check radios: tune to emergency operation frequencies, Omni, ILS on correct channel, ADF on marker.
Tail wheel locked when in position.
Check turn-and-bank while taxiing.

### Performance Notes

$S_1$ speed ———.
Minimum controllable speed ———.
$S_2$ speed ———.
Best angle of climb speed ———.
Best rate of climb speed ———.
Maximum endurance speed ———.
Maximum range speed ———.
Reduce power to ——— inches and ——— RPM after take-off.

4. Cruise

Reduce power to ——— inches and ——— RPM.
Cowl flaps closed at ——— degrees head temperature.
Mixtures leaned to obtain drop in RPM, then richened slightly.
Oil shutters set to maintain ——— degrees.
Cross feed off.
Carburetor heat as desired (or to maintain 35 degrees).
Trim tabs for level flight with *ball-bank centered,* "hands off."
Switch to auxiliary tanks.
Check cockpit:
Head temperatures: ——— degrees.
Oil temperatures: ——— degrees.
Oil pressures: ——— pounds.
Fuel consumption: checked at 30-minute intervals: ——— gpm.
Ammeters: charging.

5. Landing
   Radios on emergency channels.
   Mixture rich.
   Carburetor heat *cold.*
   Props at _____.
   Cowl flaps closed.
   Cross feed _____ as manufacturer recommends.
   Gas selector on fullest main.
   Tail wheel locked.
   Seat belts fastened.
   Gear down.
   Flaps as desired.
   Air speeds:
      Maneuvering Speed _____.
      Over-the-fence Speed _____.
      Minimum (Never-subceed) Speed _____.
6. Emergency Procedures
   Apply METO (maximum except take-off) power: _____
      inches at _____ rpm.
   Gear and flaps *up.*
   Single-engine power _____ (as recommended).
   Secure bad engine:
      Mixture, throttle, and props back on dead engine.
      Open cowl flaps on good engine.
      Switch and generator off.
      Gas selector to good engine.
      Vacuum selector to good engine.
      Cross feed off.
      Fire extinguisher set for bad engine. (*Do not pull until
         above list is completed.*)
      Trim airplane and clean up cockpit:
         Cowl flaps open on good engine, closed on bad engine.
         Rudder, ailerons, and elevator tabs as required.
         Oil shutter *cold* on good engine, *hot* on bad engine.
      Attempt to correct trouble: check fuel tanks, cross feed,
         magnetos, oil temperature, etc.
      Radio MAYDAY and land at nearest airport.
      Landing gear failure:
         Check fuse and circuit breaker.

Check generators *on*.
Gear switch *off*.
Cruise at _____ mph.
Operate manual gear-lowering lever.
Flap failure:
Check fuses.
Check generators.
Flap switch *off*.
Operate manual flap lever.
7. Secure:
Parking brakes *on*.
Cowl flaps *open*.
Wing flaps *up*.
Oil shutters *open*.
Increase power to _____ inches or RPM, move props to
high pitch.
Mixture lean.
Gas *off*.
Master switch and magneto switches *off*.
Battery, generator, and panel switches *off*.
Instruments caged.
Radios off.
Windows closed.
Controls locked.
Log flight time.
Tie down plane.

By the time you've made a checklist that's adequate, you should
know enough about your new plane to lead her gently to the altar
of take-off. You know all about her except the indicated stall speed
—which we'll find during the first flight—after which we'll paint a
red line on the air-speed indicator to show the indicated stall speed.

As for other flight characteristics, read what the manufacturer has
to say about them, and listen to what other pilots say. We'll discuss
them after we've gone through the next procedure.

## THE COCKPIT

The airlines require that pilots sit in the cockpit of a new plane
and that they learn the cockpit thoroughly before flight. Military

pilots must take a blindfold test to demonstrate that they know the location of each cockpit control; this is good insurance against pulling the wrong knob some fine dark night. It's good insurance, the premiums are relatively low, so why not invest in a policy right now?

Let's imagine that we have a single seater and that our first flight is going to be solo. If this doesn't make you more eager, nothing will. Soloing a single seater is fun, because the pilot is very much on his own. It means, also, that we definitely want to know our cockpit.

Get into that left seat. Look at the "runway," ahead and then at the panel, as though you were checking the air speed. How long did it take you to merely *find* the instrument? If it took long enough for the plane to veer off the runway, it took too long. Learn the location of the air-speed indicator, altimeter, tachometer, manifold pressure gauge, turn-and-bank, compass, and engine instruments, so that you can focus your eyes on any one of them immediately. Remember, during your first flight you're going to be so busy and so preoccupied flying the plane that you won't have time to grope visually around the panel for the information needed. The time spent in cockpit familiarization depends somewhat upon the complexity of the airplane, but mostly upon the pilot. If it takes you a long time to memorize your panel, then you must spend a long time in the cockpit.

Now go through the motions of starting, warming up, taxiing out, and preparing to take off. *Ten simulated take-offs* will virtually eliminate take-off mistakes; you can't do any better in the air—when one must both fly and think—than you do on the ground. Simulate opening the throttle, obtaining recommended power, and keeping the plane rolling straight down the runway. Now flick a glance at the air speed and back to the runway; do you have $S_1$ speed ... another glance ... do you have $S_2$ speed? If so, take off and ease the nose down in order to accelerate to climbing speed. Reduce power, check the rpm's, get the landing gear up. Notice the position of the nose and check the air speed again. Don't become so preoccupied flying the plane that you grind your way to 3,000 feet with the prop in low pitch and the gear down.

Although you probably won't experience any emergencies, such as fire, engine failure (or single-engine procedures), go through an emergency *now*. If you can't think of flaps or switches, whether to leave the gear up or down, the air speed recommended for glide, or to open your cockpit hatch at this moment, you certainly aren't ready for an actual take-off.

## THE FLIGHT

Although it's wiser to take a check pilot along on the first flight, it can be made solo. Let's assume it's solo; this will enable us to give the check pilot the best first ride he's ever had. Let's assume also he knows more about flying this new plane than we do, and inquire, "What's she like? What are the flight characteristics during take-off, stall, glide, and landing run-off? Does she tend to ground loop? How are the brakes, tough or touchy? Does the carburetor ice up easily? What are the recommended speeds?" It is better to take his comments seriously and evaluate them later, rather than to pay cash to repair a mistake.

Now, using your Checkoff List, start the engine, warm it up correctly, obtain take-off clearance, and roll her. Apply power slowly but not hesitatingly, gradually but surely, feeling any tendency of the plane to swerve because of torque or crosswind. The rudder action and the response to rudder presures give some clue as to how you'll have to react during the landing. Flick your eyes from runway to panel. (It's easy now because this is the eleventh time you've "taken off"!) Get off the ground at $S_2$ speed, accelerate, and climb at climbing speed. You automatically reduce power, adjust the props, and raise the gear without being told. The check pilot (who is certain to be there if it's *his* plane you're flying) nods approvingly. No use spending an hour of his time and sixty minutes of your money for check out.

You "clean up" the cockpit methodically, using the Checkoff List. Using a Checkoff List is not the sign of an amateur, it's the habit of a professional. With your gear up, power reduced, props set, temperatures checked and pressures verified, you clean up the cockpit rapidly. At cruising altitude level off, use the Checkoff List and get set to know the new plane better.

After the usual turns, climbs, and feeling-out of the controls comes the most important part of the flight. There is an old story in aviation annals of the World War I Ace who climbed into his new fighter, took off, circled the field, and landed—in five minutes. The story doesn't say how long he lived thereafter, because a landing is the least important part of flying a new plane. We want to know more, so we'll *execute the approach stall and the full stall, noting the exact indicated air speeds* in each maneuver.

Use carburetor heat if it is required and execute the full stall and the approach stall, power-off. (Some multi-engine planes should not be fully stalled, so be guided by the manufacturer's recommendations.) Modern planes do not, as a rule, have bad stall characteristics, but it is wiser to have the first stall occur at altitude rather than at fifty feet.

Execute the stall slowly by holding the nose on the horizon in level-flight attitude. See, feel, and listen: each of these clues will help make the landing safer. When air speed is reduced to the burble point, observe the exact indicated air speed, because *indicated* speed is what you'll be using during your approach. When the stick or wheel is fully back, note the full-stall indicated speed.

If you've been too busy to notice the altitude, execute the full stall again at a given altitude. Now attempt to recover by releasing some back pressure and by applying full take-off power. The nose may fall below the horizon, but try to recover speed and cruising attitude with minimum loss of altitude. Now subtract the lower altitude from that at which you began your stall: the amount of altitude lost is the minimum height above the ground at which you can recover from an inadvertent stall without disastrous results.

Now you are ready to complete your familiarization with this new, not quite so mysterious plane by making steeper climbs, tighter turns, and shallower glides, observing just how she looks, sounds, and feels when the air speed decreases or increases. The shallow chandelle, which is not necessarily an acrobatic maneuver, is excellent for getting the feel of the plane, and is a lot of fun besides. If you can fly through the top and bottom of the chandelle at the speeds you want, merely by checking the air speed for accuracy, you have the "feel" of the plane.

Now compute your Maneuvering, Over-the-fence, and Never-sub-ceed Speeds by multiplying stalling speed by 1.6, 1.4, and 1.2. By stalling speed we mean indicated speed, not necessarily the stall speed given in the handbook, because your indicator may have a considerable error due to Pitot-tube placement, actual instrument calibration error, or other factors. In one airplane the instrument indicates true air speed only at 150 mph; all other indications are erroneous!

## TWIN–ENGINE FLIGHT

Suppose that this is a checkout flight in twin-engines, what else must we know? As we saw previously, speed and power are two important items in flying twin engines, so let's experiment.

First, there's the Minimum Control Speed with one engine out. Knowing this speed is a must after we've had several familiarization flights, so let's shut off one engine. First, assume we apply full take-off power, should an engine fail. Next, *always* touch the gear and flaps levers; if they're down, raise them. Move the "bad" engine prop to high pitch or feather before leaning the mixture or cutting the switch, because some props won't go into high pitch with the engine shut down, and a low-pitch prop reduces air speed considerably. Move the mixture to cut-off, the switch to *off*, the cowl flaps to *open* on good and *closed* on bad engine, trim the plane, reduce power as needed, and *use the Checkoff List*.

Now ascertain Minimum Control Speed by gradually reducing speed after throttling back. Astonishing as it may sound, below a certain speed you don't have control and you can't hold altitude or climb, even with full take-off power (which is more than METO power) on the good engine. Write this speed down on your Checkoff List. Now notice that in order to regain climb speed you *must* nose over, lose altitude, gain speed, and thereby become able to climb.

Next, lower gear, or flap, or let the propeller windmill in low pitch. Again the ability to climb (in some case you'll lose altitude!) is lost; should you ever lose an engine during take-off you now realize the importance of (1) $S_2$ speeds, (2) best climb speed, and (3) the importance of cleaning up your airplane.

Second, let's find the best climb speed with one engine cut. With the cockpit cleaned up, we use METO power and time ourselves during several climbs at various air speeds. Next, we find the power required to hold altitude; the amazing thing is that a variation in speed of only a few mph results in poor performance. If we're to be expert pilots we'll have to memorize the best speeds to use for several situations, just as the Checkoff List states.

Third, review in our minds what we'd do during take-off engine failure: at $S_1$ speed we'd stop; at $S_2$ we'd take off (unless there was a lengthy runway, in which case we'd land); if failure occurred after becoming airborne, we'd continue to use full power available and attempt to accelerate to best engine-out climb speed. Finally, we realize that continuous operation at full power on one engine cannot go on forever, and we'd land as quickly as possible.

## THE LANDING

You now are familiar with the power settings, the air speeds, and the feel of your new plane. The first landing will be no different from landing any other airplane, so you approach the field and enter the traffic pattern, reducing power until you're flying at Maneuvering Speed. You feel that the plane is almost a good friend by now, but the Checkoff List is your marriage license: no aircraft ever becomes so friendly that she'll fly correctly without a Checkoff List. Get the carburetor heat set, fuel selector on fullest main, trim tabs set, prop pitch as required, and remove all mental hazards to the landing. Leave the gear and flaps to go or put them down as you wish, but all other items should be completed on the downwind leg. Turn to base leg, lower gear and flaps, and establish the glide for final approach.

The preferred method is to establish the glide by using a power approach, especially in heavier aircraft, but even in a lightplane this method is best. There is less possibility of accumulating carburetor ice, less altitude lost in an inadvertent stall, and better landing accuracy. Your control of the plane is greater, too.

Before the field boundary, or "fence," slips beneath the wings, you reduce power to obtain the Over-the-fence Speed. Should the field not have a boundary, or if it is too close to the end of the runway, use your own judgment as to when to reduce power. Some pilots prefer to lower full flaps and to ease the throttle back; the airlines prefer to add flap and make all power reductions so slight that the passengers aren't worried by power changes.

Land on the wheels: it's easier, safer, smoother, and technically easier than the full-stall landing. Now be alert and keep the nose rolling straight toward a distant point, use the brakes carefully, bring up the flaps, open the cowl flaps, and taxi off the runway. Transition from one plane to another, whether it's from reciprocal engines to jets, from low- to high-power, or from single- to multi-engine, is essentially a problem in knowing the airplane (your handbook), knowing the cockpit (your Checkoff List), and familiarization (actual flight). The manipulation of the controls is such a minor item that any pilot who has a background of smooth, precise flying can fly another airplane easily.

The important thing to remember is that your mysterious new plane may not be mysterious any longer but she's still feminine. There will always be a vague something between you and her, and that something is the Checkoff List. If you'll use it, we can end this as the storybooks do by saying, "And they lived happily ever after."

She's not unfriendly or mysterious any longer.

# 14: CURING THOSE UPS AND DOWNS

OUR program for today stars Pilot Q, a smart lightplane pilot. He's flying his personal airplane, in which there are only essential instruments, a plane that cruises at less than the approach speed of an airliner and climbs at a rate that won't crack our eardrums. But Pilot Q loves his plane and takes pride in his flying, as most of us do. When Chattanooga slips under him he reaches for his map, puts a mileage scale on it, twists his computer, and there's the ground speed: 125 mph. He'll be over the mountains and arriving at Spartanburg in short order.

For this he'll be very glad, because life—and flying—has been a series of ups and downs. Turbulence and convection currents have made flying a headache, and the altimeter was alternately above cruising altitude or below it. Pilot Q has been fighting to maintain altitude and attitude as the plane encountered gusts. With each gust the air speed changed, the trim became incorrect, and changes in attitude were accompanied by variations in rpm's, altitude, and control pressures. The flight to South Carolina proved to be more work than pleasure.

Being a smart pilot, he sought out the airport sage after he landed in order to obtain that little-heeded commodity, free advice. Pilot Q stated that his plane went up and down like a hailstone in a thunderstorm.

"Which," asked Pilot Q, "should a pilot do, maintain a given altitude during his flight or ignore changes in altitude? If it's better to hold an altitude, how should he do it?"

Better pilots than Mr. Q have asked that question and received short answers, but there is a way to hold a given altitude, despite the fact that there is no simple answer to the question and there are

148

times when it doesn't pay to hold an altitude. Many fliers have wasted time and energy in trying to hold a constant altitude when they should have taken advantage of Nature's free-power factory. Other pilots have imperiled both their own lives and the lives of others when they should have maintained a given altitude on an airway. *All* pilots can get much better performance from their planes by knowing how to eliminate the migraine headaches of ups and downs.

Take Pilot Q once again, who is flying back to Chattanooga over the same mountains and in the same kind of weather. At 7,000 feet he encountered updrafts which caused his altimeter to revolve like the sweep-second hand on the panel clock—about 1,000 feet per minute. This was power for free, and this time Pilot Q knew it. Instead of nosing down or changing his elevator tab, he gave the plane its head and soon was at 12,000 feet.

There is an old adage which states that what goes up must come down, although the adage doesn't say that whatever goes up must come down in the *same place* from which it went up. Sure enough, within a few miles Q encountered a downdraft, which unwound the altimeter faster than it had wound up. This time he fought it—not by climbing, but by turning out of the downdraft, because in his lightplane he couldn't have climbed fast enough to break even. Putting the nose down to increase his speed, he turned from his course, found stable air, and later got back on course.

To be sure, such convection currents are unusual, but so are fatal accidents. The point is that rapid convection currents, either up or down, are confined to small areas, and a slight detour will take the plane out of the danger zone. Thus, Pilot Q not only found stable air at 9,000 feet but he also had a clear profit of 2,000 feet he received postpaid from Nature's power house.

Suppose, however, that Pilot Q had encountered similar *minor* currents and the same ups and downs which he experienced on his original flight. One can't turn from course every time he finds a convection current; he can't fight the controls during a day-long flight. (Even using an automatic pilot is considered poor technique in rough weather.) What should he do if he's required to hold an altitude? When should a pilot give the plane its head and ride the convection currents?

## TRIMMING THE PLANE

The first step in curing ups and downs is to trim the plane for level flight. This is so easy that many pilots won't want to read about it, yet experienced pilots have been observed flying blissfully as they skidded their way along course. Then, other pilots have flown cross-country, burning gas and lightening the plane, cussing instead of discussing the plane for not flying "hands off" continuously, as the nose tended to rise because of decreased weight and higher air speed.

Speed and power affect elevator and rudder trim rather critically. Less critical is aileron trim, and for this reason many lightplanes do not have aileron tabs which may be adjusted from the cockpit. But they do have elevator tabs, and some have rudder tabs; how to adjust all of them is worth while knowing, because they not only help those ups and downs but add as much as 5 knots to the air speed!

The first item of importance in obtaining correct trim is the ball, called a ball-bank indicator, which doesn't indicate the bank. The only instrument that indicates bank is a gyro-horizon; the turn indicator indicates turn, and in "needle-width" turns the degrees of bank depend upon air speed. But the ball indicator (referred to by old-timers as "the bubble") shows conditions of clean, nonskid, nonslip flight obtainable only by correct tab adjustment. Get a simple ball indicator, which may be purchased for less than five dollars. It's worth it. Of course, if a pilot can tell skids or slips from the way his sensitive *derrière* sits, well and good. A ball indicator is usually more accurate and reliable.

The ball actually *is* a steel ball, inside a curved, liquid-filled, glass tube about 2 inches wide, which is calibrated from 0° to 10° (don't try to use the 30° variety, as it is curved too much for fine calibration). Install the indicator while you're on the ground, with the wings perfectly horizontal as indicated by a spirit level; then put the ball indicator on the panel so that the ball is exactly in the center of the tube. If you have a turn-and-bank indicator, the same tests for accurate installation apply. Poorly installed indicators, or aged indicators with a center depression in the tube due to wear, which causes the ball to stay centered when it shouldn't be, will nullify our efforts to trim the plane.

Learn how to use the ball. When a wing goes down and the plane is not turning fast enough for the angle of bank, the ball drops toward the low side, indicating "slip." When the plane skids, the ball goes to the high side of the tube. Now that you know this you may forget about it, because an easy rule for correcting either a slip or a skid is:

*Rudder the ball.*

Thus, if the ball is down and to the right during a right turn, indicating a slip, right rudder increases the rate of turn, stops the slip, and the ball goes back to the center of the tube. If the ball is up and to the left during a right turn, indicating a skid, left rudder decreases the rate of turn, stops the skid, and the ball goes down to the center of the tube.

Fig. 19. The ball indicator, a valuable aid in trimming the plane or coordinating turns.

Watch the ball as soon as you're in level flight at cruising power; trim the elevator tab so that you hold your altitude with hands off the stick. As you move the tab to "nose heavy" and the nose drops, the speed increases and the wings furnish more lift. As the lift increases the plane climbs, so use a little more tab; as soon as the speed becomes constant and no stick pressure is required, you're through—temporarily—with the elevator tab.

But changes in speed also affect the rudder. Usually the tab is set for right rudder during take-offs, and when you level off at cruising power the increased speed requires that you hold left rudder. The proof of this may be seen by watching the ball, which will be at left of center, indicating that we're skidding and the fuselage is flying sideways. This is not only uncomfortable but is accomplished at the expense of air speed. Rudder the ball by pressing left rudder and notice that the air speed increases and your body sits centered. Feel how relieved those stomach and buttock muscles become when you sit solidly in the airplane. It's wonderful!

You now have two choices: to fly in a skid to your destination or break a leg holding the rudder. Most pilots choose the skid. But if you have an adjustable rudder tab in the cockpit you may do neither; reach up and crank in enough tab so that the ball is centered with feet off the rudder.

But pressing left rudder usually brings the right wing up, and now right stick is required to hold the right wing down. Turn the cockpit aileron tab until the wings stay level. This is the point at which many pilots give up what seems to be a bad job; the other two tabs must now be readjusted!

The reason for this is that bringing the ball into the center has made your plane aerodynamically cleaner and, consequently, increased the air speed; with increased speed we must repeat the three steps by adjusting (1) the elevator, (2) the rudder, and (3) the ailerons. When the plane is perfectly trimmed for "hands-off" flight it not only flies faster but holds a heading. A plane can be turned only by skidding it or by banking it, either of which moves the ball off center. Therefore, with a correctly installed, accurately centered ball, the plane holds a heading instead of "searching."

Right here is where the lightplane pilot objects, "My plane doesn't have three cockpit trim tabs, and I always have to hold aileron or rudder pressure!" This difficulty can be easily remedied by resetting the *fixed* trim tabs located on the trailing edges of the aileron and rudder. The plane is flying in imperfect trim because of (1) incorrect rigging, (2) a faulty tachometer or air-speed indicator that permit speeds other than those for which the plane was designed, or (3) incorrectly adjusted tabs.

The first item, incorrect rigging, if encountered, must be checked or corrected by a skilled mechanic, a task too complicated for discussion here. Assuming that the rigging, the tachometer, and the air speed are satisfactory, let's reset the aileron and rudder tabs. What must we know in order to set the tabs correctly?

Your knee pad says, "Left wing heavy," inasmuch as you used right stick to hold the wings level. As soon as you land, adjust the tabs. If the tab is on the right aileron, your reasoning is like this: I had to lower the right wing in flight; this means I raised the right aileron. In order for the airstream to raise the aileron, I'll bend the tab *down*.

Bending the tab is easy. Walk over to the aileron and examine the tab rivetted to it. The tab is made of fairly malleable metal that can be easily bent, but how much should it be bent? The answer varies with wing area and air speed, but in general the first bending should not be more than one-sixteenth of an inch. This small amount may mean that about two more flights and subsequent adjustments may be necessary before the plane is trimmed perfectly and it flies absolutely "hands off" at a given power setting. If your plane does not have either cockpit or fixed trim tabs, a mechanic will show you how to "droop" or "raise" the aileron by adjusting the turnbuckle in the rigging cable, which may be found inside the wing after the inspection cover is removed. Or, if none of these methods is available, a small, fixed trim tab may be rivetted to the aileron.

Whatever may be required, *trim the plane*. It's worth the effort. The increase in air speed, the comfort of sitting squarely in the cockpit, and the ease of handling the plane makes flying more enjoyable.

What about the rudder? The same reasoning applies, but the direction of bend is different. Your knee pad states, "Left rudder required." You reason that in order to move the nose to the left, you must bend the tab to the right. The air will strike the tab, move the rudder to the

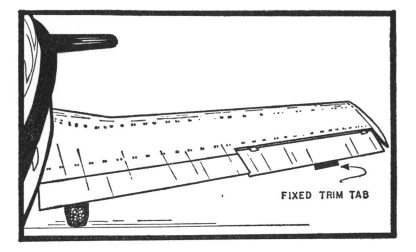

FIXED TRIM TAB

Fig. 20. If the aileron tab is bent down, the airstream forces the aileron up and the right wing moves down.

left, and center the ball. Notice that the reasoning is the same for rudder as it is for aileron, but the actual bending is opposite. The reason for bending the tabs differently is that left rudder moves the nose to the left, whereas down aileron moves the wing up.

This may seem to be complicated procedure, but when the ball is centered, the altitude and heading maintained, and the wings stay level—all with "hands off"—you've got a newer, easier handling, faster plane. Then you're ready to take off and cure those ups and downs.

## VARIABLE ALTITUDE FLIGHTS OFF THE AIRWAY

You now know that your plane is trimmed and that it should hold both altitude and heading during cross-country flight. But you may vary your altitude if you wish, and allowing the plane to fly as it pleases is both easy and comfortable cross-country procedure. It is also sloppy, and it may be downright careless, but there is a happy medium.

Utilize convection currents as outlined previously, taking advantage of the updrafts and avoiding downdrafts. But what about those minor annoyances which move the nose around? Then the air speed falls off, a wing goes down, and we start to turn. Instead of fighting these undesirable maneuvers continuously, lean back, steer with the rudders, and relax. The little skids which result from rudder flying aren't half as hard on the air speed as hour after hour of wheel flying is on you. Add a little control pressure as needed to keep the nose from getting too high or too low.

The only objectionable feature of such flying is that planes fly faster at a negative angle of attack, which is referred to as "on the step." Aerodynamically there is no such thing as "on the step," unless one is referring to a seaplane which must be accelerated in order to get on the "step" of the float during take-off. In landplanes the tail-high attitude attained at cruising speeds is also called "on the step," and it means that by flying at a negative angle of attack the drag decreases; this in turn increases cruising speed. Therefore, any time you permit the nose to rise to a higher angle of attack (because of gusts or careless flying), the cruising speed decreases.

So, giving the plane its head doesn't sanction sloppy flying or authorize us to permit the plane to pitch wildly without any control pressures, unless we simply don't care about efficiency and are willing to accept alternate increases and decreases in angle of attack—and faster or slower air speeds. A happy medium for comfortable cross-country flying is not to fight the controls but rather to keep angle of attack—and consequently the air speed—fairly constant, with a minimum amount of correction, thus taking full advantage of strong updrafts and minimizing the effort expended in fighting bumps and gusts. Result: faster speed, less fatigue, better efficiency, and more pleasure.

## CONSTANT–ALTITUDE FLIGHT

The day eventually comes when it is necessary to hold a constant altitude during VFR airways flight, night flight, or IFR flight. Within what tolerances shall we hold our altitude? Shall we constantly fight the controls?

The answer is: don't fight the controls. Any pilot who constantly manipulates them, applying rudder and aileron, alternately climbing or descending, or making other minor adjustments, is doing his utmost to arrive at his destination ready for bed. Holding an altitude or a heading within "plus-or-minus zero" is a foolish expenditure of strength except during final approaches. Expert pilots save their energy in order that they may use it when it is needed; this applies particularly when they're flying on instruments and must make a low approach, a time when their faculties must not be impaired by fatigue.

The best method is to allow a certain margin of error, say plus-or-minus 100 feet of altitude. Adjust the stabilizer tab for perfect balance in calm air, or at a slightly nose-heavy setting in rougher air. (In extremely rough air the airplane must be flown at reduced speed, the amount of reduction depending upon the roughness of the air; in rough air at slow speed almost constant control manipulation *is* necessary.)

Suppose that we're flying a lightplane (that is, a plane under 12,500 pounds), which may be single- or multi-engine, and that we have trimmed it ball-centered for level flight. We're now ready to hold a constant altitude by observing the position of the nose, the feel of the controls, and the sound of flight. When updrafts are encountered, the nose rises; then the angle of attack, lift, and drag increases. We gain altitude, lose air speed, and feel a change in control pressures. By seeing, hearing, and feeling these changes we are amply warned that corrective pressures must be applied.

Don't be in a hurry to change the elevator (stabilizer) tab, but apply gentle corrective pressure. If the updraft continues, crank or roll in a little elevator tab. Your criterion of plus-or-minus 100 feet elevation provides enough leeway so that you're not continually fighting for altitude control, and you can relax as you fly. When the heading changes, use the rudder to correct small yaws or changes of heading.

Higher standards of performance (plus-or-minus 10 feet) are fine for flight tests or in flight schools, because with more lenient standards an instructor has no criteria by which to judge performance, and strict standards show whether or not a student is apt. But when flying is your business or if you must hold an altitude during an eight-hour cross-country flight, make corrections easily within the tolerances mentioned. Then, with your plane in perfect trim, holding accurate altitudes (and headings) during cross-country flights won't necessitate any aspirin to cure the headaches of those ups and downs.

# 15: FLYING THE GAUGES

WE'RE flying in a hurry, because we want to reach the Bar-None Ranch by sunset. After sunset we have a rendezvous with a kind of femininity not connected with airplanes, so we ignore the weather. As the sun sets, the visibility seems to be less than good, and the ceiling lowers. We lower, too. The visibility becomes worse, but we push on with more hope than knowledge that the weather will improve. It doesn't.

Suddenly, we are in it. We can't see ahead or down, and there isn't anything to do but watch those instruments on the panel. Don't mind that whirling fog outside the cockpit; just watch the instruments with their flickering needles. Now the altimeter shows climb, so put the nose down and wait for the big needle on the dial to unwind. When it indicates desired altitude, ease back on the wheel and resume level flight. Easing back on the wheel increases the g's; there is a sensation of climb but after a bit it feels normal. Whoops! Now we're in a turn. We must have watched the altimeter too long, so get back to the turn-and-bank or the gyro horizon. The compass says we must turn left, so put the left wing down and start a turn.

That heavy feeling we had while leveling off seems so natural that we hold the wheel back as we continue to watch our turn. Sad to say, we feel natural but the airplane doesn't. The air speed has diminished to stalling and we're about to do something we're going to regret, like dropping in on someone unexpectedly. If this were only a dream, or a story, or an overdrawn television program!

What's so hard about instrument flight? Flying those instruments —those gauges, with their wiggling needles—isn't hard, because it's done every day. Yet our story, that of the pilot who had a compulsion to meet his rendezvous with Fate, has been told hundreds of times. He simply hadn't learned the secret of instrument flight, the easy rule that enables a pilot to get on the gauges, stay there, and relax. It wasn't the wiggling gauges, or that closed-in feeling from the enveloping fog that swirls past the windshield, or inherent lack of flying ability that erected another tombstone. It was simply the lack of a basic rule that made flying the gauges an impossible task.

When we first learned to fly we were taught to *feel* the airplane and to recognize stalls by feeling them. We also were aided by visual reference to the horizon and the ground, flying safely by this method for hundreds of hours.

He was about to drop in unexpectedly.

But when our visual references are taken away, the sense of feel becomes a false friend. The feeling of climbing, or that feeling of weightiness, is not to be trusted. Nor should we trust the feeling of turning, which can continue long after we've stopped turning, because the fluid in one's ears continues to move and gives us a sensation of turning. Therefore, we know that pilots are no longer considered wholly competent if they are limited to CAVU-VFR flight. Instrument flying—which depends upon the ability to use only the visual sense—is now included in flight syllabuses because sooner or later there comes a time when a pilot must know his instruments, a time when his safety depends upon being able to use the gauges correctly.

But there are many pilots who get into a Link Trainer and wrestle with the gauges, staring at first one and then another, only to find that instrument flying is too difficult for them. Happily, there is an easy rule, which is a must for instrument flight; it will help any Private Pilot to learn his gauges and it can aid a commercial pilot in improving his technique. Let it be clear, however, that there is no way to make instrument flying easy! It's plain to any examiner who has given flight tests that almost any student can be taught to fly smoothly and to herd his airplane around the sky, but that failure occurs because incompetent pilots don't think. Instrument flights which are flown without thinking are short, and there isn't any rule for easy thinking, not even a hard one.

If a pilot is working so hard to fly his plane that all his efforts are expended on technique, he can hardly be expected to think clearly and quickly when gauge no. 1 goes up, and while he waits for it to move downward, gauge no. 2 goes crossways. If we will develop an aid such as an easy rule and learn to use it, we'll have progressed to the category of the competent, professional pilot.

Get into the cockpit of a plane equipped for instrument flight and study the panel. Although there are many different instruments and as many different layouts, there are only four gauges which we must have in order to maintain level flight solely by reference to instruments: the turn-and-bank (also called the needle-ball), the air-speed indicator, the altimeter, and the compass. These four instruments are called "emergency panel," and must be used without other instruments by applicants for instrument ratings to demonstrate ability to control the plane's attitude.

Now add the directional gyro (also called Gyro Compass), the gyro horizon, and the rate-of-climb indicator and you have the basic group, or "full panel," used during let-downs and approaches in flight tests and required by CAR (Civil Air Regulations) for IFR (Instrument Flight Rules) operation. In addition, there are other instruments which CAR require, such as a clock with sweep-second hand, the tachometer, and so on, but these do not concern our instrument-flight technique.

Our easy rule, which applies to either emergency or full panel, was evolved after an enterprising Link Trainer instructor found that students' basic difficulty in watching the gauges was due to the fact that one cannot watch two objects simultaneously. Even if one sees the other object with peripheral vision—out of the corner of his eye —he doesn't receive the full impact of what the other object is signaling because his attention is diverted. For example, Pilot R liked to watch his altimeter, so his heading varied, but when he was told to concentrate on holding a heading, his altitude suffered from climbs and dives.

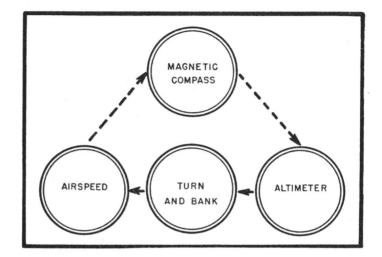

Fig. 21. The Emergency Panel. Scan the instruments in the direction of the arrows.

The instructor then had what was nothing less than a brilliant idea. He placed a series of flashlight bulbs behind the instrument panel of his Link Trainer so that each bulb illuminated a single instrument. Then, by connecting each bulb to separate contacts on a revolving wheel, he lighted the instruments in rotation: first the turn-and-bank, then the air speed, then the compass and the altimeter, and as the wheel completed one revolution it began a new cycle.

The fact that all pilots do not agree on the exact sequence of lighting (and watching) one's instruments is not important. What is important is that the method worked so well than an easy rule for flying the gauges was born, and the rule worked almost as well as the lights! The lights, moreover, were too mechanical; they didn't emphasize any particular instrument but went merrily on, one after the other. Some instruments require a split-second glance, while others should be studied for *rate* of motion.

The rule evolved is this:

*Scan the instruments systematically.*

In other words, don't stare at the air speed or the altimeter or the turn-and-bank, because the error of concentrating on a particular instrument caused the Bar-None Ranch to have a visitor drop in upon them. The rule also prevents that fierce concentration which causes a pilot to become dizzy on instruments. Often a Link Trainer instructor, deducing that his student is overconcentrating, advises him to look back over his shoulder. To the surprise of the student, the panel seems to revolve as he moves his head! As soon as he relaxes, the panel stays put.

Keeping the eyes moving thus promotes not only relaxation but constant realization of the plane's attitude. Keep your eyes moving, not just haphazardly but in a fixed pattern; start at the upper left of the basic panel instruments, go across to the right, go down, read back toward the left, and begin again. Do *not* stare at any one instrument, because the other instruments like attention too.

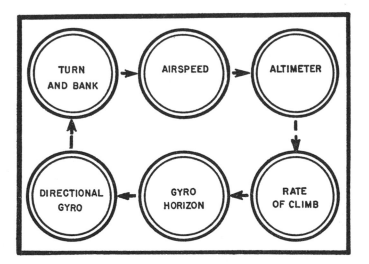

Fig. 22. The Full Panel. Scan the instruments as indicated.

How long should one scan a single instrument? The actual time depends partly on the importance of the instrument, partly on the size of the panel. Some pilots may spend only one second on an instrument, some will spend two. But three seconds per instrument is too much, because with four instruments twelve seconds are required to get back to number one, and in twelve seconds the heading, altitude, or bank can change considerably. Then, too, the altimeter is not as essential for level flight as the turn-and-bank indicator, although a sensitive altimeter is a better clue to the plane's attitude than is the air speed. Air-speed indications change slowly, due to the time required to change the plane's momentum, whereas the altimeter shows climb or descent quickly. The Instrument Landing System needles discussed in Chapter 19 are not just indicators, but must be regarded also as *rate* needles, and the pilot must see *where* they are and how fast they are going somewhere. This means that more seconds will be spent on them than on certain other instruments in the panel.

The important thing is not "How much time do I spend on each instrument?" but "Am I scanning the instruments systematically and am I completing the circuit in ample time?" Form the habit and never break it; if you have six important instruments, scan them. When you graduate to heavier planes that have more gauges, retain the habit of scanning but learn to stop the sequence occasionally in order to glance at other, less-important instruments—such as your gas gauge, your pressure-temperature group, or Omni-ILS needles. The importance of the scan habit will be seen in a moment, when we turn to our radios, our position reports, and our writing down of flight clearances.

## THINKING AHEAD

Pilot $R_1$, as mathematicians might call Pilot R's successor, learned to scan. In Chapter 24, you'll see just how the ultimate in present-day flying is accomplished. In the meantime, we've enabled ourselves to fly better by scanning, simply because it's easier to relax, think, and to think ahead.

For example, there was the ATR pilot applicant who was given a flight test and who hadn't learned to scan. He was so busy watching the gauges that he couldn't keep up his flight-progress log; if he tried to copy a revised clearance en route, he flew off course; if he was coming up on the approach leg of his ILS, he wouldn't have the ILS tuned in and checked before he got there. He hadn't trained himself to think ahead.

Suppose you have a radio call to make over a compulsory check point. You will have to radio them certain information, and in order to sound professional the information should be in a definite order. To do this well and efficiently, a pilot must think ahead and formulate the message in his mind beforehand, not as he presses the mike button. Better still, write it down before you transmit.

But keeping a flight log during instrument flight, or writing radio messages while flying, is a two-man job. Nevertheless, it can be done by one man (it has been done by students taking instrument training courses), if that man is competent and trains himself to do it as he *scans the instruments systematically.*

Pick up the chart board, write for three seconds, and scan the panel. Habit will move your eyes across the instruments, and the airplane won't leave on a cross-country trip of its own volition as you write or when you pick up the mike to call the ATCS (Air Traffic Communications Station). Write for three or four seconds, but no more than four, and scan the panel. After a while, habit will become so assertive that you'll write, scan, write, scan—each time picking up from the instrument you last scanned—and you'll not only be doing a fine job, but the job will be fun. It really is a challenge. It simply isn't necessary to let the airplane go into a dive-bombing run just because you're afraid to plan ahead, or because you're engrossed in using a pencil or talking over the radio. This, to be sure, applies to VFR flight as much as it does to instrument flight.

Write down the message to the ATCS: "Podunk Radio, this is N 777 over Podunk, zero eight (the time) at one zero thousand (10,000 feet), instrument flight plan estimating Punkin Holler (the next fix) at one four zero eight (1408, or 2:08 P.M.), Los Angeles (the destination)." The reason the pilot says "08" as his time over the fix, instead of "8 minutes after the hour" or "one-zero-eight," is because anything else is superfluous. The controller at the ATCS undoubtedly knows what time it is. The next estimate—2:08 P.M.—is given completely, because the pilot might be estimating an arrival at 3:08 P.M. The time is given in twenty-four-hour-clock numbers to eliminate the necessity of saying "P.M." or "A.M." So, over check points, give the minutes, such as "zero eight," or "three five" or "five eight," and if you don't have the correct time ask ATCS for it. As a matter of fact, if he suspects your clock is wrong he will volunteer the correct time.

Suppose at this point you have an engine failure. If the flight is a check flight in multi-engine aircraft, you can *count* on having a simulated engine failure. Now you've got the task of applying power to the good engine, buttoning down the bad engine, and "cleaning up" the cockpit. And during all this time you've got to fly the gauges! This is when scanning the gauges comes in handy. Apply power as needed, open cowl flaps, adjust throttle and props—and scan the gauges. Shut down the bad engine, propeller to high pitch or feather position, mixture lean, fuel selector off—scan the gauges. Adjust trim tabs for comfortable flying, shut down the generators, notify ATCS —scan the gauges. The heading and altitude should not vary more than a minimum during this portion of the flight test, and when the real thing comes along the procedure is routine.

The easy rule pays off because it helps us think. To be sure, the elements of instrument flying must be worked out in the Link Trainer with the help of a competent instructor, but knowing the technique is different from using it, as any coach can tell you. As stated above, almost anyone can be taught to fly smoothly and nearly anyone can manipulate the plane on the gauges, but not everyone plans his flight. The razor's edge of keenness—the ability to think and plan ahead— is the ultimate criterion of the expert, professional pilot. There's no rule that can teach us to think, but the rule of *scanning the gauges* enables us to find time to think.

All our easy rule is doing is to help us to avoid staring at a single instrument, to see them all, to relax, and to give us more time for other things. It's easier to think if part of the mind is working subconsciously, scanning the panel, and it's easier to cope with an ARTC (Air Route Traffic Control, referred to simply as ATC by pilots) instruction if a well-formed habit is taking over the job of using basic techniques and procedures. Then, when a problem or an unforeseen emergency strikes, all you have to do is to *scan the instruments systematically*, think it out, cope with the problem, and notify ATC— all the while flying the gauges with your subconscious mind.

Instrument flight today is a matter of good headwork, as we'll see in the concluding chapters. Years ago, we took an applicant to 5,000 feet and, in exchange for a simple orientation problem and a timed turn or two, wrote him out an instrument ticket which we prayed he would not use with family members aboard. Today, we insist on a flight plan, a take-off clearance that is copied in the cockpit while waiting beside the runway prior to take-off, a holding problem, and a simulated emergency that varies from radio failure, fire on board necessitating immediate landing, to a change in ATC clearance requiring flight to an alternate airport, and single-engine operation. Belligerent pilots can have all four emergencies on request—and sometimes without it—followed by a let-down to 400-1 minimums.

From this it may be seen that anyone who aspires to possess an instrument pilot rating must do more than merely know how to fly his needle, ball, and air speed. The *method* of flying is less important than certain broader aspects.

## WHICH METHOD TO USE

Despite the importance of broader issues, pilots still want to know what method is best, because they still must master the fundamentals before becoming expert. The best advice is to remember that you're flying an airplane, not the gauges. The plane flies on the instruments just as it always did; it's *you* who don't feel the same on instruments as you do in visual flight.

Whatever method is used, there are several suggestions that will improve your fundamental techniques on the gauges.

1. As soon as you go on instruments, disregard the sense of feel (that is, both touch and kinesthesia discussed in Chapter 8); use only the visual and hearing senses. The sensations of turning or climbing are invariably wrong; you can feel both and be doing neither.

2. Visualize the *attitude* of the airplane. This is difficult with only an emergency panel, but it can be done. When the needle indicates turn and the ball shows skid or slip, picture the turn. Then use both controls (aileron and rudder) and coordinate them as you do in VFR flight. Ruddering the ball, as described in Chapter 14, will move the ball to center, but a better method is simultaneous use of both controls.

When you climb or descend (use of elevators), visualize the attitude of the plane, remembering what happens in VFR flight. In climbs or descents, the air speed doesn't actually lag; it merely follows the acceleration or deceleration. After using elevator pressure, watch your air-speed meter and altimeter, not only to see what they say but how fast their needles are moving to another indication.

3. Use *Your World* in Fig. 41, and you'll never become "lost" during instrument orientation problems. For detailed problems, see Chapter 17.

In brief, fly the plane on instruments with the same procedures used during VFR weather, coordinating the controls, using your trim tabs as described in Chapter 14, and remembering that the plane won't fly erratically even if you release the controls. Sometimes it flies better if you do let go. Combine firm, prompt action with an easy, relaxed kind of flying and you'll not only be on the way to becoming an expert but your passengers will know that you are.

# 16: FLYING THE GCA

PILOT S, who had been flying cross country with great nonchalance, turned off the broadcast music to which he'd been listening
for several hours. The ground below wasn't slipping by as fast as it
should have been, and he was already overdue. The winds had been
headwinds, no doubt, and now that he was beyond the mountains
all he could see was a blanket of stratus. It was time to take inventory.

Taking inventory in a lightplane is not a whole afternoon's work.
It consists of a single glance at the fuel gauge—and if one's fuel
gauge reads empty, the firm's assets are perilously low. Pilot S's
gauge read so low that he estimated he couldn't turn back, and because he couldn't land nearby it was inadvisable to take time orient-
ing himself. He wished he'd kept his finger on his aeronautical chart,
and he hoped that Fate would be charitable by allowing him to find
an airport.

But faith, hope, and charity are not good substitutes for gasoline
in present-day engines and they aren't much help in locating landing
strips. To be sure, there was his VHF radio and the Omniradio range,
which would tell him the location of the station and the compass
heading to fly in order to get there. But how far was the station? If
he did find the station, what would he do after he flew over it? Something had to be done quickly.

The first thing to be done was to reduce power to economy cruise,
so Pilot S reduced power until he was flying at Maneuvering Speed,
60 per cent faster than stall speed. Next, hoping he could fly long
enough to reach his destination, he tuned his VHF receiver to the
Omnirange. The Omni receiver, which hadn't been checked for
months, wasn't in good working order. It is situations like these that
Mr. Paine referred to when he said, "These are the times that try

men's souls." Pilot S was about to press the panic button, when another solution occurred to him.

Why not try governmental direction-finding (DF) equipment? And, after he was located, he could use Ground Controlled Approach (GCA) for the let down through the overcast! Luckily, he knew how to use the gauges on the panel; he had scanned them during his instrument flight instruction and could fly them reasonably well, if not with the adeptness of an expert. Luckily, too, he kept a copy of *Airmen's Guide* and the *Flight Information Manual* in his map compartment, and could refresh himself on direction-finding procedures.

But had he not possessed the publications, Pilot S nevertheless could have used both DF and GCA. Clumsily perhaps, but safely. Certainly the DF would be easy, because he was in clear weather on top of a 1,000-foot overcast; possibly GCA could be worked if the weather wasn't too thick beneath the overcast. But GCA would have been so much easier if Pilot S had known a few things about it and an easy rule with which to fly GCA and reduce pilot error.

GCA requires no other flight training than knowledge of basic instrument flight and the ability to follow someone's instructions— namely, the GCA controller, who tells the pilot via radio what to do. GCA flight does, of course, require practice and training if one wishes to become skillful enough to land during weather minimums, but without an easy rule skillful pilots can work up a fairly good sweat trying to fly the plane precisely in accordance with the directions received from the GCA controller.

Switching his VHF transmitter to the emergency frequency of 121.5 mc., Pilot S called the DF homer at his destination. He was reasonably sure the range of his transmitter would include the DF homer, because VHF radios operate on a line-of-sight basis: from 1,000 feet he could transmit about 40 miles; from 10,000 feet he should be able to send or receive over 100 miles.

When a pilot uses the emergency frequency, there should *be* an emergency. Pilot S spoke into his mike, "Los Angeles Homer, this is Nan 777. Request emergency homing. Over."

This transmission alerts every tower operator within receiving range, but only the homer called will acknowledge. The homer said, "Nan 777, this is Los Angeles Homer. Transmit for homing. Over."

This was a request for Pilot S to transmit for at least ten seconds, possibly twenty. S was expected to hold his mike button down, which he did saying, "Los Angeles Homer, this is Nan 777. Ah-h-h-h-h." The "ah" was not a symptom of nervous relief, but a tone which would modulate the transmitter so that the DF operator could readily identify the signal as he swung his receiving loop antenna from maximum to minimum reception. When the loop received a minimum signal or "null," the operator had a bearing on the airplane and the course for it to fly inbound to the station. At the end of twenty seconds Pilot S completed his "ah" and said, "This is Nan 777. Over."

The information that came from the homer was, "Nan 777, this is Los Angeles Homer. Course with zero wind: one-eight-zero. Over."

One-eight-zero, or 180 degrees, was magnetic south. It didn't allow for deviation or wind! What if the wind drifted him to one side of the station? With the assets of the firm and the fuel gauge rapidly going into the red, Pilot S couldn't afford to waste time. He held the course for five minutes and asked for another bearing. This time the bearing was 190°, showing that he had drifted east of the station! By continually rechecking his position, Pilot S eventually arrived over the station after having flown a curved route, as in Fig. 23, and half the battle for survival was over.

In practice runs, a frequency other than the emergency frequency

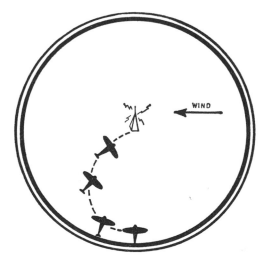

Fig. 23. Wind causes planes to drift, resulting in "bird-dogging" to the station when homing to a Direction Finder.

of 121.5 mc. would be used, and both sending and receiving frequencies would be agreed upon by Pilot S and the DF operator. In the case of Pilot S, the emergency was real enough to warrant the use of 121.5; without the help of DF he would have had to land on something other than a runway, and such landings are not usually smooth.

## THE GCA APPROACH

Pilot S was now over the station on top of the overcast, and the only way he could descend through the overcast safely was by a controlled approach. If he had had his Omni in working order, he could have obtained clearance from Approach Control and used either Omni (see Chapter 18) or the ILS (Chapter 19). But GCA is considered by many pilots superior to either.

With any type of approach, a descent from 1,000-foot tops to 600-foot ceilings is child's play, but if S had obscuration from 10,000 down to 200 feet he'd have to fly precisely and follow instructions promptly. This is the secret of GCA; it requires no special equipment, just the ability to follow instructions and to fly by instruments. GCA is, therefore, a good method for Private Pilots, and, for Pilot S, it was at this moment the only method.

After flying over the field and obtaining GCA's frequency from his map, he contacted GCA. At the field, seated before several "scopes," was the controller. He was observing his scopes closely, watching glowing images on the fluorescent glass screens. Scopes could be referred to as slow-acting television screens; that is, they retain a spot of light for several seconds. These spots are called "pips," but the pips don't look like airplanes; they are received from revolving, concave antennas many feet in diameter, which send radio signals intermittently, signals that go out with the speed of light, strike an object, and return to the antenna with equal speed. Because the GCA radio is receiving when it isn't transmitting, and because the transmitter sends intermittently, reflected signals can be seen on the scope.

This signal is seen by the controller as a bright dot, and the trick is to identify the dot. In congested areas there will be many dots that represent planes flying in the area. Controllers cannot give instructions for an approach until they have definitely identified a certain pip as the airplane they're attempting to direct.

Such identification seems impossible; each pip is moving, it glows, moves, and fades out. As it fades, the revolving radar antenna again sends a signal which strikes the plane, is reflected, and appears again on the scope. But there are tricks in all trades. After the first radio contact, the controller asks for the pilot's heading and altitude, which eliminates many pips as possibilities. Next he asks for an identifying maneuver, such as a turn. This takes time but is necessary, despite the fact that fuel is running low and the pilot is veritably itching to be brought in.

"Nan 777," says GCA, "this is Los Angeles Radar. For positive radar identification turn left to a heading of one-two-zero." During the time required for turning, the controller surveys his scope; the pip which turns to the desired heading is the pip he's after.

"Nan 777, this is Los Angeles Radar," announces GCA after he's identified the pip, "your turn observed; have you in radar contact four miles southwest of the airport; this will be a radar vector for a GCA approach to Runway 25R. The next heading will position you on downwind leg for Runway 25R. Turn left, heading zero-seven-zero." (Zero-seven-zero meaning 70°.)

Pilot S carefully acknowledges. In order to prevent misinterpretation of instructions, every pilot is required to *repeat* every GCA instruction, excepting those during final approach.

"Descend to one thousand two hundred feet," says GC. "You are now in the traffic pattern for Runway 25R."

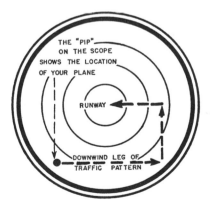

Fig. 24. How a plane appears on a GCA radarscope.

As Fig. 24 shows, the controller steers Pilot S in a pattern that's wide, much farther from the field that a normal traffic pattern. Because the GCA scopes give distance and azimuth, the controller can watch the progress of the pip, calculating speed, direction, and altitude of the plane. Suppose that Pilot S has a poorly compensated compass, or that wind causes him to drift. The controller must assume that Pilot S is holding his given heading; then, if the plane drifts or flies off course, the controller radios a corrected magnetic heading that does maintain the desired track.

Meanwhile, the controller is helping Pilot S to relax by speaking in a calm, measured voice; he asks for the pilot's name, the type of plane, his glide speed, and for other essential information. He gives the existing weather, the number of the service runway, its length, the field elevation, the altimeter setting, and other data; interspersed with the information are directions to change heading and altitude as may be required in order that the pip will continue to move toward the base leg for an approach to 25R.

"Nan 777, this is Los Angeles Radar. Now turn left to a heading of three-four-zero degrees. When you come out of this turn you will be on your base leg for Runway 25R. Over."

"GCA, this is Nan 777," acknowledges Pilot S. "Turning left to three-four-zero degrees." Pilot S is flying his gauges routinely, scanning them in a relaxed fashion. But it is on the approach leg that he'll need precision flying and a rule which will enable him to fly the glide path without first going above and then below it. He'll need also a method of holding a heading in order to stay on course all the way in. When the weather is given as "ceiling 600 feet," perfect accuracy isn't needed, because the pilot can correct his heading as soon as he's flying by visual reference to the ground. But with airline minimums of a 200-foot ceiling and ½ mile visibility, *no* variations from course or glide path are permitted. Let's see if Pilot S can make an approach under those conditions.

Now the pip on the scope shows that the plane is nearing the approach leg. It is holding heading and altitude so GCA radios, "Nan 777, this is Los Angeles Radar. Now complete your landing check, gear and flaps as desired." Pilot S completes his landing check, but leaves *gear and flaps to go*. If the gear is welded down, he will have to vary his procedure slightly, as will be shown. But he is now ready for the big part of GCA, the final approach.

"Nan 777, this is Los Angeles Radar. Now turn left to a heading of two-five-zero degrees. When you come out of this turn you will be on final approach for Runway 25R."

As S comes out of his turn, GCA again transmits, this time (possibly) with a different controller. "Nan 777, this is your final Controller. You are now on course for Runway 25R. Do not acknowledge any further transmissions. Now reduce speed to approach speed (*this instruction varies with the type of plane and the speeds used in flight, and it may be given on the downwind leg*). You are seven miles from touchdown. Your next instruction will be to assume a normal rate of descent. Please effect all corrections promptly."

## HOLDING THE GLIDE PATH

This is what we've been waiting for: the place for an easy rule. To begin with, approach speed is a slow speed, but slow flight in a GCA approach is *not* the same speed taught in Private Pilot flight tests, in which the Private Pilot is expected to fly a minimum air speed that is a coffin's breadth from the stall. This may teach the pilot how dangerous such low air speed is, but instructive or otherwise, the maneuver is *not* to be used in GCA approaches. In GCA or instrument flight, slow speed is usually Maneuvering Speed, about 60 per cent above the stall; it varies slightly according to the type and weight of plane, but the thumb rule of 60 per cent can well be used when actual engineering calculations are not available.

S adjusts his throttle, prop, and manifold pressure; with only a throttle, an accurate knowledge of the relation of rpm's to speed is essential. In heavier aircraft and approach speeds of 140 mph, other methods may be used to obtain approach speed for the glide path, but regardless of the variations of technique, the power required to obtain a certain rate of descent must be known.

In lightplanes, and particularly in twin-engine lightplanes, the following procedures result in a gratifying rate of descent. By leaving the gear and flaps to go and by flying at a power setting which results in Maneuvering Speed, Pilot S has the glide-path problem licked. When the GCA controller advises, "You are now approaching glide path. Obtain a normal descent," Pilot S is ready.

This is the moment. With a rapid motion Pilot S lowers his gear and extends one-quarter flap; now the added drag makes it necessary to put the nose down in order to maintain speed, and by putting the nose down he approximately assumes the glide-path angle. But the problem of good approaches is to hold position precisely *on glide path* and *on course*. How do we achieve such precision?

As he descends, Pilot S knows that the stratus is enveloping his plane, but he's busy with his gauges. His lightplane responds quickly to changes in power; when the GCA controller advises S, he says something like this, "You are on course, on glide path. Ten feet above glide path. Twenty feet. Bring her down, please." Pilot S reduces power and the lightplane loses altitude quickly. Then GCA says, "Good correction. On glide path . . . ten feet below glide path. Twenty feet. Bring her *up*, please." The controller is much more insistent about bringing the plane up, because below-glide-path accidents are rougher than those above glide path. Should Pilot S again change his throttle? There must be an easier method!

There is. Here is the easy rule for flying GCA:

*Hold the glide path with the elevators and hold the course with the rudder.*

This rule is so simple that it seems unnecessary, but it works. Once we have obtained the correct power setting for Maneuvering Speed, we leave the throttles untouched during our approach (except as described below). By pressing the nose down (using his elevators), Pilot S gets back on glide path, although to be sure he picks up a little speed. But with the elevator technique he doesn't "porpoise," first above and then below the glide path, thereby bringing on nervous sweats in the cockpit and driving the controller frantic on the ground. Should the plane tend to fly below glide path, gentle back pressure on the elevators will bring it "on glide path"; should we continually use pressure, a slight adjustment of the elevator tab can be made. Finally, if this results in excess speed we may add more flap; or, if we use back elevator, which results in less speed, we may decrease the flap setting.

It is far better—providing one has Maneuvering Speed—to use changes in flap setting rather than changes in throttle setting. As was shown in Chapter 4, raising flaps slightly at speeds over 60 per cent of stalling is not dangerous technique. Pilot S, in flying slightly and consistently above glide path, needed additional flaps to add drag, slow his speed, and thereby achieve the desired angle of descent.

Had he flown below glide path, removing a few degrees of flap would have increased speed and given him a shallower angle that coincided with the glide path.

The exception to the above rule occurs when speeds become much too slow or too fast. For example, in no-wind or tail-wind conditions, it may eventually become necessary to decrease power and change the throttle (power) setting; in headwinds, when the ground speed is reduced and the angle of descent is consequently increased, more power may be required. When more power is needed, add it; then go back to the easy rule of flying the glide path with the elevators. It works beautifully. A thumb rule for knowing when to change throttle is to change it only when speeds are plus-or-minus 10 mph different from Maneuvering Speed. In any case, never juggle the throttles, because the plane will porpoise along the glide path until the poor GCA controller nearly goes crazy trying to keep you on it, and if you go dangerously low he'll give you a "wave off," which means, simply, go around the field for another attempt.

## HOLDING ON–COURSE HEADINGS

So here is Pilot S, on glide path as nice as you please. The controller is talking constantly but unhurriedly, "On glide path. Now steer right to two-five-five degrees. On glide path. Now bring her back to two-five-zero degrees. On course, on glide path. Now you're swinging to the right. Steer left to two-four-eight degrees."

Without a directional gyro, such headings are almost impossible to hold. Pilot S was, in addition, banking his aircraft each time he turned! The periodic campass banked and jiggled too, and by the time it settled down Pilot S was also unsettled. Then GCA would call for a correction and the results were less than encouraging.

What better way is there? The easy rule gives it: *hold the course with the rudder.* In a heavier plane this would not be good advice, but in a lightplane it's the only advice possible. Whether one has a directional gyro or only a compass, steering GCA headings by using the rudder is the only good method. In instrument flight it's folly to bank the aircraft in order to change the heading a few degrees, because one overshoots and the compass has tremors. Even with a directional gyro the benefit of rudder correction is apparent. Remember, a small change of heading, such as 2 degrees, is enough to cause misalignment with the runway; although this is not too important for a lightplane pilot who has 600-foot ceilings and who can bank his plane close to the ground, the same error in a large airplane means a missed approach.

As for the resultant skids, ignore them; with a directional gyro and a gyro horizon, this advice is easy to take. The wings can be held level as you turn, and the skids are momentary. With an emergency panel and a periodic compass, the turn is made by using rudder, watching the turn indicator carefully, and using aileron *after* the heading has been corrected to keep the ball centered.

Now the controller's chant is encouraging. "On course . . . on glide path. Five feet above glide path." Pilot S presses the nose down, or perhaps adjusts his elevator tab. "Now turn right to two-five-two degrees." Pilot S presses right rudder for a moment, and the compass holds 252. "On course, on glide path."

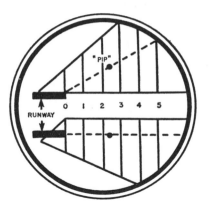

Fig. 25. When the pips are on the dotted lines, the GCA controller says, "On course . . . on glide path."

The controller watches the pip come down the glide path and follow the course line in Fig. 25 on his precision radar scope. He can tell within the first few minutes of the approach whether a competent pilot is at the controls, and he can tell when a pilot responds quickly and takes his corrections promptly.

So Pilot S broke clear at 550 feet and landed safely, thanks to GCA.

Thanks to an easy rule, he did a good job on the approach. When any pilot hears that welcome chant, "On course . . . on glide path," all the way in, until at last he sees the approach lights beckoning to him and the runway markers ahead; when he hears the final comments of his GCA controller, "You now have the field in sight; take over and land your airplane"; and when the wheels squeak down on the runway, he knows he is responsible for a job well done.

# 17: FLYING THE ADF

THE Automatic Direction Finder and a stewardess were once considered the greatest boons to pilots ever devised. While the former pointed to the station and furnished dance music, the latter supplied hot coffee. Today, we have Omnirange receivers and thermos bottles, which threaten to replace old-time aids to flying comfort. Until that catastrophe occurs, we must know something about one of them—the ADF. This chapter is for those pilots who aspire to possess an Airline Transport Pilot Certificate or an instrument rating and who must know an easy way to use the ADF.

The ADF needle is more than a diviner's wand that automatically points to the station; properly used, it will supply such information as distance to station, the direction of the wind, the drift correction to use when tracking to or from the station, and how to let down through overcast. With a little practice, anyone can use the ADF efficiently without being awed or without attributing to it supernatural powers, up to and including weather prediction.

Pilot Roxhead was so much in awe of his ADF that he never learned to use it, turning it on primarily for pointing to a station, usually a broadcast station. One day, he tuned his ADF to what he thought was the right spot, heard soothing music, and flew onward. His ADF needle (the direction indicator) pointed straight ahead, and it would have been a routine flight if the winds hadn't shifted.

Shortly before he was overdue, Rox picked up his map and tried to locate himself, but the map didn't jibe with the terrain. It didn't jibe after his ETA had come and gone either, but before his gas ran out he found a place to land. After a long walk to the settlement he'd seen from the air, Rox asked his whereabouts, to which the native replied, "No spik English, Señor." Happy to say, no international disputes came from this, and Rox managed to get back to Texas in a week or so.

Had the ADF gone wrong? Hardly. ADFs simply don't tune themselves and they can't think. They just point toward the station. This single feature is enough, and many pilots have grown so fond of their ADF that they sleep together, although sleeping in a moving cockpit is perilous. They could stay awake better by knowing an easy rule which does part of the tiring thinking for them.

The ADF is merely a radio receiver, the antenna of which is housed in a nonmagnetic, drop-shaped covering that may be located either above or below the fuselage. The antenna consists of coils of wire that can be rotated or used as a fixed loop. Such loops receive best when either end is pointed at the station; they receive nothing when the center is aimed at the station. Imagine an axle going through the loop, just as it does in a wheel; when either end of the axle points at the station, no signal can be heard.

When you switch to *Compass,* the receiver automatically interprets the signal, and an indicator needle (or pointer) swings around the ADF dial and points to the station, indicating the bearing in degrees. The ADF dial is inscribed like a compass, from 0 to 359°, 0 being the same as 360°. As the ADF dial is mounted vertically, 0 is at the top, and when the needle points upward to 0, the station is straight ahead; when it points to 90 degrees, the station is to the right; when it points downward to 180 degrees, the station is behind, and so on.

The difficult thing for many pilots to understand is that these bearings are relative, that is, in relation to the nose of the plane. Thus, no matter in which direction the plane is flying, an ADF bearing of 45° means that the station is slightly to the right of the nose. If we are flying a compass heading of south (180°), and the ADF reads 45°, the station bears 45° relative, which is 225° magnetic.

## AN EASY RULE

Obviously, an easy rule is needed to solve the problem readily. Suppose that you are flying north, to a station located at A. Because you are flying to the station and the ADF is tuned to that station, the ADF needle should indicate straight up, or 0 degrees. As you fly toward A, you find that the ADF needle drifts to the right, until it reads 010 degrees. Because nothing has happened to the station, something has possibly happened to you, but what? Where are you? What should you do to correct what has happened?

The first thing you must know in using an ADF is how to visualize where you are. This may be done most conveniently by looking at the ADF dial and considering it as your immediate "world" or locality, with the center of the dial representing the station you are tuned to, just as you did in Chapter 10. As you know, when you are flying north to the station you must be south of the station, on what is called a *radial*. Radials may be regarded as the spokes of a wheel, and the station as the hub. Place your finger on the dial south of, or below, the center, on the radial marked 180. That is where you are, in an airplane headed north, as in Fig. 26.

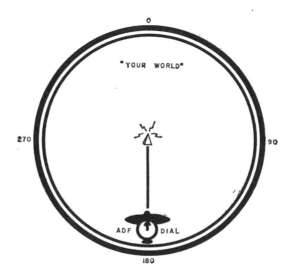

Fig. 26. You are south of the station on a heading of 0°.

When the ADF points to 010, you are no longer due south of the station on a radial of 180, but on a radial of 190, because the wind has blown you to the left. The simplest way to get to the station is to use the amateur's method of "bird dogging," which is useful but not recommended.

In "bird dogging," we turn right 10°, get our magnetic compass on 010, our ADF on 0, and thereby stay momentarily on a radial of 190. During the next few minutes the wind will again drift us to the left, until the ADF again reads 010. Then we turn to the right 10° more until we are heading 020; the ADF again points to the station with the needle on 0, and we are on a radial of 200.° By the time we finally arrive over the station, we have covered a track over the ground that looks something like Fig. 23 on page 169.

This is not a brilliant way to use the ADF. What we should do is to crab into the wind, point the airplane to the right, and fly a track of 0°. But if you crab 10° right, the ADF will point *left* of the nose to 350! How can you tell exactly what is going on?

An easy rule will tell you. Notice that in all of the following examples we use the magnetic compass (or Gyro Compass, if you have one) and not true north, because we are working with and flying compass headings. Let's begin by memorizing this simple phrase, which will be used repeatedly in all ADF work:

*Compass plus ADF equals the bearing to.*

That is, the bearing *to* the station, not the bearing away from it.

For example, in the previous problem we were flying a compass course of 0°, and the ADF needle pointed to 010°. The bearing *in* to the station, by the rule, is:

$$0 \text{ (compass)} + 10 \text{ (ADF)} = 10 \text{ degrees}$$

Now look at the ADF dial and consider it as your immediate "world," locating yourself by placing a finger on the position from which you must steer 010 to get to the station, which is always in the center of the dial. The only possible position is somewhere on radial 190, or southwest of the station, and your airplane is pointed north (360, or 0°). See Fig. 27. The airplane has a large ADF dial superimposed upon it, and the needle of the dial points to the station and a relative bearing of 010 degrees. Of course, we don't know, as yet, how far we are from the station. That will be known later on.

Now, airplanes do not always fly on a heading of 0°, or north, but for other headings all we need is a small amount of grammar-school arithmetic. Suppose that we are holding a compass heading of east, or 90°, and we tune in a station on the ADF, obtaining a needle reading of 270°. That would mean that we have the station off our left wing a number of miles. By the easy rule:

$$90 \text{ (compass)} + 270 \text{ (ADF)} = 360, \text{ or } 0°$$

We place ourselves on the ADF dial by imagining ourselves on the reciprocal of 360, which is the 180 radial south of the station, with the airplane flying east 90°, as in Fig. 28. Note that the station is off the left wing in the diagram with an ADF reading of 270.

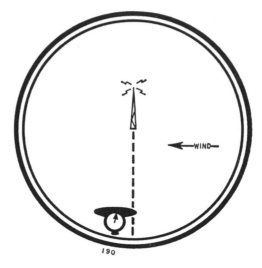

Fig. 27. After drifting to radial 190 the ADF reads 010°.

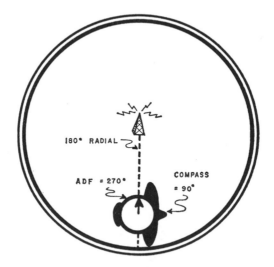

Fig. 28. Compass (90) plus ADF (270) equals 360, the bearing to the station. You are south of the station on a radial of 180, flying east.

The sum of the bearings is often a figure higher than 360°. Take the example of a plane flying west on a heading of 270. After the station is tuned in, the ADF needle also reads 270. (This example *always* causes confusion among those who do not use the easy rule.) Using the rule we obtain:

270 (compass) + 270 (ADF) = 540, the bearing *to*

But whenever we have a bearing *to* greater than 360, we must subtract 360 from it. 540 less 360 is 180, and we must fly a heading of 180 to get to the station. The only place from which we can do that is on the 0 radial, and we must be north of the station flying west, or 270, as in Fig. 29.

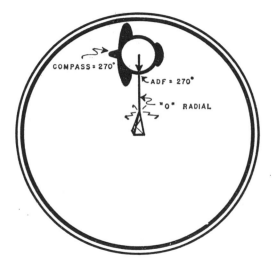

Fig. 29. Compass (270) plus ADF (270) equals 540, the bearing to the station. You are north of the station on the 0° radial flying west. Now find an easier way to solve this problem before reading on in the text.

Adding large figures is an awkward method. One easier method is to turn the adjustment knob of the ADF, rotate the dial to the compass heading, and let the ADF do the adding or subtracting for you. The results of this method have not proved satisfactory. Applicants forget to reset the dial or become preoccupied while adjusting it, usually getting into trouble. An easy but reliable method is to place a minus sign on the top left side of the ADF and call all figures on the left of zero "minus." Thus, 350° would become a —10, 315° would become —45, and so on. This method is quicker and has no penalty for forgetfulness.

Now do the previous problem again:

$$270 \ (\text{compass}) + [ \ -90] \ (\text{ADF}) = 180$$

We have obtained the correct answer without confusion or having to remove our eyes from the gauges, and we don't have to remember to reset the ADF. When a pilot is actually on instruments, the less mental fatigue he suffers the better. Place a plus sign on the right side of zero on your ADF and we are ready for the business of tracking.

Fig. 30. Consider 340° as —20°. By using this method it's easier to add any compass heading to the ADF.

## TRACKING

Tracking means to get on a radial and stay there. Suppose that the approach leg to a certain range is 270°. If you were on instruments, you'd have to get on 270 and stay there until you arrived over the station. How do you know where 270 is, the quickest way to turn in order to arrive there, and the best way to stay on it?

The value of visualizing your position on the ADF dial, or "rose," as it is called, is now obvious. We tune in our ADF to the frequency and *identify* the station by listening to its call letters. This will prevent an unplanned landing at points other than the airport. The ADF needle points to 45°, and the compass heading is 300. Where are we? How shall we get on 270?

Using the easy rule, 300 plus 45 is 345. We locate ourselves on the ADF dial by pointing to the southeast quadrant and to the position from which we must fly 345° to the station; this position has to be on the reciprocal of 345, or on the 165° radial. We are somewhere on the radial and the airplane is headed northwest, or 300 degrees. If we wish to fly to a position from which we can make an approach headed 270, that position will be on the 90° radial, which is just above our positioning finger on the ADF dial. Obviously, the quickest turn is a right turn to a heading of zero, which will intersect the 90° radial at an angle of 90 degrees.

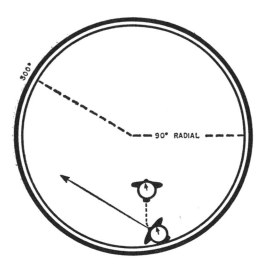

Fig. 31. To find the direction of turn to intercept a given radial, always visualize your position on *Your World* or the ADF dial. Compass 300, ADF 45: bearing to station is 345; we are southeast of the station on the reciprocal of 345 (the 165 radial) in an airplane heading 300°.

We make our turn and fly 0°, while the ADF needle swings from the right side of the dial over to the left. We fly onward until the station seemingly changes position toward our left wing; when the ADF needle swings to 270, we will be on the approach leg of 270 inbound because 0 plus 270 equals 270, the bearing *to*. But, because of the speed at which we are flying, we start our turn *before* the needle reads 270 (the exact time to turn depends upon the speed with which the needle moves), and by the time we recover from the turn on a heading of 270, the ADF needle will have moved to 0.

We are then on course, on heading, and on the approach leg. Now the question is, will we stay on it? Usually the answer is no. Suppose the wind is from our left, we drift to the right, and the ADF needle swings (it has to!) to the left and points to 350° (or −10). We know we are located at 270 − 10 or 260, on a radial of 80.

In order to fly to the station along a *track* of 270 we must get back on a radial of 90, which is on our left, and after that we must stay there. This brings up the subject of bites, of which there are many, but this is one that *we'll* take. We'll take a 30° bite, or cut, at the desired course of 270 by turning left 30° to it, or 240°. We always bite at the desired course, not at the course to which we've drifted.

Why did we turn 30°? First of all, we wouldn't correct ourselves by turning 10, because 10 is probably the amount of crab we'll have to use in order to merely counteract the wind. We didn't use 20 because it would take too long to get back on course. And we didn't use 40 or 50 because those large angles involve more or less violent maneuvering; in stronger winds, or if conditions indicate, we may indeed use 40, but not right now.

So we turn left 30° to a compass heading of 240. What will the ADF read when we are on course? Using the easy rule, we solve quickly:

$$240 + \text{ADF} = 270, \text{ the known bearing } in.$$
$$\text{Therefore, ADF} = 30$$

The ADF, which read 350 before we turned, swings over to plus 20 after we roll out on a heading of 240. As 240 plus 20 is 260, and the bearing of 260 to the station is on a radial of 80, our cross check proves our action correct. We now hold the heading and watch the ADF swing from 20 to 30. By the easy rule, 240 plus 30 is 270; we are now back on track, and it is time to turn again to the station heading.

What will be the heading? If we select 270 we'd have to do the job all over again, because we now know we have a wind from the left. (As we have no time to cross-check drift, we don't know if the wind is a tailwind or a headwind.) Instead of removing all of our 30° bite, we'll remove only 20° by turning from 240 to 260, crabbing into the wind with the ADF pointing to 010 degrees. It is here that the easy rule and the marking of the ADF with minus-plus signs is so valuable: we merely use the rule, finding that 260 plus 10 equals 270.

But that's too easy. Suppose the wind comes from the right; this is more difficult because the numbers are larger and it is harder to add them mentally. After correcting for the wind, we find ourselves crabbing to the right on a heading of 280, with the ADF indicating 350. Using the rule, we obtain:

$$280 \text{ (compass)} + 350 \text{ (ADF)} = 630$$
$$630 - 360 = 270, \text{ the } bearing \ in$$

That is not so easy. Try to do all you have to do on an approach and add those figures. Certainly there must be figures more attractive. Let's try the minus method: compass heading 280, ADF −10. Answer: 270.

As we fly inbound, the ADF needle is going to change. It is naïve to suppose that a random choice like 10 degrees of crab is going to exactly counteract an unknown wind. In the original problem we were on a heading of 260 with the ADF at 10.

If the wind is slight or the crab too great, we'll fly south of course and the ADF will read more, such as 15. We apply the rule: 260 + 15 = 275; we glance at our "world" and see that to reach 275 on the other side of the station we must be on a radial of 95, south of our track. We must now decrease the angle of crab to about 5° in order to get back on course, turning to 265 as the ADF moves to 10. Because 265 + 10 = 275, we wait until the ADF moves to 5; then 265 + 5 = 270, and we're back on track. Remember that the clue as to how much bite to take is obtained from the *amount* of needle change and the *rate* of change.

## TIME TO STATION

During ATR or instrument flight tests, the inspector will ask for "time and distance to the station." At first it would seem impossible to know how far we are from a radio station without check points, cross bearings or Distance Measuring Equipment (DME), but it can be done with good approximation—if we have a device which gives us a *bearing* to the station.

Consider Fig. 32. We're flying northward from C to B. At Point C we obtain a reading from the ADF of 270° and continue on toward Point B, where the ADF reads 30° less. The convenient relationship between the legs of this 30° right triangle is that the hypotenuse *c* is always twice the base leg *a*. Furthermore, if we regard the base leg as unity, then the hypotenuse *c* becomes equal to the cosecant of the angle of change at Point B.

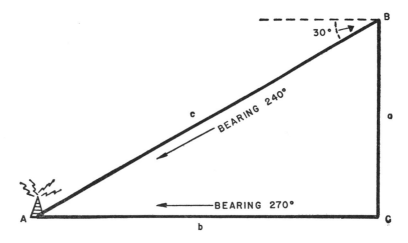

Fig. 32. In 30° right triangles, the hypotenuse c is always twice as long as a.

Now consider the interrelationship of a few cosecants for small angles. For 30° the cosecant is 2; for 20° it is 2.92; for 15° it is 3.96; for 10° it is 5.75. How may we find these cosecants easily in flight?

By inspection, it may be seen that the figures above are approximately quotients of 60 divided by the angle: thus, 60 divided by 30 equals 2, the cosecant of 30°. Therefore, the easy formula for finding *approximate* cosecants of other angles is 60 divided by the angle; likewise, if the cosecant gives us the time in for one-minute base legs, we multiply the cosecant by the elapsed time for the time *in*. Therefore, the formula is:

$$\frac{60}{\text{Number of degrees change}} \times \text{time travelled} = \text{time } in$$

For example, in Fig. 32, at Point C the ADF reads 270 to the station; we fly north from C to B and at the end of eight minutes the ADF reads 240°, a change of 30°. We then know that the time to the station from B is

$$\frac{60}{30} \times 8 = 16 \text{ minutes}$$

provided we turn inbound at *once;* by using the computer, we find that with a 110-mph ground speed we're 29+ miles away. (In instrument weather, ground speed must be estimated from the air speed.)

The rule is not usable for angles larger than 30°, but for smaller angles the accuracy is within 4 per cent, as may be observed in the next example. Suppose that in Fig. 32 we fly northward from C, but instead of continuing to B we make a computation when the ADF reads 260 (a 10° change), and the elapsed time is 2½ minutes.

By the formula, $\frac{60}{10} \times 2\frac{1}{2} = 15$ minutes; by trigonometry the answer is 14.4 minutes, but because the error is small and because the formula involves easy mental calculations, it may be used in flight. During our mental labors we begin turning toward the station, telling the inspector the time in; if he also demands the new heading, we simply use our easy rule: compass (0) + ADF (260) = 260, the bearing *in.*

The formula can be relied upon in fog and no wind, although there are larger errors possible in strong winds such as accompany storms. But knowing how far one is from the station is invaluable during approaches.

To make solutions easier, use angles that divide into 60 evenly, such as 5, 6, 10, 12, 15, 20, or 30; the angle used depends upon the time required to obtain the change. For example, a change of 10° in two minutes would be about right, but we wouldn't fly through 20° if twenty minutes were required.

Let's go back to our interception problem in which we were southeast of the station, flying a heading of 300 with the ADF pointing to 45. We have just turned north to intercept radial 90, and because we will intercept the radial at a right angle we want to do a time-in problem. Can we do it, now that we're flying *toward* the right angle instead of away from it, as in Fig. 32? Now the side *b* will be the in-bound leg, not the hypotenuse *c*. Can we do the problem? Yes, because for angles less than 20° the error is still quite small, less than 8 per cent. (The only time our formula has no error is when we solve for the hypotenuse *c* of the 30° right triangle in Fig. 32.) But because the advantage of knowing exactly where we are helps us visualize our let-down problem, let's find the time. We turn, fly north, and watch the needle. It swings from 045 to 345 because compass (0) + ADF (345) = 345, the previously computed bearing. Now wait for it to creep down to 290; when it does, take a time check and jot it on your knee pad, a time such as 15:35 (fifteen minutes thirty-five seconds). When the ADF reads 270 check the time again: 19:25, an elapsed time of nearly four minutes; start turning to the station as you solve your problem. If the inspector wants split-second timing, use your computer to find the time in. Otherwise, solve it mentally: $60/20 \times 4 = 12$ minutes.

## TRACKING AWAY

We now come to that confusing problem given in flight tests: tracking away from the station. More confusion exists over this simple feature of ADF procedures than there are ADF's. It is here that a pilot gives thanks for an easy rule by which to keep his head from spinning.

Let us suppose that we're making our approach straight in on the 90° radial at approach altitude and that we do not need to cross the station, turn around, make a procedure turn, and fly inbound the second time. We'll make our let-down after crossing the station the first time, assuming the airport runway is on the other side of the station on the 270 radial.

This is a very important part of the flight test, because we must be lined up with the runway after breaking clear of clouds at 400 feet and 1 mile visibility. As we cross the station, our ADF needle wavers, hesitates, and swings down, indicating that the station is behind us. What will the needle read?

For example, we are crabbing into the wind on a heading of 265, with the ADF reading 5 degrees. Because the let-down leg is on a heading of 270, we still want compass plus ADF to equal 270, but after passing the station our ADF says 185. Where are we? Here is where the plus and minus signs are so handy. Refer to the markings in Fig. 30: at the bottom left is a plus sign, so 185 becomes an *indication* of plus five. Then: compass (265) + ADF indication (+5) = 270, our desired track *away*. Had we added 265 to 185 we would have had organized confusion, which is just as bad as disorganized confusion.

Suppose that we have northerly winds and the ADF reads 170. Where are we, and which way shall we turn to get back on course? Here again, the minus sign is handy: compass (265) + (−10) = 255 away. A glance at the "world" shows that 255 *away* is the same as radial 255; it is to the left, or south of 270, and we must turn right. We turn to a compass heading of 275, and the ADF needle moves to −20 (160°); when it moves downward to −5 (175) we will be on track, because compass (275) + ADF (−5) = 270. The amount of correction in this example is exaggerated for the sake of clarity, but the principle applies in correcting smaller errors. Bear in mind, too, that the amount of error *and* the rate of needle change are even more important in close-in problems like let downs than they were before.

## OTHER ADF USES

The foregoing illustrates the uses of the ADF during the flight test for an instrument rating, an ATR (Airline Transport Rating), or a six-month competency check. An FAA inspector wants to see a pilot locate himself, get his time and distance, track in on a heading, and go through his let-down procedures.

There are other interesting uses which are no longer required, such as finding the time to the station by the Aural Null method. The pilot puts on his headphones, tunes to the station, identifies it, and switches to *Loop*. This method is seldom used in ADF work, but it can be helpful.

By switching his ADF to *Loop*, the pilot may rotate the loop until little or no signal is heard. This "null" may be widened by diminishing the volume control; when the loop is turned by depressing a switch, the signal fades out, and at that time the pilot reads the bearing indicated on the ADF dial.

But the loop receives equally well from either side, and the station can therefore be located at either end of the needle! By flying for a minute or so, the pilot can locate the station by watching the needle; the station *must* recede, so it is on the side of the needle that lowers. Example: the needle points to 90 (with the other end at 270). If the needle moves from 90 to 100, the station is on the right; if the rear of the needle moves from 270 to 260, the station is on the left. Then, by turning the plane to a heading that will receive a null at a right angle we can take a time check, listen to a null as we fly, and take another time check at 5, 10, 15, or 20° change.

There is another problem asked by inspectors which confuses some pilots, and that question is a variation of the 90° intercept. Fig. 31 placed us in the southeast quadrant, flying 300°, on a radial of 165. Suppose the inspector asked you to intercept the 270° *radial* at a 30° angle? The first thing to do is to locate yourself in the southeast quadrant of the ADF dial, with the plane on a heading of 300.

Obviously, this is a trick question, but trick questions are not objectionable because they prove whether or not a pilot knows his business. The inspector merely wants to know that *you* know you are already on a heading that will intercept 270 at 30°, and that you will do this on the far side of the station. Or he might ask you to intercept "a course of 270 inbound at an angle of 30° outbound." You would then see from your position on the dial that a course of 270 inbound is a radial of 90, that it is to the north of you, that a heading of 60° would do the trick, and that the shortest turn is to the right. As you would be flying away from the station, you'd read the ADF from the bottom, and when it read plus 30 (210°) you'd be on track. (Compass 60 + indication 30 = 90 *away.*)

Trick problems aren't always silly, because the approach leg could very well be located on the far side of the station, and you might have to fly to it on a 30° intercept to save time. A 90° intercept would take you far into the southwest quadrant, which is highly undesirable when the gas is running low.

## ERRORS

Whereas the amateur pilot likes an ADF during a cross-country flight, he may be tempted to depend upon it without knowing the perils of trusting his ADF implicitly. The ADF fails when it is needed most. Suppose you have been flying cross country solely by ADF, and just as you are halfway to your destination you encounter cumulo-nimbus, the thunderhead. Within a minute or so, the ADF needle can either point to the cloud, or spin like a top. Use the ADF as an aid, not a crutch.

Cross-bearings are fine, too, but many pilots do not know that the ADF dial must be calibrated, and that only two headings, 0 and 180, are exactly accurate. Other bearings can be as much as ±8° in error, and in obtaining a fix you must allow for the error. Also, readings are magnetic, so the line of direction must be corrected for deviation and variation. Finally, in taking bearings of distant stations, a further correction must be applied, a Mercator correction. Radio bearings are curved (radio signals take great circle routes), whereas Mercator charts have straight lines to represent longitude and latitude. The great-circle bearing read from an ADF may vary many degrees from the bearing plotted on a Mercator chart.

But on a routine cross-country flight over land ADF bearings can be helpful, although they are not required on the flight test because they are more radio navigation than piloting and because aeronautical charts are Lambert projections, which do give great circle routes without additional correction.

## USING THE ADF

The following are examples of ADF work that are of practical value, and although they summarize what has been presented before, they should be solved prior to using the ADF. A pilot who cannot solve these simple problems should defer his instrument flight practice to a later date. As a matter of fact, these problems should be solved before one so much as gets into the airplane or tries to work any problem under the hood.

1. The fundamental rule for finding magnetic bearings from relative bearings is: *Compass* + *ADF* = *the bearing* to *the station.*
2. Always locate yourself by visualizing your plane on *Your World* or the ADF dial, with the station in the center of the dial. Disregard the ADF needle, indicated by the arrow, for this problem.
   *a.* Problem: Aircraft flying 90°.
   ADF reads 90°.
   Find position of plane, heading, and bearing to station.

Solution: Compass (90) + ADF (90) = 180, the bearing
*to*. If we must fly south or 180 to reach the station, we must
be north of it, on the 0° radial.

Therefore: Position is north of station.

Heading is east, or 90°.

Bearing *to* station is 180°.

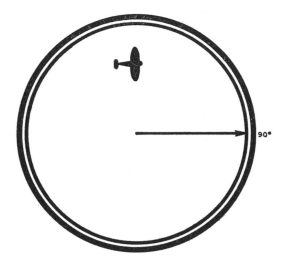

Fig. 33. Compass 90, ADF 90. You are on a radial of 0.

3. An easy way to solve large-number problems on the ADF is to
mark the ADF dial with minus and plus signs, as in Fig. 34. Thus
315° is −45°.

   *a.* Problem: Aircraft flying 135°.

   ADF reads 315°.

   Find bearing to station and position of plane on *Your
   World* or ADF dial.

   Solution: Compass + ADF = Bearing *to*.

   135 + 315 = 450.

   450 − 360 = 90 (answer).

   Or, using the minus sign, we may solve the problem easily
   and mentally:

   135 + (−45) = 90 (answer).

   Therefore: bearing to station is 90.

Position of plane is west of station on a radial of 270, flying southeast. (See Fig. 34.)

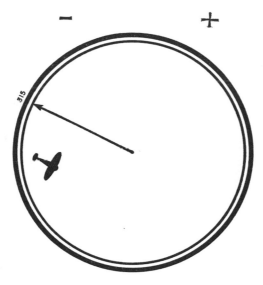

Fig. 34. Compass 135, ADF 315. You are west of the station on a radial of 270.

*b.* Problem: Aircraft flying 225°.
  ADF reads 260°.
  Find bearing to station and location of plane.
  Solution: $225 + (-100) = 125$.
  Therefore: Bearing to station is 125° *to.*
  Location of plane is northwest of station flying southwest. (See Fig. 35.)

4. Tracking *away* from the station is more difficult, but similar markings make solutions easier. Mark your ADF with a plus and minus sign, as in Figure 36, with plus at the bottom left and minus at the bottom right. Thus, for bearings *away*, 170° becomes —10, 190 is +10, and so on. Bearings *away* may be found by adding algebraically the bottom figures to the compass heading.

*a.* Problem: Aircraft flying 0° (360°).
  ADF reads 170°.
  Find bearing *away* from station and position of plane.

Solution: $360 - 10 = 350$, bearing *away*.

Therefore: Bearing *away* is 350°.

Plane is north of station on a radial of 350, on a heading of 0°. (Fig. 36)

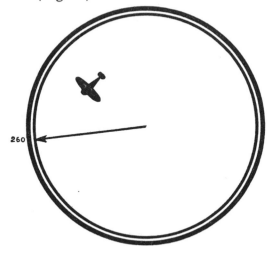

Fig. 35. Compass 225, ADF 260. You are northwest of the station on a 305 radial, flying southwest.

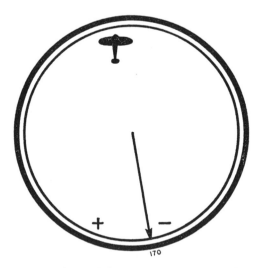

Fig. 36. You are northwest of the station, flying north on the 350 radial.

5. One should turn the shortest way to a desired track. The ADF
   dial should be used to locate the position and to determine the
   shortest direction of turn.
   *a.* Problem: Compass reads 90°.
         ADF reads 210°.
         Find position, bearing *to*, bearing *away*, direction to turn
         to intercept a radial of 80° at a 90° angle, ADF reading
         after turning, and ADF reading when on track.
   Solution: 90 + 210 = 300, the bearing *to*.
      90 + 30 = 120, the bearing *away*.
   Therefore: Plane is southeast of station headed east.
         Shortest turn is left.
         Heading upon completion of turn will be 350°, which may
         be verified by a glance at the *World*. ADF will read 310°
         upon completion of turn, which may be checked from
         the rule: Compass (350) + ADF (−50) = 300°, the bear-
         ing *to* the station. ADF will read 270 when plane reaches
         the 80 radial, which is verified by the rule: Compass
         (350) + (−90) = 260, the bearing *to* the station. (See
         Fig. 37.)

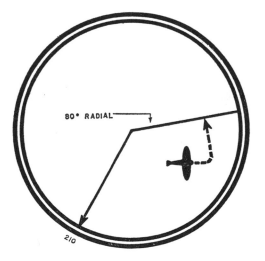

Fig. 37. ADF reads 210, compass 90. Which
way do you turn to intercept a radial of 80?

*b.* Problem: Compass reads 90°.
    ADF reads 0°.
    Find position, and direction to turn to intercept a radial of
    80°, without flying over the station.

Solution: This is a trick question, but does involve a practice
    problem which occasionally is given when the pilot is on
    one side of the station and the approach leg is on the other.
    Position is on a radial of 270, or inbound to the station on
    90, west of the station. Pilot must fly a heading of 170 for a
    period of time depending upon the traffic over the station,
    turn left to 80 and fly for X minutes (when he is abreast of
    the station the ADF will read 270). He then flies four min-
    utes farther, turns left to 350, which will intercept the 80°
    radial at 90°.

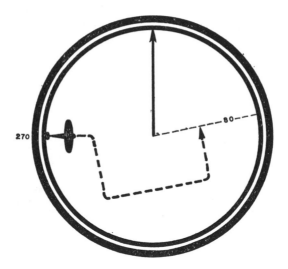

Fig. 38. How to intercept a radial without flying over the station.

*c.* Problem: Compass reads 300°.
    ADF reads 30°.
    Find the direction to turn to intercept radial 270 at 30°.

Solution: This is a trick question, and the ADF reading of
    30° has nothing to do with the solution. Locate yourself on

*Your World.* The bearing *to* is 300 plus 30, or 330 *to,* which places the plane in the southeast quadrant on a heading of 300°. We now can see quite easily that we're already on a heading which will permit us to intercept 270 at a 30° angle, but we will make intercept at a point *beyond* the station.

Knowing how to solve problems like this is particularly useful if the 270 radial is also the approach leg, and we wish to arrive at the point of intercept more quickly than we would have with a 90° intercept. By now you should be able to determine what the ADF should read at the point of intercept.*

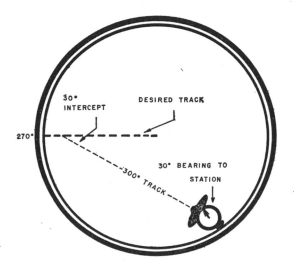

Fig. 39. Watch out for trick intercept problems. A plane in the southeast quadrant on a heading of 300° will intercept a radial of 270 at a 30° angle—on the *other* side of the station.

* Answer: 150°.

# 18: FLYING THE OMNIRANGE

YOU'RE flying cross country from San Diego to Los Angeles. The coast is clear and easy to follow because the visibility is unlimited. You can see Catalina Island 30 miles to your left and by straining the imagination you can almost hear the band playing "Avalon." But by the time Long Beach appears beneath the nose, something happens to the visibility. The Los Angeles Chamber of Commerce doesn't like this, nor do you, but neither of you can do much about it. Because Los Angeles International Airport is practically on instruments, hidden behind the Smog Curtain, you decide to turn on your Omni receiver.

Finding your bearing to the airport with the aid of an Omnirange is easy. Where the antiquated four-legged ranges with their confusing A's and N's were ambiguous, the Omni always indicates the magnetic bearing to or from the station, no matter where you happen to be. You may so much as turn through 360°, but as long as you remain on a radial the Omni will read the direction to the station. Because it reads *magnetic* rather than *relative* bearings, the Omni is much easier to use than the ADF described in Chapter 17. There are, however, some phases of ADF work that are helpful and which may be applied to the Omni procedures presented here.

The Omni is truly a marvelous aid to the Private Pilot. If, like the ADF, Omni cannot be used for weather prediction, it can nevertheless tell you the time and distance to the station, how to fly from one position to another, and how to let down through solid overcast—if one knows how. Just because the word "Omni" is derived from the Latin word meaning "all," or because VHF Omni-directional Range (VOR) implies the meaning "all magnetic bearings," is no reason to infer that we know *all* about Omni.

The Omnirange receiver is so simple, light, and relatively inexpensive, compared to airline equipment such as the Instrument
Landing System (ILS), Distance Measuring Equipment (DME),
or the Automatic Direction Finder (ADF), that most Private Pilots
do have Omni receivers. The panel installation, with its three com-
ponents plus tuner, is simple, convenient, and easy to operate. It
can even be used for a partial ILS approach, as described in Chapter 19. From simple cross-country work to cross-bearing checks,
knowledge of the Omni and how to use it is a must.

You can almost hear them playing "Avalon."

When the visibility is such that Los Angeles is apparently on
instruments, we're not dismayed because our Omni will get us to
the runway. As we find the frequency of Los Angeles Omni on the
chart, we are confident that we can fly our Omni expertly because
we know a rule that makes such flying easier. Tune the receiver to
113.6 and listen to the identifiers, LAX; after the station is identified, it's a matter of seconds until you'll have the direct bearing to
LAX.

First, there's the course selector (Fig. 40A), which is marked like
the compass, in degrees. Rotate it until a certain degree of setting
causes the needle of the flight path deviation indicator (FPDI)

(in Fig. 40B) to become centered. Next, glance at the TO–FROM indicator (Fig. 40C). If it reads FROM, rotate the course selector 180 degrees; then the TO–FROM indicator says TO, and you read the bearing to the station directly from the dial of the course selector. If your Omni utilizes other methods, the result is the same. You obtain a bearing to the station in a matter of seconds.

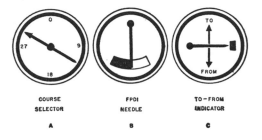

Fig. 40. The Omni group: (A) the Course Selector; (B) the FPDI (deviation needle); (C) "TO–FROM" indicator.

Next, you call Los Angeles Radio on the VHF frequency to see if Los Angeles is on instruments. They advise that Los Angeles does have adequate visibility and you may fly VFR; if the visibility were less than VFR minimums, you'd need an IFR clearance and an instrument rating. A glance at the chart shows there is a fan marker known as La Habra 25 miles east of LAX, which would be an ideal location from which to make an approach because it is practically on the approach radial of 69° given on FAA's VOR Instrument Approach Procedure Chart. All one must know are such items as: How far are you from the station? How does the Omni work when you're flying from one radial to another? Is it possible to tell when one is over La Habra if he has only an Omni receiver? And, how do I tie down a radial?

## HOW TO TIE DOWN A RADIAL

You look at your needle. It is swinging to the left, and the words of your instructor come to mind. He said to fly toward the needle when flying course-selector headings, so you turn left. But how many degrees shall we turn? And suppose we do get back on course: how do we tie down a radial?

This is when knowing another rule prevents confusion. Let's take our Omni in hand, so to speak, and find the operational procedures. First there is our aeronautical chart with its 4½-inch circle around the Omni radio station. The circle is numbered every 30 degrees and every degree in the circle may be considered a spoke of a wheel, radiating outward, called a *radial*. An even simpler way to remember what radials are is to consider all FROM bearings as *radials*.

For example, we turn the course selector so that the pointer indicates FROM. The course selector says that the course *from* the station is 120°, which means that we're on the 120° radial. This simplifies matters considerably. By looking at *Your World* (which is repeated here in Fig. 41), we locate ourselves southeast of the station, somewhere on a radial of 120 degrees. The radials are *magnetic* bearings; notice the arrow on your VOR circle on your areonautical chart. It points to zero, but zero is 15° to the east of true north because 15° is the magnetic variation in this particular part of the country.

Next, rotate the course selector until the TO–FROM needle says TO. Now the selector reads 300°, our bearing *to* the station and the compass heading we'll fly that will presumably take us to LAX. But what about compass deviation? What about wind? It is true that these errors will cause a plane to fly off course, but the OMNI FPDI needle will indicate when we're off course by moving to the right or left. In flying the Omnirange, one may remain on course merely by keeping the needle centered, even if he had several degrees of deviation and a 50-mile crosswind. If the needle were kept centered, the plane would have to crab in order to remain on track to the station.

Therefore, keeping the needle centered is the first problem. We check the needle, which has drifted to the left, indicating that we must fly left to get back on course. Let's see where we are now. Rotate the course selector until the needle is centered: it now reads 290 *to*, and a glance at the *World* shows us that in order to fly 290 to the station we must be on a 110 radial, a little to the north of 120. We change our heading by turning *left* and await developments;

here is where we must learn how to tie down a heading accurately, as we must do during let downs on final approach.

Let's apply the easy rule for flying glide path, localizer, or Omni needles. The rule is to fly toward the needle, but for Omni we add a few extra words:

*If the compass heading and the course selector reading are the same, fly toward the needle.*

We make a left turn of 30° and hold this heading until the needle again is centered. As in previous chapters, we want a large, standard bite when we tie down a leg, because it gives us information we need promptly and because it is large enough to offset wind or compass error immediately, without having to go through the monotonous and confusing procedure of taking a ten-degree bite, then five more, and so on until a pilot doesn't know what he's doing. Finally, 30° bites seem to be just right: large enough to correct for drift and small enough to be convenient. The only objection to 30° bites is that they are not to be used during final approach, when one must use small bites such as 2 or 3 degrees, and during cross-country flights when such corrections would wear a pilot out.

## YOUR WORLD AGAIN

As the needle drifts to the left, we review our knowledge of bites as discussed in previous chapters. We know that we're going to turn left 30°, and we recall that a bite is always taken against the *desired* course, not against the one to which we've drifted. If 290° is the desired course and if the course selector is set to 290°, we must turn left toward the needle. Let's check this by referring to our homemade compass rose, or *World* (in Fig. 41), which is almost indispensable in working orientation problems.

If the rose is our immediate world and if the station is in the center of it, then we're southeast of the station in an airplane headed 290°. We wish to turn left toward the needle, and because 260 is 30° left of 290, 260 is the bite heading. This method of figuring bites and headings, or in computing headings to intersect a given radial, will forever prevent you from flying incorrect headings, such as 290 + 30 or 320. Similar errors have been made on flight tests by supposedly competent applicants. The resultant failure of the flight test is not half as bad as what happens to a pilot who makes such a mistake under actual instrument conditions.

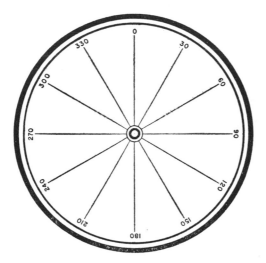

Fig. 41. *Your World.* As indispensable for Omni problems as it was for compass work. The station is always in the center; thus, if the Omni indicates a bearing of 120° *from,* you're on a radial of 120. Place a finger on 120, locating yourself southeast of the station. To fly toward the station you'll fly 300° (with the Omni reading 300 *to*), so 300° is the compass course *to* the station. For intercepting radials, such as a radial of 150, it's instantly apparent that you must fly southwest; and in order to intercept 150 at a 90° angle, the heading is 240°.

We fly our new heading of 260 and watch the needle, which moves either slowly or quickly back to center depending upon the velocity of the wind, our distance from the station, and the amount of course error. In any event, it is the *position* of the needle and the *rate* of change that we must watch. If the needle moves quickly, we must anticipate the needle by removing almost all of the 30° bite before the needle is centered. On the other hand, if the needle moves slowly, we'll allow the needle to become practically centered before we remove the bite and we'll leave more of the bite in the new heading. For example, with a slow-moving needle, we'll turn

right from 260 to 280, thereby flying a course correction and crabbing into the wind 10 degrees.

For purposes of illustration we'll continue on to the station at
high altitude. As we near the station we should have the heading
tied down to within a few degrees, and we fly over the station
making good a track of 290. The TO–FROM pointer and the needle
waver, oscillate, and reverse themselves, the red flags indicating
"poor reception" above the station come up, waver, and go back
down. Finally, the Omni settles down with the TO–FROM pointer on
FROM, and at this point the FPDI needle usually moves to the right
or left because of wind, instrument error, or sloppy flying. Which
direction shall we turn to center the needle and to go outbound
on the 290 *radial?*

The easy rule still holds!

*If the compass heading and the course selector reading are the
same, fly toward the needle.*

Thus, we wait thirty seconds to see if the needle centers. If it
does not, we fly toward it a few degrees—not many, because we're
very close in and the radials are narrow. Regardless of the fact
that we are flying *outbound* and the TO–FROM pointer is indicating
FROM, the rule applies.

If we were actually on instruments we'd reverse course, fly outbound on the heading given on the VOR chart, let down to approach minimums, make a procedure turn, and fly inbound on the
approach heading; during the inbound flight we'd let down to our
minimum altitude, hoping to become contact at that time. This
will be described later.


## FINDING TIME AND DISTANCE FROM STATION

Now let's go back to our original position on the 110 radial,
from which we'll fly to La Habra and make a simulated instrument approach. As readers of Chapter 17 know, time and distance
problems are simply a matter of flying the base leg of a 90° triangle.
We wish to fly to La Habra and get on the 69 radial; which way
shall we turn? How may we solve the problem of time-distance to
the station and how may we find La Habra?

The needle is centered, so we are on the 110 radial; we visualize our position on the *World*, noting that we are southeast of the station. Because the 69 radial is north of us, we'll fly to the north. In order to have a 90° triangle, we'll turn 90 degrees. But 110 plus 90 is 200! And 200 is to the south! To prevent confusion we again glance at our *World*, which would be worth its weight in gold if this were a flight test. We see instantly that the 20° radial is across the circle from 200, so we turn north to 20° for our new heading.

As you start turning right to 20°, take a time check, jotting this time on your knee pad, and fly for at least two minutes. Now you may work with either *to* bearings or *from* bearings. Most pilots prefer *from* readings in time and distance problems because all *from* bearings are radials. Whichever you use, remember that you are flying counterclockwise and that all the bearings decrease. Now take a time check at a 5-, 6-, 10-, 15-, or 20-degree change by rotating the course selector until the needle is centered. Suppose that it reads 104°—a change of 6° in one minute and fifty seconds.

Using the formula we used in Chapter 17, we obtain:

$$\frac{60}{\text{Degree of change}} \times \text{time} = \text{time required to fly to station}$$

$$\frac{60}{6} \times 1.8 = 18 \text{ minutes to the station}$$

If you're flying at 110 mph, your computer tells you that you're about 33 statute miles away. This figure is only approximate because the formula is accurate only for a 30° right triangle, but the accuracy is sufficient for practical purposes.

You now know that you're about 33 miles southeast of station on a radial of 104, and the aeronautical chart shows that this position is south of La Habra about 15 miles. La Habra is a fan marker, 4 miles wide and 10 miles long—can we find La Habra?

The answer is that La Habra is a *fan* marker, not a radio *beacon*. The first is on 75 mc. and the other on low frequency, for use in ADF work. In actual instrument work we would be required to hold at a position more accurately defined, but for a VFR approach we can find La Habra accurately enough by using what is known as cross bearings, and obtain a "fix" or position of the plane.

## CROSS BEARINGS AND FIXES

This requires that we find another Omni station located from 60° to 90° from La Habra and LAX. Break out the chart again. There's Long Beach; no need to use a protractor, as a glance at the Omni rose shows La Habra lies on the 12° radial of Long Beach. When we get on the LAX Omni radial of 69, we'll see if we're near La Habra or not.

La Habra is north, so after finding the distance to LAX as described above, turn left to true north. But, as you learned in Chapter 10, the compass doesn't point north. Now you may be glad to have learned another easy rule, a rule that works in the cockpit when you need it: *From compass to true ... add east.* If you stopped the turn at 0°, then compass (0) plus variation (15) equals 15, which is not true north. Turn left to 345 and you're flying true north to La Habra. For further accuracy, check the deviation card, but in this problem we'll assume no deviation.

Now, because we don't have to fly toward or away from the needle, we'll use radials in flying from our previous position to the 69 radial. Turn the course selector to 69, with the pointer on FROM; don't bother about flying toward the needle, because the rule doesn't work when the compass and the Omni differ more than 90°. Make a recheck by looking at the *World.* You should be flying north from radial 120 to radial 69, so your computations were correct. Watch your progress toward radial 69 by checking the Omni occasionally; do this by turning the course selector and centering the needle. After radial 100 slips by, you check again at a setting of 90; finally, you turn the selector to 69. When the needle is centered again you're on radial 69, somewhere in the vicinity of La Habra.

We're now ready to tune in Long Beach and obtain a cross-bearing check in order to obtain our position, or fix. Find the frequency, tune in the Omni, and listen to the identifiers, LGB. Rotate the course selector until the pointer says FROM (we're still dealing with radials) and take a reading. The selector says 14°, so we're slightly east of radial 12, almost exactly where we'd planned to be. The point where the LGB 14 radial intersects the LAX 69 radial is our fix, and this method of obtaining fixes is ideal for cross-country work.

## HOLDING

Under actual instrument conditions, we'd probably have to "hold" at a given altitude and position while awaiting our approach clearance from Air Route Traffic Control (referred to as ATC in radio parlance). ATC expects pilots to be inbound at approach time; in fact, they more than expect it—they demand it. With both an Omni and a marker-beacon receiver, there are many places to hold, but with only an Omni we'd have to hold over an Omni station on a given radial.

Let's suppose we're holding on radial 69 in a one-minute holding pattern. A one-minute pattern means that we fly one-minute legs. Thus, it requires four minutes to complete the pattern: fly to the station, allow one minute to turn 180 degrees, one minute outbound, one minute to turn 180 degrees, and one minute inbound. This means we must regulate the pattern in order to be at the fix at the time ATC said to be there.

For example, from our position at La Habra (if it had an Omni), we'd turn west to a heading of 249 on the 69 radial. Now be alert. If your Omni course selector says 69 with the compass reading 249, the rule no longer applies. This is where many Omni pilots attempt to learn a new rule and consequently go astray. *Don't try it.* Your compass heading is 249, but with the Omni selector set to 69, you must learn a new rule, such as flying away from the needle. This is good information to forget because it is poor learning technique and because safe flying is easier when you know *one* good rule well. Simply turn the selector to 249: now the compass and your Omni read the same, so *fly toward the needle!* When one is on instruments, he mustn't be confused with new or different rules.

We arrive at our fix; the Omni reverses (or the marker-beacon light on the panel flashes), and we check the time: two minutes to go! We can't fly a complete pattern of four minutes, because that will make every pilot behind us two minutes late. We therefore make a standard, two-minute turn, arriving at the fix on time and making everyone happy.

## THE OMNI INSTRUMENT APPROACH

If this were an actual Omni instrument approach, we would first have to obtain a definite fix by radio—not by a cross-bearing fix but by locating a beacon or radio transmitter below us. With only an Omni receiver, we'd obtain this by flying inbound and crossing the station; we'd then reverse course, make a descent to approach altitude, execute a procedure turn, and fly inbound to the field. This is not as hard as it sounds if we use the techniques already learned.

Set the course selector on 249 and fly inbound, tying down the high approach in order to learn what kind of winds you are likely to have during the low approach. Cross the station at a given high altitude, reverse course and fly outbound on the 69 radial for four minutes. As you fly outbound you have the choice of two methods: Use the easy rule and reverse the course selector so that it reads the same as the compass (69), or try to be a mastermind and fly away from the needle on FROM headings. But remember: one moment of forgetfulness on the part of the mastermind may cause much unhappiness. Why not reverse the selector so that it reads the same as the compass? Then merely fly toward the needle and make this approach easy! As you fly, descend to the approach altitude given on the VOR approach chart: 2,000 feet. At the end of four minutes, make a procedure turn according to the chart; for the LAX range it's on the south side of course.

Procedure turns may be conventional or otherwise. The conventional procedure turn consists of a 45° turn off course, a one-minute leg, a 180° turn, and flight back to the radial. This involves complicated arithmetical additions. An easier procedure turn is made by turning off course 80° and then rolling immediately into a turn in the opposite direction; this brings the plane back on the radial headed inbound. The advantages are that no complicated additions, subtractions, or timing must be computed in reversing one's heading. The only arithmetical addition is course heading plus 80 degrees.

As we roll out of the turn *inbound* on 249, we rotate the course selector until it also reads 249. Now all we have to do is tie down the leg during our approach. When we're on course, we reduce power to obtain a 500 fpm descent; from 2,000 feet to our minimum altitude of 500 feet is 1,500 feet, so we should be clear of clouds in three minutes. Begin to tie down the needle by taking a small bite at the course heading. When the needle drifts to the left, turn to 246°; when the needle comes back to center, leave a little bite in the heading. Just as we learned in previous chapters, it is not only the position of the needle but also the rate of movement that must be considered in making corrections and in holding headings.

Keep your eyes moving systematically around the panel, checking your altitude during the descent. Make those small heading corrections with the rudder and, as the radial becomes narrower, remember that a little correction makes the needle move faster and sooner.

At 500 feet or so, we have visual contact with the ground. Advise approach control, get clearance to land, and stay on the Omni needle, because we're over 2 miles from the runway (two minutes at approach speeds under 65 knots), and the runway cannot be seen as yet with 1-mile visibility.

## CHECKING YOUR OMNI

Was the approach lined up with the runway? If it was, good; if it was not, your Omni has an error which should be calibrated. There are hundreds of Omni check points, and it pays to check your Omni regularly. There are two places to do this, in the air and on the ground. By referring to the Flight Information Manual, the location of the Omni and the ground-air check points may be ascertained. Find the sites, turn on your Omni, and check the readings.

With the FPDI needle centered, the bearing should be plus or minus 4 degrees on the ground or plus or minus 6 degrees in the air. Enter the corrections on your Omni calibration card: For 30° steer 33°, etc. Don't attempt to repair the receiver if the error is greater than instrument flying tolerances, because an Omni receiver is a very high frequency receiver and is extremely delicate.

Flying the Omnirange is not only easy but fun, providing that you have an easy rule. Just remember to keep *the compass heading and the course selector reading the same,* and to fly toward the needle. With that method you'll never go wrong.

# 19: FLYING THE ILS

WHEN we tuned in the Instrument Landing System, our passengers were amused. The cockpit might well have been a scene from a magazine advertisement captioned, "They laughed when I sat down to play my ILS." The fact that we didn't have a complete ILS in the airplane might have been one reason they laughed; another reason was that they considered the ILS, with its blue-yellow sectors, much too difficult for an average lightplane driver.

As we watched the Omni needle come to life and swing to one side, we knew what we were going to do, because our Omni was equipped to receive an ILS localizer and we did have a VHF 75-mc. marker-beacon receiver. Now our critics began to look perplexed. The needle was in the blue side of the dial, and that meant we were in the blue sector and must turn toward—at this point their mental gears ground furiously. Which sector *were* we in? Should we turn this way or that-a-way?

If our kibitzers turned at all, it should have been to turn over a new leaf, because their ground school had been neglected. As Omni pilots know, all needles may be flown by the same rule, *fly toward the needle*, providing the course selector and the compass heading are similar. But this is only part of the technique of flying the ILS, and there are other important factors to know in flying the system which airline pilots use. These other factors can be made easier if one doesn't have to think about colors and which way to turn, how much to turn, or when to turn. Then there is the other half of the ILS, the glide path. Certainly, we use the same rule and fly toward the needle, but what is the best way to stay on a glide path? And may we make an instrument ILS approach without a glide-path needle?

Nowadays, with so many Private Pilots possessing equipment

which enables them to use part of the ILS, and so many believing that flying the ILS is difficult, the time has come to learn a few facts.

Not every plane has both ILS and a refrigerator, but if they were so equipped there would at least be ice cubes handy. If one has the equipment, he should know how to use it instead of letting it lie idle.

At least we'd have ice cubes handy.

"But," someone objects, "how can I fly a glide path when I don't have a glide-path receiver? Or a marker-beacon receiver?"

The answer is that you *can* fly the ILS without the glide path, but the marker-beacon receiver must be used because it is the only means we have of determining our exact position en route to the station. Then, *if the Omni receiver is built to receive the ILS signal,* we tune in the *localizer,* which is the main signal of the ILS.

The *localizer* is the name given to the radio signal that is in line with the runway and enables one to *locate* his plane on the center line from the runway. The portion of this beam that is right of the ILS approach course is called the blue sector, while the other half is yellow. Now that you know on which side you may find blue, proceed to forget about it on inbound headings. There is an easier way to locate yourself.

The other part of the ILS is the glide path—also called the glide slope. It is a signal beamed from approximately the touchdown part of the runway at an upward angle of about 3°, although there are spurious glide paths at greater angles. This means that approaches above 3° should not be used, and one must stay precisely on glide path. But the 2½ to 3° angle of the glide path is the average power-on gliding angle for planes with approach speeds of 70 to 150 knots. For example, on a 2½° glide path at 90 knots in still air, the rate of descent is 400 fpm, at 150 knots the rate of descent is 665 fpm. It has no color system, but the method used to fly the glide slope is exactly the same as for flying other needles, and there is a technique for flying the glide path that enables one to stay on glide path much more easily.

Let's make a run on Los Angeles ILS. Bring along an ILS instrument approach chart for Los Angeles (available from the U.S. Coast and Geodetic Survey). This chart contains, among other bits of invaluable information, the ILS heading, the distance of markers from the airport, the altitudes at which to cross markers, and the frequencies of the ILS, markers, and beacons.

Glance at the top of our ILS chart and find the frequency: 109.9 megacycles (mc.). Turn on the radios, tune to 109.9, and identify Los Angeles by the code signal given on the chart: LAX. The Morse code signal actually says "i-lax," the "i" (two dots) being used to distinguish ILS from other LAX signals like VOR. We check the needle, and prepare to take off.

This brings another dissent from someone. "Wait! What about the glide slope?" This is, indeed, a nice point; we certainly want the glide-path needle working. But if we have complete II S equipment, the glide path was turned on at the same time we turned on the ILS. Glide-path receivers are simultaneously tuned to glide-slope channels. Thus, if you tune in the LAX localizer on 109.9 mc., you have also tuned in its glide path on 333.8 mc. In switching to Long Beach ILS, 16 miles away, you'd also automatically change the glide-path receiver to 335 mc. Because other localizers and glide slopes are paired in a similar manner, all that is necessary is to turn on the ILS and tune to the localizer frequency of the ILS which is going to be used.

If we do *not* have complete ILS equipment but have purchased a separate glide-path receiver, we must indeed tune it separately, and in this case we must obtain both localizer and glide-path frequencies from the approach chart and tune the receivers accordingly.

After taking off, fly outbound from LAX in order that we may make a straight-in approach. There are other approaches authorized, but the procedures are similar and they all must be made after a transition from certain positions, or fixes, at which the aircraft "holds" by circling a given position. This position is always a radio fix, and that is another reason why we must have a 75-mc. marker-beacon receiver for this type approach. Therefore, we'll fly to a position about 15 miles east and call Los Angeles Approach Control on any of the frequencies given on the upper-left corner of the ILS chart.

This is mandatory. With traffic as congested as it is today, we want to avoid the big airliners which arrive so frequently. The only benefit one receives from hearing four fans vibrating directly over-head is that the reaction tightens flabby stomach muscles. By contacting LAX Approach Control, we advise them of our position, obtain clearance, and become recognized as part of the traffic problem.

Those four fans overhead tighten flabby stomach muscles.

Approach Control grants permission with a reply something like this: "Nan 777 . . . Los Angeles Approach Control clears Nan 777 to the Downey Radio Beacon; maintain three thousand feet, cross Downey at three thousand, hold east of Downey in a non-standard, one-minute holding pattern. Expect approach clearance at two-four. Over."

You repeat the clearance to Approach Control (this is essential because it assures Approach Control that you have received and *will follow* the instructions). You note the time—you *must* have the correct time on the panel clock, and if you doubt the clock you must ask Approach Control for the correct time. You observe that the time is now thirteen minutes past whatever hour it happens to be (the exact hour is omitted in position reports).

You take up your chart to find Downey; it turns out to be a dumbbell-shaped fan marker with a circle in the center. The circle represents nondirectional beacons on low frequencies, used by pilots who have Automatic Direction Finders. Fan markers, however, are on 75 mc. and emit a signal which causes a panel light to flash dots and dashes. Downey, for example, sends an "a" or "dot-dash." This is the primary reason for having a marker-beacon receiver: so you can hold at a fix and tell exactly when you are over any one of the three 75-mc. markers we're going to use during our approach (the Downey Marker, the Outer Marker, and the Middle Marker).

But Approach Control said to hold east of Downey. From the Flight Information Manual, you learn that to hold in a non-standard holding pattern east of Downey requires that you fly inbound on the localizer, turn left 180°, fly one minute outbound, turn back, and fly one minute inbound—a total of four minutes. This may complicate matters if you find yourself over Downey at :21, when a four-minute pattern would cause you to be a minute late in leaving Downey for LAX. How we'll get around this difficulty will be seen in a moment.

### FLYING THE LOCALIZER

We cross Downey inbound at :17 and the marker beacon flashes dot-dashes (or we may listen to the a's). We turn outbound and begin flying our holding pattern, *disregarding* the needle because the rule no longer applies and because we are south of the ILS leg. We turn inbound and again fly toward the needle, getting back on the leg. During the straightaway portion is the time to compute our ETA at each marker beacon between us and the station. The ILS chart shows Downey to be 7.8 nautical miles from the Outer Marker (shown as OM on the chart), while from OM to the Middle Marker (MM) is 4.7 miles. We're holding in pattern at our Maneuvering Speed of 80 knots, which is also the speed to be used in the approach. A twist of the computer gives us a time en route of six minutes from Downey to OM and three and one half minutes from OM to MM.

Adding these to the time of our Downey departure (presuming it will be :24) we get an ETA of :30 at OM and :33½ at MM. Jot these on your knee pad or progress chart for future reference.

The fun begins when the panel clock reads :21 and we've just crossed Downey inbound. Now we'll have to vary our one-minute pattern, because our departure time is expected to be :24 and that means we must *leave* Downey inbound at :24. It isn't difficult to clip thirty seconds from each leg: one minute in a standard turn outbound, thirty seconds outbound, one minute to turn inbound, plus another thirty-second leg, equals three minutes, and that places us at Downey at :24. The important fact to remember is that we are expected to be on time; if we are one minute late, every other plane holding above us will also be delayed one minute or more. In order to be at Downey at :24 we must adjust our pattern so that we will be there on time.

We reach Downey inbound. The panel light flashes, and if the pilot ahead of us was on time for his departure, Approach Control radios, "Nan 777 ... Los Angeles Approach Control clears Nan 777 for a simulated ILS approach. Report inbound over the Outer Marker. Over."

We acknowledge and repeat, making preparations for the run. We want everything to be set up for landing, so we complete the Checkoff List, leaving gear and flaps to go as usual. In some planes, one-quarter flap has been used during Maneuvering Speeds to increase the stability of the airplane, and in this case a slight modification of glide-path technique—described later—is required. In the acknowledgment, you tell Approach Control that you're leaving Downey inbound, thereby enabling Approach Control to direct any plane behind you to begin holding at Downey.

At your altitude of 3,000 feet you'll be well below the glide path, as a glance at the ILS chart will verify. Also, the horizontal (glide path) needle will be above center, signalling that the glide path is above us.

The time has come to get on the localizer and "tie it down." Usually, the vertical needle is initially off to one side. Which way shall we turn, how much shall we turn, and when do we turn in order to center the needle?

The easy rule is, of course, to fly toward the needle, as we did when flying the Omni. We also observe (1) the position of the needle and (2) the rate of change. Both needles may be flown without thinking about color if one remembers the rule:

*When the compass is the same as the approach leg heading, fly toward the needle.*

Both needles may be flown by flying toward the needle, but what is overlooked by many beginners is how far and how fast the needle moves. Notice how far the vertical needle is from center. We have just passed Downey, which is about 13 nautical miles from the runway, so the ILS beam is fairly wide at this distance. If the needle is three dots (about an inch) from center, we'll need a big bite, or heading correction, to re-center the needle. We therefore turn left toward the needle.

*Turn 30 degrees,* just as for any other drift correction. This standard bite will quickly bring us back on course, where the needle will be centered. It is large enough to correct for wind, and you know from experience what it will do; a smaller bite might be sufficient only to compensate for wind drift. When we're closer in, we'll use a much smaller bite. What is the new heading? Glance at the *World* you used in other chapters: if the ILS approach leg heading is 248°, then a heading to the left of that is 218°.

As you fly 218°, watch the needle for *rate of change.* This is going to be your important clue in flying close-in headings. Glance at the other gauges, just as though you are on actual instruments, scanning each briefly, never staring at a particular one for more than a second or so. Now, if the ILS needle moves rapidly back to center, we are correcting rapidly and must uncorrect rapidly. The action of the needle is exactly as it is when flying the Omni. With rapid needle action, we must turn back to the ILS heading of 248 shortly before it becomes centered; with a slow-moving needle, we'll wait until the needle is practically centered before changing heading.

Now hold a drift correction heading of a few degrees. The needle will probably move from center, but the *rate of change* tells you what's happening to the airplane: a slow needle means a gradual drift from course and a small correction may hold us on course. By the time we arrive at the Outer Marker (:30), we must have the heading fairly well tied down, because at that time we'll have to make our let down.

## THE GLIDE PATH

If we have complete ILS equipment (both localizer and glide path) we can intercept the glide path by flying inbound from Downey at 3,000 feet (our holding altitude). In the event that ILS charts of other stations direct that we intercept at a lower altitude, we must descend when leaving our holding position to the specified altitude, level off, and make intercept at that altitude.

After leaving Downey at :24 we maintain Maneuvering Speed (which is also our approach speed) and watch for the horizontal glide-path needle to come down and the 75 mc. marker-beacon light to flash. As the horizontal needle approaches center, observe the rate of change: if the needle moves slowly, we have a low ground speed and a headwind; a rapid movement denotes higher ground speeds. The faster the needle moves, the more we must anticipate the needle by making immediate changes in configuration (such as wheels and flaps); if the needle moves slowly, we may be more deliberate in obtaining an approach configuration.

Exactly how rapidly must we let down? The chart tells us that in no-wind conditions on LAX's 3° glide path (which is steeper than other glide paths to permit higher approaches by noisy jet aircraft) a plane flying at 100 knots descends at 530 fpm. By working a simple ratio problem on our computer, we find that at 80 knots we must lose about 485 fpm. This rate may be obtained by the same technique used in other approaches, namely by lowering gear and flaps, which automatically adds enough drag so that the plane descends at *approximately* the correct rate for maintaining position on the glide path.

When the needle begins to move downward, we watch it carefully for *rate* of movement. We judge the needle movement to be normal, so shortly before it reaches center we lower gear and flaps; by the time it is centered we're on glide path with the rate-of-climb indicator showing about 485 fpm down. Now try to hold the glide-path needle centered without any change of throttle, because power changes almost always result in a porpoising effect, with the plane flying first above the glide path and then below it, as we found during our GCA approaches. Porpoising invariably results in pilots fighting their needles or watching them so intently that they can't hold either the glide path or localizer accurately. In actual instrument ILS approaches, with weather minimums of 200-½, large errors in glide-path altitude can mean an overshoot or an attempt to build a tunnel under the runway. In four-engine planes such errors cannot be corrected quickly, and the result of also being a few degrees off the localizer is a missed approach, in which the pilot climbs, goes back to OM, and does it all over again.

Therefore, if the plane goes above glide path, push the nose down and get the glide-path needle centered; release elevator pressure and see if the needle remains centered. If continuous pressure is required and the speed builds up, don't change the throttle but add a few degrees of flap, which increases drag and the rate of descent. Soon you'll be holding the glide path easily, with small forward or backward movements of the wheel, and staying precisely on the glide path.

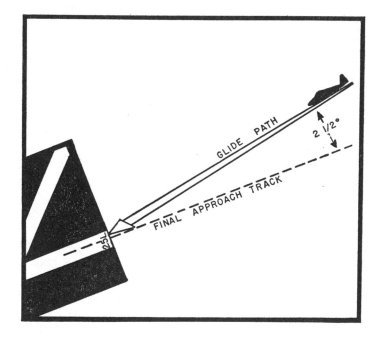

Fig. 42. On course, on glide path.

This invites the usual objection. "Ah," comments our favorite objector, "what if I go *below* the glide path? One can't fly upward to the needle indefinitely without adding power!" True, he cannot, and the method has this limitation, but he can remove a few degrees of flap *before* he adds power. Adding power is a must if the air speed diminishes more than 10 per cent of Maneuvering Speed, but, in general, a leeway of plus or minus 10 per cent air speed is permissible in holding the glide path before we change the throttle setting. It should be understood that the throttle setting (rpm's with fixed propellers, or manifold pressure with constant-speed propellers) must have been originally set correctly, a setting found by experimentation and practice. The basic rule, don't change power until you have to, still holds.

## APPROXIMATING THE GLIDE PATH WITH LOCALIZER ONLY

But suppose that we have no glide-path needle and are making a partial ILS approach with our OMNI-ILS receiver. Our ILS chart tells us that the glide path intercepts the Outer Marker at 1,830 feet, so we descend to that altitude immediately after leaving our holding position at Downey. We get the vertical needle (localizer) nicely tied down in the center of the dial, and arrive at OM at :30. Can we get on glide path?

The answer is that we can only approximate the glide path, and for this reason an approach and let down with only an ILS localizer and a marker beacon receiver would limit us to the VOR minimums given on the VOR chart: 500-1. We could obtain assistance in staying on the glide path by asking for a monitored approach from the tower, in which case the tower gives us intermittent comments during the final approach regarding our deviations from glide path— comments which are made as the radar operator watches the pip of our plane on his GCA radarscope. But the final approach *can* be made without tower assistance. When the light flashes at :30, giving us a fix over OM, we lower gear and enough flaps for final approach.

Now we must descend from 1,830 feet to below cloud level, which is supposedly at 500 feet *above the ground.* The chart tells us that field elevation is 126 feet, so we should be clear of clouds and have visual contact when the altimeter reads *about* 626 feet—which again emphasizes the importance of setting our altimeter as described in Chapter 7. (For a complete ILS approach with a 200-foot ceiling, we'd expect to have contact when the altimeter read 326 feet, or just after reaching the Middle Marker at :33½.)

We must therefore lose 1,200 feet of altitude (or 1,500 feet with complete ILS) in 3½ minutes. At 485 fpm down, this is easy. Now we remember Approach Control's instructions and advise them that we're over the Outer Marker inbound, and are told that we are cleared to continue our approach. We watch the needle(s), scan the instruments, and wait for 626 feet indicated (or 326 feet for complete ILS), where we should be clear of obscuration at 500- or 200-foot ceilings, respectively. If we have not made contact at those minimums, we'll follow our missed approach procedures by climbing to 2,000 feet as specified on the ILS chart.

With either full or partial ILS approach, we have tied down the localizer heading. As soon as we left the Outer Marker we began to hold the heading with the rudder and to use ailerons only in bringing up the wings as needed. The reason for this is that it's easier to correct the heading 1 or 2 degrees by using rudder. We are holding a gyro heading of 248, the needle drifts to the left. Remember, we aren't interested only in where the needle is but also in the rate with which it moves. This needle moves fairly rapidly so we steer 244, hold it, watch the needle move back, and turn to 246. With the gyro compasses now required for instrument flight, it's easy to hold the heading within a tolerance of 1 degree. Had the needle moved quickly back to center, we would have uncorrected promptly to a gyro heading of 247; the closer we get to the Middle Marker, the narrower the localizer becomes and the more imperative it is to take little bites quickly.

At :33 we break clear of clouds at 500 feet and advise Approach Control that we're "contact" (with a 200-foot ceiling we'd stay on the instruments, watch for the beacon light to flash over MM at :33½, and become contact at approximately :34 at 200 feet). The approach lights loom up ahead and, thanks to a precision approach, we are nicely lined up for a landing on 25L. We make the usual power reduction, obtain Over-the-fence Speed, and land our airplane.

Some pilots prefer to use other methods in flying the ILS, but the method we've used has been found to be the least confusing to applicants during flight tests. One objection to "flying the needle" during the ILS approach is that it doesn't work in flying the reverse course. For example, in flying the reciprocal of the approach heading (68°) one must fly away from the needle, just as we did with the Omni when the compass was not the same as the course-selector reading. But reverse courses on either Omni or ILS are seldom used, and the simplicity of the rule, fly toward the needle, greatly offsets the objections.

We touch down after our almost perfect approach, with that good feeling which comes after doing a job professionally. We realize that flying the ILS is not quite as hard as we thought it was, and that they shouldn't have laughed when we "sat down to play our ILS."

# 20: FOR BATS ONLY

YOU'RE an expert Private Pilot en route to the West Coast, flying late into the afternoon on what was to be a routine cross-country flight. As you fly over your check points, it becomes apparent that there are much stronger headwinds than were given you by aerology. With a twist of the computer, what was once a suspicion becomes belief. Your new Estimated Time of Arrival is now *after* sunset, which darkens the picture exceedingly—you simply don't *like* to fly at night!

Take another example, the dilemma of Pilot V, who didn't believe in using a "confuser" to compute ground speed. He hadn't prepared for a night flight, and because he could see the sun at 10,000 feet he thought it was still daylight at 1,000 feet. He was also flying into a headwind, and by the time he got to his destination, there was darkness outside and inside the cockpit. He didn't have a flashlight, he didn't know anything about night flying, and he wished he were home in bed. The cockpit became a strange, unfamiliar place; he couldn't find switches, regulators, or cockpit lights without fumbling. After lighting the cockpit, he was light-blind for many seconds, and at that point he reached up and pressed the panic button.

His fear of the dark was not entirely a personal idiosyncracy. Go to any airport and interview ten pilots picked at random and in the daytime. They may all cheerfully aver they just love night flying, but their log books will prove that only two of them fly at night. Night flying, at least for the other eight, may be wonderful, but they consider it more pleasant in an automobile.

Why do 80 per cent of pilots regard night flying as a pastime for bats only? If a bat can do it with only auditory sense to guide its flight, why shouldn't we (with our Omni, two-way radio, running lights, and reliable engines) also fly at night? Night flying is easy, it's fun, and night pilots call it beautiful. Let's turn on the landing lights and take a brighter view of night flying. Let's see why night flying is feasible and safe for a Private Pilot.

Knowing how to fly at night will eliminate the necessity of making that famous, life-saving 180° turn back to the nearest airport, or the possibility of flying into trouble, like Pilot V. Knowledge, plus a pointer or two and a few night flights with a competent instructor, will eradicate those imaginary obstacles that keep Private Pilots on the ground.

He reached up and pressed the panic button.

The first obstacle that deters one from flying at night is lack of confidence, which is a kind of fear. This fear may be physical. Many pilots simply believe they cannot see well enough to avoid hazards, but with reasonably good night vision this particular fear is unfounded. Or, the fear may be mental. Some pilots mistakenly believe that night flying is difficult because they do not have well-defined reference points by which to keep the airplane right side up. This is only partially true. The basic difference between night flying and daytime flying is that darkness causes the horizon to have less definition. Certainly we must concede that with total obscuration (especially at sea), VFR night flying is impossible and the pilot is forced to fly on instruments. Aircraft-carrier pilots are ordered to use instruments following carrier take-offs at night when there is no horizon, because the sea and sky seem to be as one, and a pilot can be climbing or gliding and not be able to tell the difference. In such conditions he goes on instruments thankfully.

But with starlit skies or on moonlit nights this objection vanishes, because it is possible to see the horizon and night flying is easy. Level flight, climbs, approaches, and landings aren't much more difficult than they are in the daytime, and the panel glows in the darkness with either illuminated or phosphorescent dials giving altitude, air speed, and temperatures.

The second objection to night flying is that Private Pilots anticipate getting lost. It is true that without a radio night flying is no cinch, because one is practically out of visual contact with the ground except in the vicinity of large, brightly lighted cities. But on cross-country flights, the lights of one village, town, or city look much like those of another, and to fly a dead-reckoning course toward a distant airport without radio aids is certain to become a guessing game. Today, with that invaluable aid to private flying, the Omnirange receiver, staying on course is simplicity itself; with the aid of cross bearings we can approximate our progress en route, and although such bearings will not pin-point our location because of Omni course errors, we can easily find the airport at our destination.

The final hazard in the minds of non-night fliers is that of engine failure. This is a very minor point unless it happens to us, in which case it's a major calamity. But modern-engine failures are as rare today as they were common yesterday; the statistics of engine failure have diminished to the point where the chances of having the engine fail on a particular flight are less than those of winning an Irish sweepstakes. But these failures are not sudden, and a good gauge-watcher can land with partial power failure before his engine quits entirely. Even those landings with power failure are not as drastic as one may think. Here again, statistics prove that it's not the field that damages one's airplane so much as pilot error in getting into the field and making a safe landing. A pilot can glide into a field and walk out, but to fall into it, after stalling, eliminates the walking.

If the above answers to common objections don't satisfy you, simply *try* night flying. But before you do, let's go over a few easy rules that make night flying simple in CAVU weather.

## USING THE EYES AT NIGHT

Let's go back to our expert pilot who is flying westward at sun set. You turn on your running lights thirty minutes before sunset. Soon the sky is black behind you; ahead is twilight that deepens into darkness, and the lights of the city flicker like candles. But, being an expert, you've prepared for this eventuality by making preparations for the flight.

You've darkened the back of the propeller so that it will not reflect light into the cockpit and partially blind you; you've checked the running lights, memorized the position of cockpit controls so that you can locate any switch or lever blindfolded; you've cleaned the windshield thoroughly because even faint film makes objects hazy; you've checked the battery, radios, fuel, and landing lights (although good landings can be made without landing lights, as will be described later). Finally you've changed your cockpit lighting effects to *red*.

Red light is known to be the least visible of any color, and the frequency of this light does not affect our eyes like white light. For example, wear a pair of red goggles the next time you go to the movies; upon entering the dimly lighted theater, you'll have night adaptation and see plainly. You therefore have covered the usual cockpit lights with red cellophane, leaving the switch-on light uncovered (white) for emergency use. Now, as you fly, you'll have night adaptation all the time; even the flashlight is covered with cellophane, but in such a way that the red paper can be easily and quickly removed should you need white light. Remember not to turn on the white light, because a single flash destroys night adaptation and several minutes will be required to recover from light-blindness, or as much as half an hour to regain complete adaptation.

You have pasted narrow slips of luminous Scotch tape on the important instruments: over the stall speed of the air-speed indicator, the cruising rpm's of the tachometer, and the temperature limits of the oil-temperature gauge. They're pasted in such a way that they're apparently lined up with the needle, allowing for parallax and the position of the pilot to the left of center.

You've tied a loop of cord around your flashlight and pencil so they won't get behind the seat just when you need them most. Hanging them on a hook or around one's neck is better than having to look for them.

If rule one for the protection of the eyes is to use red illumination, then rule two is don't stare. Never focus directly upon an object at night and don't stare at it. In focusing the eyes, we place the image of an object in the center of the retina, which is not as sensitive as the edge of the retina. By looking slightly to one side, we see an object more clearly; for example, the next time you star gaze ask your companion to first look directly at a star and then slightly away from it. She'll admit the star seems brighter when one doesn't look directly at it.

By not staring at an object, the eyes are more relaxed. Moving the eyes is an excellent method of relaxing them, whereas staring keeps eyes muscles tense and eventually the eyes water. Dry those tears by moving the eyes; you'll see better and you'll see more, because by moving the eyes you pick out objects that otherwise are not noticed. Hunters use this rule to good advantage. Finally, shifting one's vision and scanning the sky continuously is important in the daytime but at night it is vital; in these days of rapidly moving aircraft, a plane can appear out of nowhere very quickly.

Be alert for *moving* lights. Sometimes remembering the location of the colors helps. Recall the old jingle, "Port wine is red," and be reminded that red lights are on the port, or left, wing. Running lights are required by law to be visible from only certain forward angles, so if you can see red and green lights the plane is certainly coming toward you.

## CROSS COUNTRY AT NIGHT

So here we are, flying westward at sunset with perfect equanimity. As the dusk deepens, our night adaptation increases until we can see objects plainly. In the red-lighted cockpit we retain adaptation by using white light only in extreme emergency. Twinkling lights appear from the towns below, but at night one town looks much like another. Where are we?

According to our Omni we're on a certain radial, so we're on course. Now we'll use the method described in Chapter 18 and obtain a fix by cross bearings. With hundreds of Omni stations on our airways, it's easy to find one that is nearly at right angles to our course, tune it in, identify it, and obtain the bearing *from*. Draw a line on the *radial* of this Omni; where it intersects our course is our approximate position.

Take up the progress chart and jot down the time and position. Do the same thing on the aeronautical chart; you now have a fix which helps answer the question, "Where do we go, should we have an emergency?" Locate the nearest field on the chart, repeating the procedure as frequently as you think you should. The next time you get a fix, use your computer in determining ground speed and thereby determine the accuracy of your ETA. In short, cross-country flying at night is similar to daytime flying, the primary difference being that you're busier. To be sure, the answer to where to go in case of complete engine failure is "Down!" But such failure is rare, and your engine almost always will give warning of impending failure by changes in instrument readings. Be an instrument watcher at all times, but be a better one at night than you are in the daytime.

"Sure," objects someone, "I know that engines seldom fail, but what if I happen to be there when the engine does quit!" This, indeed, is the great shortcoming of statistics. When the one in that million-to-one is *you*, you've got to know what to do. It's dark down there, we don't know what the winds may be, and we can hardly distinguish a pasture from a wheat field. But there are roads, clearings, and other fields that may be used, and the important point to remember is this: a landing at stalling speed is infinitely better than a crash from a stall-and-spin. We'll therefore assume Over-the-fence Speed, select the best possible site, and go into it at the Minimum, or Never-subceed, Speed. Even with flares (which are not installed in the average lightplane), we can do little better than this.

When it comes time to switch tanks, turn on the heat, regulate the by-passes, turn on the passing light, or tune the radios, we reach directly for the correct switch or lever because we previously memorized their location. We maintain our progress chart, keep track of the ETA, advise the airways communication stations as we fly over them by making routine radio reports, and enjoy the beauty of the twinkling lights. The revolving beacons amaze us—there are thousands of them, it seems, but they don't tempt us. Flying lighted airways was once possible, but today you can fly any direction you wish by watching the beacons, none of which is exactly on the desired course. Stick to the Omni and you'll get there better.

This night flight, while keeping us busy, has been so much fun that before we know it we're making the let down in order to arrive at the field with traffic pattern altitude. Let's call the tower and get permission to land. Can we make this night landing a good one?

## NIGHT LANDINGS

As we watch the lights of the city come into sight, we notify the tower, giving them our altitude and location, receiving landing instructions, which include the altimeter setting and the service runway. Should the airport be small and on the outskirts of the city, we'd find it by flying an Omni radial; in that case we'd need either flare pots, floodlights, or landing lights in order to land.

But the pointers of previous chapters help us. We correct our altimeter, go through the Checkoff List, and get into the traffic pattern with Maneuvering Speed. At towerless fields we'd check the tee or wind sock for wind velocity, gusts, and any possible crosswind. As we fly the pattern we keep our eyes moving constantly, being very alert for moving lights. The only apparently nonmoving light that is dangerous is the white tail light of the plane we're overtaking.

Night time is when these precision approaches feel good, because we know we're going to land precisely on Point X, at the near end of the runway. We hold Maneuvering Speed until we see the fence, ease the power back, add more flaps, and cross the fence at Over-the-fence Speed. Now look out far ahead and ease her down to the runway. Here is where the wheel landing feels good and is good; whether or not you have landing lights, flare pots, or floods, it is no trick to find the ground. Most pilots make better landings at night, either because there are fewer distractions or because they are more careful at night. By looking far ahead rather than down, height can be estimated better, and when the wheels touch use easy forward pressure to hold them on the ground; remove the last bit of power you may be using, raise the flaps, and keep the plane rolling straight down the runway.

As you taxi back to the hangar, close your flight plan and go through the Checkoff List: cowl flaps open, flaps up, oil shutters closed, radios off, landing lights off. It's been fun and not at all difficult; you'd like to try it again, and why not? You're now a full-fledged member of that exclusive organization of night fliers whose motto is, "For Bats Only."

# 21 : THE JETS ARE COMING

TOMORROW, when you step into your private jet, you're going to fly faster, more smoothly, and more quietly than ever before. The jets are coming, and with them faster speeds, less complicated operation, and easier handling. It is a jet—not a jest—that will make possible a morning take-off in New York followed by a landing in Los Angeles before breakfast.

There may be other forms of travel; looks into the future are always made through a crystal ball, darkly. But if we are to fly a jet, what kind will it be? A ramjet that flies faster than sound? The turbojet now used by military aircraft? Or the turboprop airplane used by commercial airlines? And what will be the effect of these speedy aircraft on the flight techniques and the words of wisdom written so seriously and read so painfully in the preceding pages? Will we have to eat our words chapter by chapter or just page by page? When jets come for the Private Pilot, will we really say good-by to romance and become careless about taking it off, using flaps, knowing stalls, making precision approaches, and applying precision techniques in trying to fly expertly, in a professional manner?

Quite the contrary. With higher speed we'll need even more precision, and Quality X will be more important than it is now. When the day of private jet planes arrives, you pilots who are expertly professional will be ready to fly jets, so let's see what jets are all about.

To begin with, what's the difference between rockets, ramjets, turbojets, and turboprops? How does one take off and fly a jet? What is the difference between jet and reciprocal engine operation? It's time that we knew the difference, because jets are not exactly new, inasmuch as they were invented in the pre-Christian era.

Long before Nero kept his lions on a diet, Hero of Alexandria designed and constructed a machine called an *aeolipile* (ee-oll'-ih-pile). It has been called the first steam engine, but it should have been called the first jet.

It was simply a hollow metal ball which was mounted so it could revolve. There were two bent pipes inserted in opposite sides of the sphere, pointed in opposite directions. After water was heated inside the ball, steam issued from the pipes, which then became small jets, and the sphere revolved. For this Hero became a hero, although the jet wasn't used during the intervening 1,900 years except to open temple doors. History doesn't explain how the doors were closed, and one can think of a quicker way to move doors—so this may account for the little use made of Hero's invention.

The next important part of the turbojet—the turbine—was invented later. It was driven by water, not steam or gas, and it came into being after a smart inventor placed buckets on each side of a vertical wheel so that the buckets would always be top-side-up on a particular side of the wheel. When the wheel was placed beneath a waterfall, it revolved merrily and became popularly known as a water wheel. It could have been called a water turbine because it used the principles of the turbine.

That ended the brave beginning of the jet, and the aeolipile was just a curiosity for 1,900 years. Then two engines were invented almost simultaneously: the gas turbine and the reciprocating engine. It seems almost incredible that of the two machines the more complicated would be developed first. But the reciprocating engine, with its intricate timing and its intake, compression, power stroke, and exhaust cycle was favored because what Mr. Ford and the Wright Brothers needed was a low-power, low-speed engine rather than the turbine with its fantastic speeds. Only after the reciprocating engine was developed to its fullest extent, and still higher speeds were desired, was the jet to be favorably looked upon.

## THE ROCKET

Rockets, jets, and toy balloons operate on one principle. Engines which operate on this principle are faster than piston engines because the faster they go the easier it is for them to go faster. There is a limit to their speed, of course, the limit being the velocity (or pressure) of the escaping gases.

For example, fill a balloon with air and you have air under pressure, called compressed air. Release the balloon, and compressed air escapes from one end as it presses against the other end. Result: the balloon is pushed across the room in twisting circles. Affix a stick to the mouthpiece or nozzle of the balloon and it will fly straight. Now find a way to have the air burn fuel and form high-pressure gas to move the balloon faster; you may set the house afire but you'll have a simple rocket.

The rocket is ancient and so is the principle it uses. Some people think that the outrushing gases push against the air in our atmosphere, but the atmosphere actually restricts the gases. For example, if the air outside the rocket is at the same pressure as the gas inside, the gas can't go anywhere, and neither will the rocket. Rockets, jets, or toy balloons perform better without the pressure of any atmosphere at the tail, because the high-pressure gases can escape easier. When the pressure outside the rocket decreases to zero (as it does at hundred-mile altitudes), maximum efficiency is obtained.

Another explanation of rocket operation is to consider what happens when the mouthpiece of our toy balloon is clamped shut to prevent air from escaping. Then the inside pressure is equalized inside the balloon and nothing happens. Now release the mouthpiece: the pressure becomes less at one end and is thereafter greater at the opposite side, so the compressed air pushes against the top of the balloon, forcing it to move away. It might be said that the balloon moves while the air stays behind, or that for each action there is an equal and opposite reaction.

The rocket, therefore, moves because expanding, high-pressure gases push against the rocket, not against the atmosphere. Because rockets contain both air and fuel within them, they are suitable for travel in airless space where a jet literally suffocates.

## THE RAMJET

Jets, like rockets and balloons, utilize the same principles of propulsion. The ramjet is the simplest form of jet because it contains only fuel, getting air with which to burn the fuel as air is rammed into the jet during forward motion through the atmosphere. It has neither turbine nor compressor to force the air into the combustion chamber and therefore cannot fly from a standing start.

But once the ramjet has speed, it really moves. By speed is meant velocity faster than the speed of sound; at this speed, a turbine inside of the jet would actually impede its progress. The usefulness of the ramjet is limited because it not only must be in motion before it can operate, but it must have outside air; this limits its practicability in airless worlds or for space travel.

But the very simplicity of the ramjet makes it useful on helicopters, and for this-world travel—provided that it's first put in motion by other means of propulsion. After it is moved, air is rammed into the nose, or "divergent nozzle," combined with fuel, and ignited; the burning fuel expands and emerges from the tail, or "convergent" nozzle.

The future of the ramjet is debatable, but imagine what could happen if ramjet engines were installed in planes that were first flown to high speeds by other means. We could fly faster than the sun apparently travels, flying westward into yesterday or eastward into tomorrow, a subject better left to science-fiction experts.

But place liquid air in a rocket or guided missile, combine it with fuel, ignite it, and you've got a high-speed device that can go to the moon or anywhere else we wish to send it.

## THE TURBOJET

Suppose that we now devise a means of utilizing atmospheric oxygen, compressing it, and mixing it with the fuel our jet carries. Then we'll burn the mixture in a combustion chamber and jet it through a tail nozzle. The burning gas forms higher pressure at the front, or top, of the chamber than there is at the tail, thereby pushing the jet forward. This push is called "thrust."

But the air compressor must be powered somehow, and this is where the turbine is used; its only function is to rotate the compressor, not to make the jet fly. As the burning gases expand and move toward the tail, they pass through the blades of the turbine and cause it to revolve at high speed. Because the turbine and the compressor are on the same shaft, they both rotate.

As the compressor revolves, it sucks in air from the outside and pushes it rearward into the combustion chamber, where it is mixed

with fuel; it ignites, burns, and passes out the tail. The only thing
lacking in the picture is the starter. By turning the compressor with
an electric starter, air is forced into the combustion chamber, mixed
with fuel, and ignited; the turbine turns the compressor, and
from that time on the jet can take off when ready.

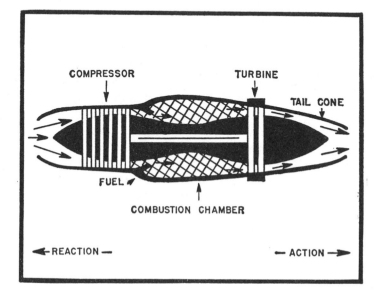

Fig. 43. The expanding gases press against the front of
the chamber, which moves away from the expanding gases.

## THE TURBOPROP

At last we come to the turboprop, which is only part jet; more
accurately speaking, it's mostly turbine. It should really be called
a propeller turbine, but the term turboprop is more imaginative
and is now in general use.

What happens is this: we have the same compressor driving the
air into a combustion chamber, burning the fuel, driving the turbine, and going out the tail of the jet. But, in addition, the turbine
not only drives the compressor but also the propeller. Thus, when
one component turns, they all turn.

But propellers revolve at mere hundreds of revolutions per minute, whereas turbines revolve at thousands of rpm's. This means that in the nose of the engine there must be installed gears which permit the turbine to spin rapidly while the propellers spin comparatively slowly. And, although most of the power of the turbo-*jet* is comsumed when the gas "thrusts" against the jet, most of the power in a turbo*prop* is spent in turning the turbine. About 80 per cent of the power goes into the turbine, but the other 20 per cent isn't wasted because it's used in pushing the airplane.

And that's the beauty of it. Here we are, flying a turbojet at 20,000 feet. Not even the soup appears nervous—it's as calm as we are. We know our plane is not only smooth and fast but economical to operate; it's more efficient than a reciprocating engine and, except for the whine of the turbines, it's much quieter. It combines the best features of the latter plus the high speed of the jet.

## FACTS DEPARTMENT

Here are a few items for those who don't know the facts of jets.

*Fuel.* Jets usually burn a low-volatile kerosene, which is much cheaper than gasoline, although Diesel oils or gasoline have been used. The smoke one sees trailing a jet is unconsumed kerosene, or carbon. Sometimes this unconsumed fuel is further burned in a tail compartment called an "after burner," which adds to the power output or thrust of the jet.

*Turbo compound.* This is like calling a tall man "shorty," because the turbo compound isn't either a turbine or a jet. It is simply a reciprocating engine which has small turbines in the exhaust that produce power from the exhaust gases, thereby getting something for nothing, so to speak, because exhaust gases are usually wasted in other type engines.

*Speed.* Speed in jets is measured by Machs. Mach 1 is the speed of sound at a given altitude. The speed of sound is 761 mph at sea level, while at 35,000 feet it is only 660 mph. Thus Mach 1 at 35,000 feet is slower than Mach 1 at sea level. The term derives from Professor Mach, an aerodynamicist of Austria.

*Thrust.* Because more thrust is developed when there's less pressure outside the jet, jet engines have more effective power at greater altitude. Therefore, horsepower isn't used to denote the power of a jet. For example, a pound of thrust equals 1 horsepower at 375 mph. In our turboprop airplane, the propeller might develop 1,500 horsepower from the prop but only 350 pounds of thrust from the jet.

*Pulse jet.* The German buzz bombs of World War II were not just ramjets, but also pulse jets, because the fuel and air were burned intermittently. The resultant vibration was not the only reason why buzz bombs were headache stimulators, however.

If Leonardo da Vinci, who designed a turbine-type wheel that utilized hot chimney gases, were to see a jet, he would nod sagely—not merely because he approved of the jet principle, but because Leonardo would be over 400 years old. We doubt if it will take that long for Private Pilots to fly jets, so let's see what it's like to fly one.

### FLYING THE JET

Ask any passenger in a jet airline about flying a jet. He'll tell you there's nothing like it. The reduced noise and the smoothness of flight make jet flying superb. For pilots, there's ease of operation, a less complicated engine, and *speed.*

For example, check points creep past in your propellor-driven plane, but when you're sitting in a jet they flash by. What do these variations mean to the pilot?

Let's get into a jet trainer and find out. We've got a simpler panel, with fuel-pressure gauges, oil-pressure indicator, and flowmeter instead of the assortment needed for reciprocating engines. We press the starter, which energizes the compressor, and the turbine comes to life as the fuel ignites. During the time of taxi, we'll have warmed our jet enough for take-off. We check the speed of the turbine by the tachometer (which indicates the *percentage* of take-off rpm) and the tail-pipe temperature, which is an indication of the temperature of the gases passing through the turbine. The speed and temperature tell us when we have the thrust required for take-off.

Use the Checkoff List, set the flaps, hold the brakes, adjust the throttle or power control for full take-off power, and release the brakes. Because there is no torque, don't hold right rudder to roll straight down the runway. The acceleration is slow so we'll use lots of runway, but once we get into the air be alert. We're already flying fast and starting to fly faster; if we don't get the gear up promptly the air pressure at high speed may damage it. Watch the air speed.

Flaps should be raised promptly, and as they come up a small amount of lift is lost, which we can compensate for by increasing the angle of attack. Now, at climbing speed, ease back on the stick and climb. The altimeter begins to wind like the hands of a broken watch, making 6 rpm. Level off (in two minutes!) at 12,000 feet and set a course for San Francisco, 400 miles away.

*You're going to be there in 40 minutes.* Suppose you are flying dead reckoning without radio aids. A 5-degree error in heading will fly you rapidly off course and you'll arrive at a point about 35 miles from San Francisco; each minute you fly off-course places you about 1 mile from course. But the consoling feature of this speed is that you can get back to your destination in three and one-half minutes!

The check points slide under you rapidly, and you're busy changing radio frequencies. You decide to circle the town below and roll into a gentle 30-degree bank. At 600 mph you don't seem to turn; as Fig. 44 shows, a 30-degree bank requires five minutes for a complete turn, at the end of which you'll have flown 50 miles. You steepen the bank to 60 degrees, feeling the 2g force sucking you into the seat. At this steep bank it will take you a minute and one-half to circle the town. This is the reason that jets are always banked steeply: at medium banks they simply turn slowly.

You head for your destination, but there is a cloud layer ahead. Not wishing to make an instrument approach, you put the nose down to get underneath the clouds; this doesn't work because the jet picks up speed and approaches the sound barrier, so you extend the dive brakes and lose 6,000 feet in a minute or so, thereby getting under the clouds before you fly over them.

But the plane is as cold as the upper-air temperature, and as it descends into lower, warmer layers it acts like an iced drink in the summertime; the windshield becomes fogged with precipitation and moisture, and you're thankful for those windshield blowers that evaporate the condensation.

When San Francisco is still out of sight but only a few minutes away, we make preparations to land and get clearance. Now is the time when the techniques of precision flying we've studied and practiced are invaluable. The jet must be brought in precisely, with accurate approach speeds, and with *high power.*

The high-power setting is required because the acceleration of a jet is slow; we keep the power on but lower the dive brakes enough

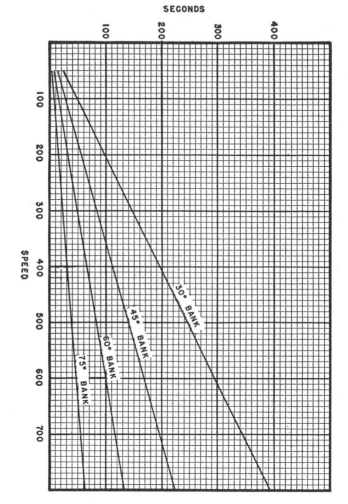

**Fig. 44.** Fast-flying jets turn slowly. In a medium (30°) bank, a 600-mph jet takes five minutes to complete a turn. The time, in seconds, required to make a 360-degree turn at various speeds and degrees of bank may be obtained from this graph.

to obtain approach speed. The reason for this is that we can always raise the dive brakes and go around the field if we have to; with only partial power during our approach we'd be in one of those embarrassing situations. We obtain a lower touchdown speed by landing slightly nose-high in our wheel landing, then cut the power and taxi in.

Was this jet flight too difficult for the average Private Pilot? Perhaps. But is it beyond the ability of the expert Private Pilot? Certainly not. Mechanization is commonplace in the twentieth century, and the application of precision technique in lightplane flying may be applied to the high-speed jet. But after one has mastered techniques and learned the rules he *still* must have Quality X and the ability to think ahead of his plane. The faster one moves, the farther ahead he must think, and the more accurate must be his thinking.

If this can be boiled down to a single sentence, that sentence would read, "Think and act, do *something*, and after you've done it make a recheck." For a final lesson, let's consider The Legend of Sitting Bull, whose sitting is discussed in the next chapter.

# $22:$ THE LEGEND OF SITTING BULL

IF anyone has read this far, he's read quite a bit about professional flying. The hints and easy rules for take-offs, precision approaches, and instrument flying—it is hoped—have made him a better pilot. And in learning the business of flying he has even retained some of the romance, such as the beauty of night flying and the excitement of speedy jet airplanes.

But the question of Quality X still remains. There are questions in our minds such as, What kind of pilot am I? Supposing that I am using the previously suggested techniques, have I developed Quality X? And, if I do think ahead of the plane, how can I consciously apply such thinking in a practicable manner?

Consider for a moment those pilots who just sit in the cockpit for as many hours as Fate allows and who never try to improve their flying. They fly in a certain manner and differ from their more competent brethren in that they either do not have Quality X or they do not indicate they have it. They go through flight training and take flight tests, gradually acquiring pilot ratings but never getting that finishing touch of the expert pilot.

Such fliers could be called "sitting" pilots, and they present themselves regularly to any inspector or flight examiner; examiners can recognize them by their habit of just sitting. If a check pilot were to write a book about them, the most appropriate title would be *The Legend of Sitting Bull.*

Read about Sitting Bull, who is not the villain in a cowboy-and-Indian movie. As he flies cross country, we notice that he's calm and unperturbed, a quality greatly to be admired, but we wish he'd do something. There are mountains ahead, and the peaks seem to reach up like a probing hatpin. We don't like hatpins beneath us and we wish that Sitting Bull would climb higher *before* we get to the moun-

**242**

tains and thus place us in a less vulnerable position. By the time he starts his climb, we're helping the engine with every muscle we can tighten, wishing he'd done more climbing and less sitting.

As we fly onward a weather broadcast comes in, advising that the weather ahead is good for crops but not for pilots. Sitting Bull now has another decision to make: should he execute that most difficult cross-country maneuver, the 180° turn, or continue to his destination?

Sitting Bull had mountains ahead.

When the ceilings begin to lower, we descend to an altitude a few hundred feet above the terrain. This is bad enough, but, as time goes on and gas runs out, a simple twist of the computer shows that we'll reach the destination only by using a power-off glide, a method we're reluctant to recommend.

Still no decision from Mr. Bull. If he had read about Quality X he isn't giving any indication of it, because thinking ahead of the plane must be evidenced by prompt, decisive action. In this situation he could not have gone on instruments because there wasn't sufficient fuel for an alternate airport, and he couldn't proceed with his flight plan for the same reason. His only correct decision was to land at the nearest airport, but in order to do that he should have been planning as he flew, pin-pointing himself during the flight, and *acting* upon his decisions.

For instance, he could have made the decision to climb over the mountains sooner; when the weather closed in he would have immediately changed his flight plan; and when headwinds made it impossible to continue the flight to the original destination, he would not only have thought ahead of the plane but would have acted promptly and turned to an alternate airport.

Prompt decisions are usually difficult to make, but if one has the skills which have been described in other chapters, plus the all-important Quality X, he is better prepared to make decisions—and he still has to make them. Because making a decision implies a choice between doing something and doing nothing, and because doing nothing is easier, some pilots do just that until the time for putting the decision into effect has passed.

How can we tell if we're acting promptly? What can we do to train ourselves so that we may never follow the vapor trails of Sitting Bull?

Test yourself by solving the following problems. Like all tests, they prove nothing conclusively, but they do indicate something. The decision you make is one part of the problem and the time taken to put the decision into effect is the other. And despite the fact that our tests are not at all conclusive, they'll furnish a small clue as to *how* you are using Quality X.

Before you study the next illustration, note the time and check yourself on how long it takes to reach a decision and to *act*. Each illustration is quite simple and there are no tricks; merely study the problem, then begin timing yourself as soon as you look at the picture. The time factor is just as important as your solution.

In the next figure, you're flying the plane crosswind, and just as you approach Fields A and B you have engine difficulties and must land immediately. You have only enough altitude to land in Field A upwind or Field B downwind; either field is long enough for a landing with a 5-mph wind blowing.

Do not read below the figure until you have decided upon the solution and have acted, at which moment check the time you required to decide and act. Begin timing yourself *now*.

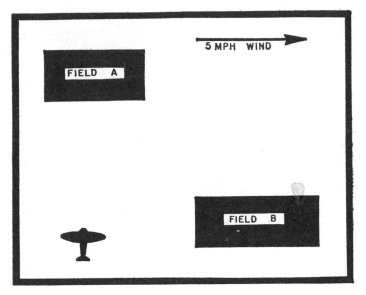

Fig. 45.

This problem is the kind that tempts pilots into a long deliberation. There is Field B, nice and long, very convenient, and downwind. Should we, or shouldn't we? You know that downwind landings are not recommended, but the field is so long and it's handy. By this time it's too late to go into Field B, so you look at Field A, which is into the wind. But now you've got to maneuver sharply, flying away from the field and making steep turns close to the ground. It would have been much easier had you turned with the intention of landing in Field B in the first place.

So it seems that you could have landed in either field safely if you had decided at once and acted promptly. Just what "promptly" is in terms of seconds is debatable, but the point is that *you* know whether you deliberated too long; and if you did, you probably need practice in analyzing problems quickly and acting promptly.

In the next figure we have a variation of the problem. Here you're flying toward a mass of cumulo-nimbus. To the right is solid overcast, while to the left are rugged, 10,000-foot peaks. Decide whether you're going to turn right, climb, stay on course, or turn left. Do not read below the figure until you have decided, at which moment see how long you deliberated. Begin timing yourself *now!*

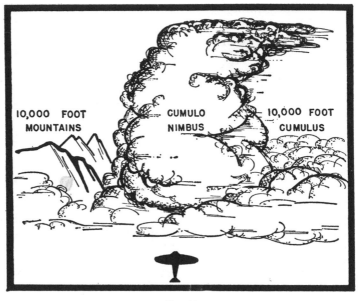

Fig. 46

This also tempts pilots into a lengthy deliberation. Certainly we wouldn't fly through cumulo-nimbus and into those violent updrafts; we wouldn't attempt to climb over it in our lightplane. But which way to turn? If we turn right we'll have smooth flying "on top" and we can easily get back on course after we've passed the clouds. But we don't know what's beneath the clouds, and such flying with a single engine bothers some pilots, despite the reliability of modern engines.

As for turning left, we know that there'll be updrafts and downdrafts in those mountains, but at least we'll be CAVU. If we turn left we'll therefore have to climb higher and possibly detour farther, because the anvil of the cumulo-nimbus indicates that the winds are from the left.

During this deliberation we've flown closer to the clouds, and now it's evident that we should have decided sooner and acted more promptly. It wasn't so much which way we turned (because either route is feasible) as it was the *time* we consumed in contemplating our alternatives. How long did it take to reach a decision? Again, it must be you who evaluates your ability to think to a conclusion and take immediate action, because it is you who knows if you procrastinated unduly before you turned.

If these inadequate tests prove anything at all, it is that we must force ourselves to act promptly after evaluating the pertinent factors of a situation. *Think through to a decision and take action promptly.*

If a trained pilot merely *acts* he has a better chance of acting correctly than he would if he does nothing. But making decisions is difficult—it's those mental problems which cause nervous breakdowns, not the expenditure of physical strength.

If we're thinking ahead and if we've trained ourselves to act promptly in routine flights, making decisions is no longer a difficult mental problem. By making decisions of lesser import when there is plenty of time, it becomes possible for one to act quickly in emergencies when there is hardly any time.

Thus, as an average pilot develops Quality X while perfecting techniques, and as he gradually moves into the expert category, the ability to think ahead almost invariably has to be accompanied by prompt actions *because* he's thinking ahead.

## CHECK IT!

As your flying hours increase, you're going to develop those admirable traits of alertness, correct thinking, anticipation, and prompt action. When you come to simple problems like that of selecting Field A or Field B, you see the answer clearly in a few seconds, an indication of alertness and the ability to act promptly. It could also be that you're over-confident, a trait which could be called the kissing-cousin of heedlessness.

Take, for example, Check Pilot W, who had many thousand hours of safe, conservative, careful flying in his log book. One day he was giving a flight check in multi-engine aircraft, sitting on the right side in the co-pilot's seat. The flight was excellent: the turns, climbs, orientation, engine-out procedures, and missed-approach procedures were top quality; the 400-1 shot was so good he permitted the applicant to complete the approach, make a landing, taxi to a stop, lock the controls, and shoot Sitting Bull. Both Check Pilot W and the applicant felt very confident about the flight, so they taxied rapidly into position and took off—without using the Checkoff List.

Halfway down the runway and at transport category $V_1$ speed, the applicant found that his controls were immovable! Check Pilot W, who didn't have his hands on the controls, didn't know what had happened; he was surprised when the applicant snapped his throttles back just in time and remarked, as he burned his brakes, "That was pretty close." It was, indeed, very close—to the end of the runway. The applicant then taxied back and used his Checkoff List.

At this point the control tower operator became curious. "What's the matter?" he asked. "Are you in trouble?"

Check Pilot W, who was in the co-pilot seat, picked up the microphone and gave himself full blame for the near accident. "Oh, no," panted Check Pilot W. "I just have a green co-pilot."

These veteran pilots may have felt green, but both of their faces were quite red. They knew that there is no excuse for not using the Checkoff List, but at least they had Quality X, were alert, and *acted promptly*. They had practiced developing Quality X during each hour of flying, and by prompt action had obviated the necessity of calling out the local fire department.

These veteran pilots could make excellent decisions but had grown so overconfident that they no longer doubted themselves, and they had forgotten that the perfect pilot has yet to fly an airplane. They had also forgotten that the final rule in the rule book is *Check it!*

Take for our final example another close one in which Check Pilot W was again the star performer. He was on final approach after a flight check with an equally competent applicant on the left side, a pilot who should have had full responsibility for the safety of the plane. But Check Pilot W was the senior pilot, so if anything happened to the plane it would be he and not the applicant who would be featured in any chapter added to The Legend of Sitting Bull.

There they were on final approach, "gear down, cleared to land," or so the switches said, because both the gear and the flap switches were in *down* position. But the Checkoff List called for *visual* inspection of the gear. Both pilots were supposed to peer downward, see a wheel, and say, "I got a wheel," a statement more satisfying than grammatical.

Check Pilot W, who had learned his lesson the day before, had an overwhelming desire to check something; a quick look at the Checkoff List confirmed his suspicions that no one had *looked*. At the very last moment he decided to look himself—and saw no wheel! Opening the throttles, he climbed to altitude and checked the equipment: a fuse had blown. Therefore, the gear had not been lowered when the switch was thrown, and the landing would have been made wheels-up. Yes, the tower should have warned him, and yes, the red light on the panel should have glowed, but the tower operator hadn't noticed and the red light was burned out. This freakish double-malfunctioning couldn't happen more than once in a million times, but when that one time is our time, it's too much.

After cranking the gear down by hand they landed, both of them confirmed believers in the value of *Check it!*

If we now summarize what has been stressed in this and previous chapters, we'll have a definition of an expert pilot who flies in a professional manner. He has Quality X; he has the skills and techniques heretofore described; he makes decisions quickly and acts promptly; and finally, he has acquired the habit of checking and rechecking as he flies.

But even expert pilots pick up new habits, not all of them good. To stay at a high level of proficiency we must check not only the airplane but ourselves. Let's take a flight check and see how we're doing, in the next and concluding technical chapter.

# $23\colon$ CHECKING FLIGHT PROFICIENCY

YOU and another expert pilot are on final approach. He flies in a professional manner because he has to—he's an airline captain. You want him to fly expertly—you're one of the passengers. Still, as a Private Pilot, you take pride in smooth technique. You watch and listen as he makes his let down to the runway: very smooth, nice power reduction, and an accurate precision landing.

"Not bad," you say to the stewardess.

"Naturally," says she, sniffing. She probably has as many hours in the air as you have, all of them in the coffee department, and therefore knows all about flying. "He just had his six-months proficiency check."

"Did he pass it?" you crack, but she is not amused at such levity. Neither are you, because you suddenly remember that it's been a long, long time since you had a flight check. Just how necessary is it for you to be checked? You banish such an unpleasant thought from your mind by resolving to take a check the day after next year.

Because you own a lightplane and use it in your business, it's only a day or so later that you're rolling your plane from the hangar. You check it thoroughly, file a flight plan, warm up, and get taxi clearance from the tower. While waiting for take-off, the words of the airline stewardess come to mind, "He just had his six-months proficiency check."

Come to think of it, how long has it been since your last check? You are an expert pilot who flies in a professional manner, but even experts can acquire bad habits. When you obtain clearance and push the throttle forward, you roll down the runway a bit more cautiously than usual. Instead of leaving the ground precisely at $S_2$ speed, you hold the wheels on the runway longer and bump the gear, doing a few grinds for good measure.

That wasn't so good, and you know it. Maybe a flight check would help, but to arrange for a check takes half a day of your time, and you're very busy. Besides, do flight checks really prove anything? What good does it do to demonstrate steep turns, eights, stalls, and spot landings? Is there any correlation between proficiency in these items and flight safety? How can a check pilot possibly estimate that hard-to-define Quality X?

She knows all about flying.

As any check pilot will tell you, flight checks are an attempt to estimate both safety and proficiency. In thousands of flight tests, all I could do was to evaluate technique and literally guess at an applicant's level of thinking ability. If he met minimum standards for certain maneuvers, and if I could not detect any suicidal tendencies, the applicant got his ticket. If he was obviously clumsy, he did not.

With more advanced pilots or during routine proficiency checks, we check pilots can suggest the practice of certain maneuvers; sometimes we can detect bad habits which have been acquired during years of solo flight. But in advanced flying, pilots are assumed to possess Quality X! Therefore, although routine flight checks do help, they're not the last word.

It seems to me that any pilot who has reached the professional level is his own best check pilot. So, as you circle the airport, you suddenly realize that you do have a few bad habits. With a wing low, you come up the groove for a landing, forgetting to hold a constant air speed and to reduce speed over the fence. You land without precision, halfway down the runway, taxi to a stop, cut the switch, and climb out—all in one piece, the criterion of a successful flight. But there's that annoying self-criticism, the feeling that you're not doing your very best.

Why not check yourself on the next flight and regularly thereafter? If you've been flying a few years without a check, you've undoubtedly developed flight habits, not all of them good ones. You're inclined to pay less attention to details than you did once, and if you wouldn't fly in an airline with an unchecked pilot, why trust your own private airline?

Let's use some of the information in the preceding chapters to check ourselves.

## YOUR SIX-MONTH PROFICIENCY CHECK

Every six months you can check yourself during routine cross-country flights ordinarily taken for business purposes. There are two broad phases to consider: the actual maneuvers, and judgment —that Quality X of flying.

Write down the following essential items and grade yourself strictly, recalling that one can fool all the people some of the time, but one can't fool himself all of the time. Use the system of 1 for excellent, 2 for above average, 3 average, 4 below average, and 5 for failing. In each maneuver, grade yourself first on technique, then on judgment—Quality X.

*Take-offs.* Roll into the take-off position, apply throttle smoothly and fully in one continuous motion. Now, with prompt but gentle pressures on wheel and rudder, hold the nose down just long enough to get $S_2$ speed; keep the plane rolling straight without achieving those bumps and grinds of Chapter 3. At $S_2$ speed, get off the runway, nose over to get climbing speed, and then climb precisely at climbing speed. Grade your technique.

Now grade Quality X, your ability to plan and think. Did you check both sky and runway for traffic, in addition to the control tower's clearance? If there wasn't a control tower, this is essential. Did you use the best available runway? Were you relaxed enough to check the air speed during your take-off run? At every moment, as you climbed, did you know where you'd go in the event of engine failure? Did you remember to raise the landing gear when you began to climb? Did you reduce power and adjust propeller rpm's before churning to higher altitude?

Grade all items strictly. If you forgot any of them, give yourself a low score; a low score on Quality X is worse than a low score on technique. By writing your score you avoid being lenient with yourself. Give yourself a failing grade on the entire test if any grade on Quaity X is below passing. A slight error in technique is not always hazardous, but bad judgment will sooner or later get you into trouble. As we've said before, anyone can herd a plane around the sky, but a competent pilot is one who thinks, plans ahead, acts promptly, and continually checks himself.

*Climbs.* Your first turn should be in the traffic pattern unless the tower has authorized a straight-out climb. Watch your technique: is the turn medium banked, and are you climbing at climbing air speed? Take a look at the ball-bank indicator: if you are holding the correct amount of right rudder, the ball will be centered, indicating that you are neither slipping nor skidding. Should the ball be off to the left in a left turn, you are slipping in more ways than one. Rudder the ball into the center by pressing left rudder for left ball, right rudder for right ball, just as we did in Chapter 14. A precision, ball-centered climb merits a 1 for technique.

Did you remember to look ahead and behind for other traffic before turning? Are the panel instruments indicating the correct pressures, temperatures, rpm's, power, flap position, wheel position, and cowl flap opening? Are you using a routine system of checking the gauges as described in Chapter 15? If you have done all these well, grade yourself accordingly on Quality X.

*Stalls.* At cruising altitude, level off and get on the compass heading for your destination. Get set for cruise by "cleaning up the cockpit" according to your Checkoff List. Now reduce power and execute a few stalls with power on and power off, maneuvers which may add as much as a minute to your flight but which are so very valuable. There are pilots who seldom stall their plane and who assume that the indicated stalling speed is the same forever. It isn't.

Stall speeds vary with the condition of the plane and the air-speed indicator, which (like their owner) don't stay young. Jot down this new speed: it must be used in computing new $S_1$, $S_2$, climbing, Maneuvering, and Over-the-fence Speeds described in Chapter 5. If the indicator shows excessive error, have it checked or repaired; your air-speedometer is the primary instrument used in precision flying, and is essential in making precision take-offs and approaches.

Watch your technique in these stalls, and be sure that you're feeling it and can recognize the burble point. Note the altitude, recover with the recommended technique of Chapter 8, and check the altimeter. If you lost over 75 feet, or if the nose wandered, you're not as expert as you think. Give yourself a grade on technique.

What about thinking ahead? Did you look for other planes around and below you? Did you apply carburetor heat? Even if the stall technique was perfect, failure to plan ahead gives you a 5 on the maneuver.

*Turns.* Apply power and get back on your compass heading. We've lost about a minute so far, and the next maneuver will take a minute more. Put the plane into a steep bank (more than 45°) and hold it for two complete turns. Use the method described in Chapter 8: look at the chord line of the downward wing, feel the control pressure change, and listen to the engine. Now, if you're still flying in a professional manner, you will hold your altitude within 5 or 10 feet, which is good for a 1. But what about the ball? If it's not centered you don't deserve more than 3; what's more, an expert pilot uses his ball indicator only as a *reference*, because his sense of feel (Chapter 8) tells him at once if he is skidding or slipping. A few degrees of ball doesn't mean a pilot is unsafe, but he isn't smooth and he certainly doesn't deserve a mark of 1.

Grade thinking and planning: did you carefully check the area before turning? Did you use enough power for the degree of bank? Were you aware of the instruments, other planes, and your recovery heading, or did you stare fixedly at the lower wing?

*Emergencies.* Modern engines are so reliable that when they do quit, the silence is not golden. That's why check pilots love to give simulated emergencies during steep turns, or during S turns at low altitude.

Emergencies always happen when one expects them least. This

has never been proved, but I will guarantee that it's true. Cut your throttle somewhere in this turn, or merely simulate it if you're in a hurry. Where's the best field? Where's the wind? Have you forgotten how to pick a field promptly, as described in Chapter 6? If you are confused or too deliberate, don't give yourself 1 or 2. If this high-altitude emergency is not completed to low altitude, it tests only Quality X so no grade on technique is warranted.

*Cross-country technique.* In just 3 minutes you've had an excellent beginning on a proficiency check, and you've learned more than a check pilot could tell you in 30 minutes. Clean up the cockpit by setting cruising power, adjusting rpm's, regulating the mixture, and checking the temperatures, pressures, cowling, or other items on your cruising Checkoff List. Because you are still in familiar country, pick out a landmark and find it on your chart. Pin-point yourself and jot down the time in minutes.

It is the first leg of a cross-country flight that is so important. Only by pin-pointing yourself can you verify ground speed, drift, heading, and the accuracy of your ETA. Check the course on your chart, and glance at the compass. Do you know instantly what is the true course? If not, a review of Chapter 10 will help. Be sure you are flying a compass *heading* into the wind, not a compass *course;* as you fly toward the third check point, continually notice landmarks and stay on course by making the *track* (over the ground) coincide with the course on your map. If the map looks like the landscape below, you're holding your map correctly; if it doesn't, look at Chapter 11 after you get home instead of television.

Keep the plane trimmed for level flight, hands off, as we did in Chapter 14. You thereby fly faster and have less fatigue. Now, knowing your speed, location, fuel reserve, and weather at destination, you've earned a 1 for technique.

But what about Quality X? Are you just sitting there, or are you thinking ahead? Suppose the engine quits, the weather changes, or other emergencies arise. Can you turn almost immediately toward the nearest airport on the map? If there isn't a nearby airport, can you turn almost at once to the nearest and best field? Suppose you arrive over your check points at increasingly later intervals, which tells you of adverse headwinds. Can you obtain your new ETA from your computer instantly, and promptly decide whether to continue, land, or turn back? An expert pilot has thought out much of this beforehand, and he deserves an excellent grade for *not* "just sitting there."

When your ETA is plus 20 minutes, begin to plan your let down. Some pilots arrive at their destination with 10,000 feet of altitude, because they're not planning or thinking. Be sharp: use your computer, estimate how far out you must begin your let down at let-down air speed in order to arrive in the traffic pattern with traffic-pattern altitude. At the proper time adjust the elevator tab nose down, pick up speed, and begin your descent.

Now consider all these items in grading your cross-country work. If you've arrived on time, made good position reports, stayed on course, and planned each move correctly, you've not only gotten 1's but it's been fun, and the romance of flying is still with you.

*Maneuvers.* Suppose that your airfield is *not* in a congested area: plan the let down during this six-months proficiency check to arrive a few miles from the airport at 500 feet altitude. Veteran pilots seldom spend any time on low-altitude work, but 2 minutes doing S turns across a road will tell you volumes.

Glance at Fig. 47 and read the caption. The S turn across a road is the best low-altitude maneuver for judging performance because there are so many criteria. You must fly the plane over a given track, keep the ball centered, shade your turns to compensate for wind, maintain a constant altitude, and be alert for other planes . . . simultaneously.

It is also a wonderful maneuver for awakening pilots, so give yourself a cut gun and surprise yourself. If you've been alert and have been thinking ahead, you'll turn into the wind and toward the best field. Grade yourself: could you think, as well as fly?

*Approach and landing.* Climb back to traffic-pattern altitude, call the tower, and get set for your final maneuvers—the approach and landing. But good landings depend greatly upon the approach, so we'll consider it a single maneuver.

By the time you're in the traffic pattern you have the plane nicely stabilized at Maneuvering Speed. Now you have several minutes to get used to the feel of the plane at reduced speed, and to accustom yourself to the changed sound of this speed. You run through the Checkoff List, leaving gear and flaps to go as described in Chapter 6, and when you arrive at your base leg, everything is checked.

This entitles you to a good grade for both technique and planning.

See if you can get a perfect score for the final approach. Leave the power setting as it is, but lower gear and flaps as you turn to base leg. Try not to touch the power until we get to the fence. By watching the nose you can tell how you're doing: we want an accurate approach as described in Chapter 6, with a landing on

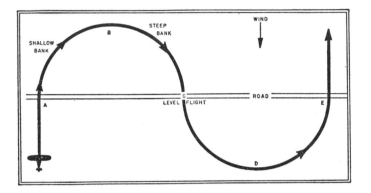

Fig. 47. The S turn is the best single maneuver for checking manipulation of the controls, planning, alertness, coordination, and use of the senses. Select a road or line 90° to the wind, flying at an altitude commensurate with air speed, i.e., from 500 to 800 feet in a lightplane. Begin maneuver by crossing the road in level flight, upwind, at Point A. Plan to arrive at Point B after a medium turn. Now make the *track* from B to C similar to that from A to B by increasing the bank to allow for wind drift. Check altitude, co-ordination, and traffic; cross Point C in level flight. Fly from Point C to Point D, making the curve similar to ABC by banking steeply to allow for wind, and use a medium bank from D to E for the same reason. Check altitude, coordination, and traffic. Cross Point E in level flight. AC should equal CE. Simulate a forced landing at any point to test alertness.

Point X. If the nose creeps downward because of high wind velocity, you turn toward the field sooner; if the nose creeps upward because of no wind, turn later and add flaps as required. Take a critique of yourself: are you relaxed and confident? Do you apply more flaps when the nose creeps ahead, or do you juggle the throttle in little bursts of power? If the wind is excessively strong and gusty, do you use flaps judiciously and smoothly increase power? What speed will you use across the fence in gusty winds?

Are you flying the plane in a constant angle of power glide, or is the air speed continually changing? An accurate approach is impossible with variable air speeds; try to gain the fence before making the final power reduction because your score will be higher if you do.

When the fence comes into view you ease the power back in order to have Over-the-fence Speed at the fence, neither before nor beyond it. Now, if the runway is clear, you lower flaps as needed and realize that you're committed to the landing. Look out ahead, ease the nose up slightly in order to provide the extra lift needed at the slower speed, get close to the runway, and let the wheels touch. Get the flaps up, taxi to the hanger, and close your flight plan.

Now, at the hanger with the switches cut, give yourself a technical grade: was the approach handled smoothly? Was the approach made without changes of power? Did you have accurate speeds during the approach? Did you land on Point X? If so, mark down a good grade.

But what about Quality X? Were you thinking ahead and considering the roll-off, or did you just sit there when the wheels touched? Did you remember to raise the flaps at touchdown, or did you taxi half a mile with the tires throwing rocks through the flaps? Did you look behind before taxiing? If you forgot all those items, your ability to sleep can hardly be exceeded.

Put the plane in the barn and check over your score sheet. Several 1's for technique mean that you're still an expert and can handle your plane smoothly, efficiently, and well. But what do you find under Quality X? If there is a single 5 there, you need practice and a review of these chapters.

Now that we've seen how we may fly expertly and professionally, our technical work is finished. But there is a small part that hasn't been covered: the picture of how it is done by pilots who hold Airline Transport Ratings (ATR), the highest type of pilot certificate.

Flying cross country under perfect conditions is one thing—flying in instrument weather is another. Perhaps you're interested in becoming an ATR pilot, so let's see what it's like to fly cross country under Instrument Flight Rule (IFR) conditions.

Ready? Then get under the hood and fly the final chapter, a short chapter that's a combination of fact and fiction—a story about *you* piloting the plane in the captain's seat on the left-hand side.

# 24: 10,000 SECONDS UNDER THE HOOD

"AT 12,000 feet we were still climbing, and the pilot looked at the check pilot on his right with a question mark in his eyes. There was no oxygen aboard the plane, and to fly higher than 12,000 feet for long periods was not recommended. Ahead were solid clouds mushrooming upward interminably, and somewhere in those clouds Mt. San Jacinto reached up, while on the right was snow-capped San Gorgonio, 11,502 feet above the level of the sea."

The above, at first glance, might seem to be a portion of a particularly bad script written for a Class Z movie on television. That is bad enough, but what is worse is to be in the script with a pilot who shouldn't be there. Suppose that you're not only in the script but are sitting on the left side, flying the gauges under a blind-flying hood. Only the check pilot can see what's ahead. What would you do if you were the pilot?

"Turn around," you say, and that is a good answer, particularly if you don't realize that 10,000 seconds under the hood requires that you know certain things. What about voice procedures, position reports, clearances, and let downs? What is it like to make an approach at a busy airport when the surrounding country has instrument weather? How can one fly the gauges and use a computer, estimate time over the next fix, handle the radios, and fly the plane? What happens if an engine quits (presuming you have more than one)? Can one man do all the work?

He not only can, but many pilots have done it. As a matter of fact, the first paragraph is part of a true-life picture. The entire episode actually happened.

Suppose you are that pilot. On the right side you'll have the check pilot, a man with a fiendish sense of humor, that perennial prerequisite of check pilots. You and he are completing a simulated-instrument cross-country flight check, and are now returning westward to Los Angeles. High above Palm Springs, the check pilot gets a radio report and picks up his mike. Inasmuch as the blind-flying hood is remarkably efficient (you cannot see out at all), you are not surprised when he says there is actual instrument weather ahead. You are merely dumbfounded.

**On your right sits the check pilot.**

The pilot—that's you—doesn't like it, because as an applicant you've never been on the gauges except under the hood, and those clouds up ahead make you pause and consider. Pausing, in an airplane, is merely a figure of speech. A pilot can't pause—he roars onward. You'd like to perform that well-known 180° turn, but this won't do at all, so you begin to sweat a little. There is a subtle difference between flying when you know you can pull the hood down to take the pressure off and flying in the soup when you know you can't. But instrument flying is fun, perfectly safe, and entirely feasible, providing one knows the rudiments of flying and can *think*—a point which has been stressed in the preceding pages. A pilot who can merely keep his plane on course at a given altitude has no business getting fogbound until he gets the fog out of his head.

You look over at the check pilot for a change of heart, but he is busy lighting a cigarette. He hasn't been much help since the flight began, over two hours before, for what was to be a routine, simulated-instrument flight check. While you compose a strong but tactful objection to flying through the clouds, Mr. Check Pilot radios ARTC and the clearance comes back, "Nan 777, ATC clears Nan 777 from present position to Los Angeles. Climb immediately to one-four thousand, cruise and maintain one-four thousand until further advised."

So at 12,000 feet you're still climbing and at 14,000 the shiny aluminum nose goes down, the props are pulled back to cruising rpm, the throttle adjusted to recommended manifold pressure, mixtures leaned out, cowl flaps closed, and the controls trimmed until the plane cruises along nicely in level flight with "hands off."

Almost hands off, that is, because you seem to have your hands full of airplane. The plane, which is a fine airplane and a great favorite, is not noted for any tendency to hold an attitude when flown on the gauges. As you reach down to pick up your progress chart, she whips off on a new heading at a new altitude, seeming to have a built-in tendency to wander from any given heading or altitude. The knowledge that you'll soon be on actual instruments doesn't help you to relax; airplane jockeys are like anyone else when the pressure is on, and you'd rather be VFR.

VFR flying, with visual reference to the horizon as it stretches interminably around the aircraft, is easy. A pilot can steer, eat lunch, smoke, and keep up his progress chart, but once the aircraft enters clouds and the pilot begins to concentrate on his instruments to maintain level flight in a given direction, he is busier than ants in marmalade.

So you—the pilot—fly on toward the cloud bank, only half a mile away. There'll probably be icing, turbulence, and the unknown in those clouds, which is not enough to dismay a seasoned veteran but

You fly blind toward the cloud bank.

is nevertheless a bit rough for a pilot taking a flight check. Entering a cloud mass, however, is not like diving into cold water; the pilot wouldn't have known the change if the check pilot hadn't told him. "You're in it," he observes casually. You visualize the fog that the check pilot sees through the hood louvres, fog that swirls off the wing tips, condenses on the windshield, gray and impenetrable. The bumps start to come, and you gently touch the wheel to bring a wing up, pressing rudder to move the nose back to 256°, the magnetic heading from Palm Springs to Los Angeles. You've been taught to fly planes like this mostly with the rudders and not to fight the wing dips. This reduces tension during instrument flying. In a larger plane you'd keep it level with the ailerons (use of wheel), relying upon the mass of the plane to hold a heading (little use of rudder).

When the gyro horizon indicates that the wings and nose are level, the pilot reaches down to pick up his progress chart. The chart gives the ETA over Riverside as 1356, or 1:56 P.M. But between Palm Springs and Riverside is the Banning Marker, a radio signal that will flash a white light telling him he is over Banning and 25 miles from the Riverside range station.

As the white light begins to flash the pilot notes his time: on schedule. He is carefully jotting this on the progress chart when the check pilot interrupts, in the characteristic manner of check pilots. He had been guarding the frequency of ATCS (Air Traffic Communications Station) while the pilot listened to the range.

"ATCS is calling you," he says helplessly, as if he couldn't answer them himself. The pilot, who had been watching his Omni-ILS needle, hurriedly reaches for his mike with one hand as he flies with the other; he wonders if there are other worries besides traffic, delays, bumps, or icing in the clouds. He tells ATCS to go ahead and transmit.

ATCS radios clearance. "ATC clears Nan 777 to the Downey Radio Beacon; climb immediately to one-six thousand, descend immediately after passing Riverside to cross La Habra at five thousand, cross Downey at three thousand, maintain three thousand, expect approach clearance at one-six (2:16 P.M.). Over."

The pilot, who had been carefully copying this clearance and simultaneously trying to hold a heading, repeats the clearance to ATCS. Then he looks over at the check pilot. "*Sixteen* thousand! And no oxygen?"

The check pilot shrugs and motions to the throttles. "Let's go! When ATC says 'immediately' they don't mean five minutes later."

During all this repartee, the plane had descended slightly and veered off the heading. Now the pilot eases her back to 256°, opens his cowl flaps, enriches the mixtures, increases power and resets his props to 2,000 rpm. The aircraft commences to climb to 16,000 feet.

Flipping his radio switch, the pilot gets back on the Riverside range, picks up his progress chart, and wipes the sweat from his brow. Up, up, up, watching the instruments with routine, systematic flicks of the eyes from altimeter to compass, gyro horizon, Omni-ILS needle, ADF, temperature gauges, and around the panel—starting the procedure over again, never gazing steadily at one particular instrument. Momentarily checking fuel, amperes, oil pressure, head temperature, watching for 16,000. Then to level off, reduce power, reset the props, lean the mixtures, close the flaps; watch for the Automatic Direction Finder (ADF) needles to dip and the panel light to flash for indication of position over Riverside. Check the progress chart, keep her on 256, pick up a wing, ease the nose to the left, use computer to get the ETA at La Habra and Downey. Jot down the times so that his Position Report, when radioed in over Riverside, will sound professional.

The check pilot, who doesn't seem to be worth having along, slouches in his seat and tries to light a cigarette, but the unlighted match falls to the deck. He reaches down to pick it up, unconcernedly making a minor adjustment en route. Check pilots should be watched carefully for moves like this, but the pilot had troubles of his own.

The clock on the panel reads 1356, and the pilot watches the sweep-second hand tick relentlessly past the minute; he listens to the range signal increase in volume, wondering if he has missed his estimate. Perhaps the winds have changed. Just as he is beginning to itch, the green ADF needle (one ADF is usually green, the other red, for easy reference) swings down and the white light flashes: Riverside! And only forty-five seconds late—lateness that is due to the change in air speed during the climb to 16,000, which the pilot had forgotten to allow for. The time is over Riverside at five-seven.

Flipping the radio switch, the pilot gets ATCS and makes his position report. "Riverside Radio, this is Nan 777 over Riverside, five-seven (not one-fifty-seven) at one-six thousand, Instrument Flight Plan estimating Downey at one-six, Los Angeles. Over."

ATCS merely replies, "Stand by." The pilot eases his throttles back and begins to descend as ordered: 15,000 . . . 14,000 . . . on course, on heading, everything okay. Just as he emits a sigh of relief, it happens. With a tired shudder, an engine coughs and dies! The plane veers to the right, the rate-of-climb indicator swings downward and the altimeter begins to unwind. The pilot jerks as if Mt. San Gorgonio had reached up and jabbed him, applying left rudder; had he been climbing, the loss of power would have required full left rudder.

The pilot apparently has St. Vitus's Dance. He moves quickly, and from force of habit and long training fire-walls both throttles (full throttle) and enriches both mixtures; a more experienced pilot would have immediately identified the dead engine as "right," because of the left rudder required, and he would have used less power, since he was descending and didn't need full power. After identifying the dead engine, he pulls the prop to high pitch (or feathers it if he can), because lightplane twin-engine aircraft do not perform well until they are cleaned up. He next pulls back the right throttle and mixture control, and adjusts power on the left engine to regulate his descent. He cuts the right switch, closes the fuel selector, the vacuum selector, and sets the $CO_2$ fire extinguisher bottle to *Ready*. He "cleans up" the good engine by setting manifold pressure (throttle), rpm (prop pitch), opens the left cowl flaps, kills the right generator, adjusts the stabilizer and rudder tabs, and corrects his heading to 256 degrees.

It was hard work, but inasmuch as asking for help from the check pilot was useless if not inadvisable, the pilot calls ATCS himself. "Riverside Radio, this is Nan 777 leaving one-three thousand, zero-one (2:01 P.M.), Instrument Flight Plan estimating Downey one-six, Los Angeles. Right engine dead. Request straight-in approach from Downey. This is an emergency. Over."

The operator at ATCS said, "Roger, wait." The plane was losing altitude easily with only one engine operative, but what about the 15-mile pull from Downey to Los Angeles Airport? What if you, the pilot, miss your approach and have to climb out, hold, and go in again, all on one engine? The first approach has to be the right approach—very literally the "final" approach.

The pilot has to lose altitude rapidly to cross La Habra at 5,000, but he sees his ADF needle swing down just as the plane passes through 5,000. He keeps his heading of 256 and rejoices that

Downey is a cinch at one-six. He radios he's leaving La Habra and 5,000, but ATCS doesn't answer.

"What now?" asked the check pilot curiously. "Your radio must be out."

"The regulations say we must keep going according to the clearance," says the pilot, switching from OMNI frequency to ILS in order to be ready, after leaving Downey, to get on the localizer. Then he tunes the green ADF to Downey, the red one to the outer marker, and in the meantime systematically scans his instruments, with routine glances at the oil temperature, oil pressure, and head temperature gauges.

The Downey ADF needle swings down, the light flashes. The pilot grinds in the Outer Marker by turning the "coffee grinder" crank on the ADF, picks up his mike, and switches from ATCS frequency to Approach Control. "Los Angeles Approach Control, this is Nan 777 over Downey one-six at three thousand. Leaving Downey. Request straight-in ILS approach. Over." He had forgotten to declare an emergency!

But his luck charm was working. Approach Control came right back and authorized a straight-in approach. Why the radios seemingly were functioning now, no one ever found out; had they remained out, the approach would necessarily have been continued anyway. In a few minutes, the horizontal needle of the ILS dropped to the center of its dial, indicating that the plane was on glide path. The vertical needle had been centered at Downey, showing that the plane was on course.

If he'd had two engines and approach speed, the pilot would merely have lowered a quarter-flap and his wheels to obtain speed and glide angle to stay on the glide path. With only one engine operative, he lowers one-quarter flaps (for stability) and adjusts the left engine power to maintain approach speed and glide angle. The plane stays on the glide path with only small corrections of elevator, and on course with small applications of rudder, as the pilot flies toward the ILS needle.

Now he calls for the Checkoff List and gets ready to land, with "gear to go." The green ADF swings down and a purple light flashes; that will be the Outer Marker. He grinds in the Middle Marker and advises Approach Control he's leaving the Outer Marker. Approach Control further clears Nan 777 for a straight-in approach to Runway 25L. Now the pilot knows it is time to tie down his ILS and make the approach perfect. When the ADF swings down over the radio beacon, he watches the ILS needle; it swings to one side, showing that he is drifting off course. With a little rudder pressure he moves the nose until his gyro shows a change of 2 or 3 degrees, picking up his wings as needed, keeping the vertical needle centered. When he flies below glide path he eases the nose up slightly, always flying toward the needle. His eyes also scan the gauges rapidly: the air speed, altimeter, gyro, ADF.

The check pilot begins to call out air speed and altitude: "800 . . . 100; 700 . . . 98; 600 . . . 100; 500 . . . 102; 400 . . . Contact!"

At the magic word "Contact," the check pilot begins to earn his salary. He reaches over with one hand to lower the gear, reaches down with the other to turn on the fuel selector beneath his seat and revive the right engine; he is disconnecting the blind-flying hood when a yellow light flashes on the panel.

"Middle Marker," says the pilot, and looks up. "Why, it's CAVU," he shouts.

"Full flaps, gear down, I gotta wheel," says the check pilot. "I'll give you the right engine after we land, in order to taxi."

The pilot—that's you—doesn't know whether to be glad or mad, but you taxi to a stop and cut the switches. Then you look at the check pilot.

"That was a good flight," says the check pilot, "about three hours long—that's 10,000 seconds under the hood, more or less. We were on time all the way, the voice procedures were good, instrument technique passable, but your single-engine work shows you can think, and that's what counts. Couldn't have done better myself, come to think of it.

"By the way, we left that cloud bank at five-eight, just before I cut your right engine this side of Riverside."

### . . . AND IN CONCLUSION

Perhaps it was reprehensible to let anyone believe he was on the gauges after running out of clouds; it is possibly worse, on a flight test, to fly with one engine inoperative as low as 400 feet. More than likely this was done for story purposes, but the truth is that single-engine instrument approaches and landings have been made when conditions were very much worse.

If, in real life, no check pilot would leave an engine out so long a time or at such low altitudes, the story illustrates instrument techniques if nothing else. The point is that a good pilot expects the unexpected to happen and is not surprised if it does. To be under the hood for 10,000 seconds is not phenomenal, but if nothing extraordinary happens in 10,000 hours, *that* may be considered phenomenal. This does not imply that any time one goes on instruments he may expect a breath-taking episode. It merely means that each instrument flight is different and is flown under varying conditions requring some change of plan or an unanticipated action.

A three-hour instrument flight is ideal for observing just how many things a pilot forgets, or how many necessary items he can remember after it is too late. For example, assume you're the inspector on a flight check. You have a pilot who never computes an ETA until after he's called the communication station, at which time he grabs his computer to figure it out. He never looks up the frequency of the station he's calling until after he calls the station, he runs a tank dry before he changes tanks. Should you sign his certificate of competency to pilot aircraft on instruments? Would you like to fly with him?

Such mistakes may not be disqualifying, but after a check pilot has witnessed either these or similar errors, he has definite ideas as to whether he should give an "Up" or a "Down" on the check, no matter what he may have to sign according to law. An inspector can't deny a man a license if he performs, in a minimum-standard way, the required maneuvers, but he can pray that he never has to ride behind the man he's certifying.

So here we are, right back to Quality X and the perennial question, "What kind of pilot am I?" In answering the question you are the best judge because by now you probably know a few easy rules to use in order to fly with correct techniques in an alert manner, doubting yourself enough to make rechecks and making full use of Quality X.

In trying to describe the essence of expert flying, we've come a long way and it is hoped that we've pinned it down. It seems, to add a final thought, that positive action is better than inaction, and that the kind of thought required in flying is not the pensive kind. A trained pilot who thinks and acts has a better than average chance of being right, whereas the pilot who does nothing is usually wrong. The pilot who is firm with himself and adheres to a high standard of performance, who wants to improve his flying and who uses a few easy rules to make his flying better and easier, is rolling his take-off like an expert, climbing out of the field with the ease which comes only from competence and assuredness.

We watch him climb and disappear in the blue of the sky, knowing that he's planning his flight, making decisions promptly, and checking himself exactly as we've urged him to.

And that makes us feel good, and when you're feeling good it's time to quit, so let's put the airplanes in the hangar and lock the hangar doors.

...and lock the hangar doors.

# INDEX

## ABOUT THE AUTHOR

John R. Hoyt has been flying twenty-five years and has logged 6,000 hours in military and civil aircraft. After receiving his bachelor's degree at the University of California, Los Angeles, and doing graduate work at the University of Southern California, he learned to fly in 1933. He later spent four years on the *USS Lexington* flying dive bombers and fighters, and was on active duty in the Bureau of Aeronautics. He has been a CAA inspector in charge of inspector flight refreshers, and has served as a commander in the United States Naval Reserve. He is an Associate Fellow of the Institute of Aeronautical Sciences. Mr. Hoyt has written three books and has published more than 200 magazine articles.